WOMEN, EMPIRES, AND
BODY POLITICS AT
THE UNITED NATIONS,
1946–1975

Expanding Frontiers:
Interdisciplinary Approaches
to Studies of Women,
Gender, and Sexuality

SERIES EDITORS:

Karen J. Leong
Andrea Smith

Women, Empires, and Body Politics at the United Nations, 1946–1975

Giusi Russo

University of Nebraska Press

LINCOLN

Portions of the introduction originally appeared as: "The UN and the Colonial World: New Questions and New Directions," in *Journal of Contemporary History*, April 2022, copyright © 2022 SAGE Publications, DOI: https://doi.org/10.1177/00220094221084150; "'Freedom of Choice Is a Western Concept': Equality, Bodily Rhetoric, and Feminist Fears 1964–1974," in *International History Review* 42, no. 6 (2020): 1210–28; and "Contested Practices, Human Rights, and Colonial Bodies in Pain: The UN and African Women, 1947–1965," in *Gender and History* 30, no.1 (2018): 196–213.

The University of Nebraska Press is part of a land-grant institution with campuses and programs on the past, present, and future homelands of the Pawnee, Ponca, Otoe-Missouria, Omaha, Dakota, Lakota, Kaw, Cheyenne, and Arapaho Peoples, as well as those of the relocated Ho-Chunk, Sac and Fox, and Iowa Peoples.

♾

Library of Congress Cataloging-in-Publication Data
Names: Russo, Giusi, author.
Title: Women, empires, and body politics at the United Nations, 1946–1975 / Giusi Russo.
Description: Lincoln: University of Nebraska Press, 2023. | Series: Expanding frontiers: interdisciplinary approaches to studies of women, gender, and sexuality | Includes bibliographical references and index.
Identifiers: LCCN 2022049656
ISBN 9781496205810 (hardcover)
ISBN 9781496234438 (paperback)
ISBN 9781496234933 (epub)
ISBN 9781496234940 (pdf)
Subjects: LCSH: Women's rights—History—20th century. | Women—Social conditions—20th century. | United Nations. Commission on the Status of Women. | Decolonization. | BISAC: POLITICAL SCIENCE / International Relations / General | SOCIAL SCIENCE / Women's Studies
Classification: LCC HQ1236 .R877 2023 |
DDC 305.4209/04—dc23/eng/20221222
LC record available at https://lccn.loc.gov/2022049656

Set in Arno Pro by A. Shahan.

To my parents, Giovanna Ruggeri and Luciano Russo

Contents

Illustrations

Acknowledgments

I started to work on this project during my graduate school days in Binghamton, New York. There my advisor, Jean Quataert, contributed to the shape of my ideas. Like her I was trained in European history but then became fascinated with the history of bodies, empires, and internationalism. I thank Jean, who unfortunately passed away before the completion of this project but who always encouraged me to produce scholarship that united my interest in theory with my historical training.

I am grateful to my supportive work environment at Montgomery County Community College, where colleagues and administrators have accompanied the development and completion of this project. The college has continuously supported my participation at conferences where I could discuss the ideas that came to form this book.

The completion of this study required archival research in different locations. At each, I found knowledgeable archivists and librarians to whom I owe a great debt of gratitude. Specifically, I want to thank Lynn Thitchener at the Cornell University Library, Adele Torrance at the UNESCO Archives in Paris, Marie Villemin Partow at the WHO in Geneva, Remo Becci at the ILO in Geneva, Romain Ledauphin at the UN Headquarters in New York City, and Julia Greider at the Schlesinger Library.

My numerous collective projects with scholars scattered across multiple continents have shaped my ideas on human rights, universalism, empires, and bodies. I want to thank Simon Lewis for our work together on postcolonial nostalgia, a project that helped me to understand the nuances of imperial histories. Thank you also to Marco Zoppi and the project on Europe and Africa, in which I could expand on my ideas on the history of the body in an African context.

Thank you to the University of Basel group on colonial violence, which helped shape my thinking on the role of intergovernmental organization and the intimate, two phenomena whose interconnections had previously seemed remote to me.

Thank you to my friends Kirsten Ernst, Olivia Holmes, Alex Otieno, Charles Peterson, Andrew Sholtz, and Roberta Strippoli for their constant encouragement. Also, thank you to Eileen Boris, Roland Burke, and Leigh Ann Wheeler for their support. Thank you to my editor Emily Casillas who has believed in me and this project.

A special thank you to my partner Tom whose affection and enthusiasm to debate for multiple hours on bodies and empires have been instrumental for the success of this project. Whenever I feel discouraged his "stick with it" reminds me that writing is like sculpting and that numerous modifications are necessary to the continuous improvement of a project.

I dedicate this book to my parents. To my mother, Giovanna Ruggeri, who rebelled against tradition by hiding pants and miniskirts from her parents—an act that today seems modest but that in 1960s Siracusa, Italy, was revolutionary. And to my father, Luciano Russo, who was born and raised in an Italian colony and told me and my brothers the contradictory stories of colonialism.

Abbreviations

CSW	United Nations Commission on the Status of Women
DEDAW	Declaration on the Elimination of Discrimination Against Women
ECOSOC	United Nations Economic and Social Council
GA	United Nations General Assembly
HRC	United Nations Human Rights Commission
IWY	International Women's Year
ILO	International Labour Organization
LN	League of Nations
SSW	Secretariat Section on the Status of Women
TC	United Nations Trusteeship Council
UN	United Nations Organization
UNESCO	United Nations Educational, Scientific and Cultural Organization
WHO	World Health Organization
WIDF	Women's International Democratic Federation

WOMEN, EMPIRES, AND
BODY POLITICS AT
THE UNITED NATIONS,
1946–1975

Introduction

During a 1955 UN Commission on the Status of Women debate, the Polish representative Zofia Wasilkowska claimed that her delegation "had taken up the cudgels on behalf of the indigenous peoples. It was a matter of general knowledge that the women in those territories were doubly oppressed, both as women and as indigenous inhabitants."[1] The debate was part of a long series of interventions on the modification of the female body for cultural purposes, a practice often termed *female genital cutting*. In her speech, the word *indigenous* meant the people in the dependent territories of Africa. In her understanding, colonial powers as well as native men oppressed native women. Moreover, she took responsibility for the task of giving voice to women she perceived as voiceless and assumed the role of their guardian.

The location of Wasilkowska as a "second-world" state's delegate complicates this picture and provides a multilayered analysis of women's rights activism at the United Nations. First, her language recalls Victorian imperial feminist tropes; depicting the pain of the racial "other" in sensationalist terms, portraying the other as oppressed, and ultimately declaring a firm intention to rescue "the other." Second, her affiliation with the Soviet sphere of influence might suggest a self-assumed role of guardian in order to produce a stance in opposition to first-world colonialism. Historians have shown how the Soviets presented themselves as an emancipatory and anticolonial power.[2] In both instances, however, her words reflect an imperial feminist position in the sense that she constructs "the other" through binary terms and provides a series of hegemonic assumptions.

The geographic distance implicit in the Polish delegate's words, along with her need to give voice to the voiceless, shows the pre-1960s partial representation of the global female experience at the UN, a picture that became more complete as new members from former colonies joined the organization. Through her intention of rescuing the racial other, Wasilkowska also implied that Eastern European women were comparatively more advanced. Ultimately, since this was a debate about bodily harm—part of a long series of similar speeches—Wasilkowska and the other participants recast the body as the center of female oppression, an objectified body that they could discuss without directly referring to it, or that they could address through emotions of outrage and sensationalist language.

Wasilkowska's words were not unique within the Commission on the Status of Women (CSW), the UN body in charge of women's rights. Through a collaborative imperial feminist effort, delegates at the CSW created a discursive category of woman in the dependent territories. This was a specific kind of woman: a victim of her culture, often represented as an abject creature. The rescuing trend shifted when those who had been represented and narrated became part of the UN in the form of women delegates from post-decolonization nation-states. Even in these new national formations, however, scrutiny of the postcolonial female body showed how intersections between international human rights and the local setting revealed a set of tensions.

In the UN language of women's rights, the discourses around the body, of colonized women first and decolonized women later, had a central role that went from mere condemnation to a quest for technocratic solutions. A persistent observation of the African colonial world in transition identified the private sphere as a site of violence; a trope that later expanded on a global scale (violence against women became part of the mainstream discourse on women's rights at the Vienna Conference of 1993). This process started through the UN's intersections with the dependent territories. I present in this study the unexplored contributions of the early stages of the CSW and its imperial feminist bodily tensions, a historical and theoretical trajectory that allowed for a more complex understanding of discrimination in women's lives. The history of the CSW is dominated by a quest for organizational agency that commissioners, self-consciously or not, struggled to build (doing so without questioning the status quo), working around patriarchy, empires, and the nation.

Women, Empires, and Body Politics at the United Nations 1946–1975 tells the story of how the female body was at the center of the international politics of promotion and obstruction of women's rights in the postwar period and how traditional European empires' locales were instrumental in the formulation of UN gender politics. Observing the status of women in the dependent territories produced a clear shift in the commission's politics; from a commitment to national laws as an indicator of women's equality to a focus on actual practices that, in their view, perpetuated discrimination against women. This shift is foundational to my argument, because what appeared as a hegemonic politics, through which Western delegates assumed their superiority, contributed in reality to a definition of discriminating practices for women everywhere. Women from the Global South pushed back, showing that expressions such as "backwardness" did not help the plight of women's rights but instead contributed to separations and hierarchies. Moreover, they were the ones who observed that women were oppressed everywhere. All commissioners had to face, however, the limitation intrinsic in human rights, which were considered universal and women's rights, which were thought of as a different category, in need of constant adjustments. In a concentric dimension, women first and women in the colonial world later became groups in need of extra elements to be inserted within the fabric of international human rights.

The UN category of women's rights emerged from a dialectical and diplomatic process that saw first the inclusion of sex equality in the UN Charter, followed by the creation of the UN Commission on the Status of Women. Most UN constituencies had to be convinced of the goodness and viability of a category of human rights only for women. The politics at the basis of women's rights revolved around women's bodies or a reinforced bodily understanding of womanhood. The rhetoric to build international provisions for women regarded them first as entrapped outside of the political arena, as the bearers of war sacrifice, and as professionally constrained. Later, conceptions of women's rights were connected to more private and specifically bodily dimensions, exemplified by displacement, trafficking, and, ultimately, reproducing the nation.

The most central locale for bodily dimensions was the empire, in its expanded understanding of colonial and postcolonial spheres. Dependent territories—either de facto colonies or territories under international administration—offered the sensationalism UN representatives needed to create a sense of urgency for the establishment of international women's rights. In a crescendo that rose from struggles and justifications resembling nineteenth-century women's suffrage rhetoric to more sophisticated representations of bodily pain, UN women's delegates were able to sensitize international audiences to a whole spectrum of problems identified within the colonial world. Like their nineteenth-century predecessors, in fact, the empire in its different configurations allowed them a prominent role as rescuers.

Empire meant many things within the UN setting. The UN Charter divided the colonial world into trust territories (under international administration) and non-self-governing territories. With the separation came a violence-free colonial language geared toward modern management and development. Along the lines of John Robinson and Ronald Gallagher's popular work on formal and informal imperial control, at the UN there were also multiple instances that resembled colonialism; the occupation of Japan, the partition of Palestine, the expansion of Soviet power into central Asian countries, and U.S. internal racial and legal segregation.[3] Besides these instances of informal control and the internationalization of colonialism, the charter also included new principles that allowed for the formulation of women's rights.

The UN language on equality created a set of binaries connected to the categories inscribed within the charter articles. Sex and racial equality specifically shaped a dialectical politics of man versus woman and white versus nonwhite in Western empires, which epitomized ideal rhetorical and physical sites onto which to contest such tensions. Within these interconnections two different trajectories emerged, both belonging to the postwar moment: cultural relativism and technocracy, both modern and progressive, but also antithetical to each other. Cultural relativism and technocracy are opposite, but they worked together against women. From one side the UN promoted assessing, measuring, planning, and recommending; on the other side, when it came to women, it promoted realism based on the assumed lack of Western understanding of non-Western cultures. Not understanding appeared as modern as anti-Eurocentrism and new, an alternative to the old civilizing mission. The female body became the terrain on which the UN played out this modern dichotomy. For example, polygamy was first declared a demeaning evil for women but was later sanctioned and accepted by the

UN because of economic realism. Similarly, so-called rituals that allegedly harmed the female body were first sensationally rejected and then declared cultural practices and not medical ones, according to the cultural relativist assumption that culture does not harm.

The history of the emergence of postcolonial nations allows me to focus on differences among newly formed and existing states in relation to the status of women. Decolonization highlighted substantial disparities in economic growth between postcolonial states and the rest of the world. Commissioners participated in the debate of how to promote and implement development plans. What is original and compelling in this analysis is the association between the lack of economic growth in former colonies and the goal of fighting discrimination against women. Through this tandem interpretation of development and equality, commissioners carefully combined their work on the 1967 Declaration on the Elimination of Discrimination Against Women (DEDAW) with the attention to women's place in the larger international project of economic development. Ultimately, the transnational interaction between women from the Global North and Global South and their joint efforts to change women's lives globally is crucial for understanding how the commission envisioned the changing status of the postwar gender order.

The UN Commission on the Status of Women

Founded in 1946 and still operative today, the United Nations Commission on the Status of Women (CSW) was created to promote and implement international measures to raise the status of women worldwide. Through its ambitious goals of identifying and ending the inequality constraining women's lives globally, the CSW inaugurated a sustained relationship between the new UN international system of human rights, empires, and women.

First conceived as a subcommission of the Human Rights Commission (HRC), the CSW was created instead as a full commission dependent on the Economic and Social Council (ECOSOC). This shift might appear purely logistic, but it highlights the problematic relationship between the universalism of human rights and the special attention that women's and gender issues required. At that time some state representatives, Eleanor Roosevelt among them, thought that a commission solely dedicated to women's rights would duplicate the HRC and perpetuate the subaltern status of women's issues in the newly formed international organization. Conversely, other delegates, such as the Danish Bodil Begtrup and the Dominican Minerva Bernardino, insisted on the formation of a separate entity in charge of women's rights because they feared that within a larger framework, women's issues would be ignored. The new commission had both organizational support within the UN and legal justification through new international legal instruments. First the UN Charter and later the Universal Declaration of Human Rights provided the international principles underpinning the commission's work, as for example, the above-mentioned "sex equality clause" in the charter.

From its creation until the mid-1950s, the CSW worked on political rights and the public sphere. From the late 1950s to 1975, the commission worked on the private sphere and economic rights, promoted the participation of women in development, and also worked for nondiscrimination in all aspects of women's lives. The turning point, the best-known and most effective activist moment, was the proclamation of the International Women's Year (IWY) in 1975 and the preparation for the Mexico City Women's World Conference, the first international gathering of what became the Decade for Women, 1975–1985.

Since the early stages of its operations, the CSW placed a special emphasis on the colonial world.[4] From the very first meeting, commissioners claimed that the audience and beneficiaries of their advocacy were "the women of the world." The UN membership was based on the status of nationhood; dependent territories, with the exception of India and Pakistan, which became independent soon after the creation of the UN, did not enjoy full membership.[5] Assuming the women of the world as the constituency of the CSW encouraged animated debates on women living under imperial rule and the question of extending UN resolutions, conventions, and declarations to dependent territories.

The CSW drafted four conventions in the initial decades of its existence: the Convention on the Political Rights of Women (adopted in 1952), the Convention on the Nationality of Married Women (adopted in 1957), the Convention on Consent to Marriage, Minimum Age for Marriage, and Registration of Marriages (adopted in 1965), and the Declaration on the Elimination of Discrimination against Women (adopted in 1967).

In the 1950s the commission attempted to draft a convention on the elimination of dowry, bride-price, sati, and child marriage. The CSW along with the HRC led the debates over these issues, especially in light of the later controversy (1959) with the World Health Organization (WHO) over the practice of female genital modification. For most commissioners, this practice endangered women's lives. Nevertheless, for the WHO, the matter was cultural and not medical. This topic represented another problematic aspect as well: for new postcolonial members of the commission, with their charged colonial pasts, such scrutiny challenged the boundaries between the commission's operations and the principle of self-determination. In an interview, former British UN delegate Margaret Bruce claimed that during a UN seminar in Togo (1964), commissioners abandoned the topic of gender and traditions in the developing countries when African women expressively requested that only non-Western women deal with the subject in question (family law).[6] This example shows how the commission became a useful tool for postcolonial countries' delegates to manifest dissent against intrusion into their local culture. Tension between commissioners from different areas of the world increased once national development became the new focus of the CSW.

The economic boom of the 1960s encouraged new studies on the possibilities of expanding the benefits of development to disadvantaged areas of the world. Development became a "trend," and the UN was deeply involved in experimentation and projection of economic growth for destitute countries. Women as a group were excluded from development projects because both international aid organizations and recipients of international aid considered men the exclusive agents of development. Women in the Global South, however, pushed to have a bigger role.[7]

The CSW participated in the debate over development and challenged the exclusion of women. This time signals a shift of focus in the commission's work: from political to economic rights. The role of the CSW in the gendered debate over development offers two different sides: the function of gender in the passage from political to economic rights and the category of development as creator of new North/South differences in terms of knowledge, technology, and the condition of women. Conceptions of development produced new hierarchies between women from developed and underdeveloped areas and a sort of neo-imperial feminism, but this time with resistance from the formerly "voiceless."

The 1967 DEDAW, for example, is representative of the commission's activity in promoting measures in favor of women and development; it also captures tensions among the commissioners. One of the aims of the declaration was to "abolish traditional norms and practice that prevented women's equality." This goal introduced traditional norms as a loaded issue and encouraged questions on how the commission negotiated the relationship between gender and development for women in general and especially within former colonies. The case of DEDAW's purpose in matters of cultural norms opened a window onto the contested discourse of the relationship between women and culture within the national and international order. The UN and the commission acted in this historical context as new external definers of culture, norms, and gender roles.

Narratives of the Commission on the Status of Women

Producing a history of women and empires at the UN means being in dialogue with different fields. I draw here on different bodies of scholarship because of intersections between events within and outside of the UN. Specifically, I look at works on the CSW, on the global women's movement, and on decolonization.

Through a realist approach, canonical texts provide a solid chronology of the commission's activity and, sometimes, a direct account, as most authors participated in actual international policy making.[8] Historians have focused on either inserting the CSW into the wider history of the global women's movement or on analyzing a specific country's attitude toward the commission.[9] Ultimately, recent works problematize the contribution of the CSW to issues of labor, issues of violence against women, or a specific convention. A recent edited collection by Rebecca Adami and Dan Plesch focuses on specific women and the UN at large and encourages more gender equity in contemporary international organizations.[10] While all accounts have merit and are useful for building inquiries around the commission, some contribute more to the questions I formulated for this study because of their engagement with the Global South, be it within the context of the Cold War or decolonization.

One example is Eileen Boris's chapter titled "Equality's Cold War: The ILO and the UN Commission on the Status of Women, 1946–1970s," which through careful archival research in multiple countries, analyzes the tension of expertise on economic rights between the International Labour Organization (ILO) and the CSW. Boris shows the central role of the debates between liberal and protectionist discourse on women's labor—a separation that emerged for bodily reasons, which constrained women's labor and which recalls the multiple tensions universalism created since man was the universalized category.[11] In a more recent monograph, Boris engages more with women in the Global South and shows how the ILO was a space in which the creation of the category "woman worker" intersected with other dimensions such as race and class.[12] When reading both works, one gets the sense of how labor and the category of working woman are instrumental to understanding the impact of the Cold War in the creation of independent nation-states.

Important accounts on specific countries and the CSW have been contributed by Helen Laville on the U.S. and Britain, Jan Lambertz on the CSW and Europe in general, and more recently by Lisa Baldez on the U.S. and the 1979 Convention on the Elimination of All Forms of Discrimination Against Women (CEDAW).[13] Laville argues that rivalries among U.S. women's organizations contributed to different political positions on the creation of the CSW. She also looks at a shift in the British government's attitude toward the CSW. In Laville's opinion, this change was due to the effective activism of British women's organizations. Similarly, Lambertz claims that in post-1945 Europe, war-led emergencies did not leave as much space for a women's rights agenda. Specifically, she refers to the displacement of people, Cold War antagonisms, and the continued presence of empires facing decolonization. These two contributions are central for understanding contentious local attitudes toward the CSW. Baldez instead looks at the CSW's work in the history of the UN instruments that fought discrimination against women. She shows how Cold War competing politics pushed American representatives at the UN to devalue the role of the commission, where the Soviets were instead pretty active.

Other scholars in economics and legal studies have engaged with the CSW to trace either the long history of development within the UN or the challenges of self-determination for the indigenous populations. Devaki

Jain's monograph looks at the CSW as a part of a longer process, the history of women and development within the UN.[14] Her work clearly shows women's agency in a process that led to the recognition of the gender component in the discourse of development. Jain places women delegates from the Global South at the center of the process that brought and reinforced the politics of development. Karen Knop's work on self-determination and minorities is fundamental for an understanding of the commission's work in the colonial world.[15] In the context of the CSW, she shows how the Trusteeship Council conceived of equalities from a Western point of view. Knop highlights how the CSW shifted from promoting UN-led self-determination to advocacy for decolonization as a general goal, independent of the UN.

Histories of the women's movement, be they global or dedicated to a specific geographic area, do mention the CSW and are useful for tracing a parallel trajectory that goes from white middle-class Western women who participated in the movement to transnational Black women, women from the Global South, and women from Eastern Europe. *Breaking the Wave* has been especially useful for identifying the presence of Black internationalism, previously analyzed from a male perspective by Penny Von Eschen and Carol Anderson,[16] but now deepened with more recent archival research that traces the central role of women of color in internationalism.

Written from the UN perspective and with an intention of decolonizing the archives, Rebecca Adami's work focuses on the participation of women of color in the drafting of the Universal Declaration of Human Rights. Adami rightly observes that power obscured the voices of women delegates from the Global South (specifically, India, Pakistan, and the Dominican Republic) who instead contributed to a universal definition of human rights. In her view, the final product reflects "their different religious and cultural values" and includes them in the Declaration.[17]

Jocelyn Olcott and Katherine Marino show different phases of Latin American women's engagements with women's rights.[18] Olcott focuses on the results of women's political divisions across traditional Cold War lines at the UN Conference in Mexico City. She claims that women's international groups had to let go of the official and agreed on script/agenda to allow representatives to freely disagree and dismantle the rigid conference organization; this adjustment to the participants and their needs contributed to the first global feminist event. Marino's book talks about an earlier time, but it is salient for assessing the contributions of Latin American women to the global women's movement.

Along the trend of decolonizing knowledge is the work of Francisca de Haan.[19] She argues that Cold War prejudices have had a role in the historiography of the women's movement and charges feminists in capitalist countries with failing to question the role of the West in colonial practices that kept the Global South underdeveloped. In a way, de Haan is encouraging a decolonization of the history of the global women's movement, one that also strips this history of stereotypical images of Soviet Bloc women who blindly promoted communism. Her point about the politicization of UN representatives is especially observable through the sources of this study. There was a clear double standard on what "political" meant in the diplomacy of intergovernmental organizations. Women representatives were expected to be "proper," and "proper" meant pushing for formal gender equality, which never questioned the structures of specific political and economic systems. Kristen Ghodsee's scholarship on the contribution of the Soviet Union to questions of economic rights is a concrete example of how to transcend Cold War categories when analyzing the history of women's movements.[20]

Useful for the larger context in which the commission operated are works on the UN and decolonization since they look at the power dynamics between anticolonial groups and traditional colonial power. A significant example is the chapter by Gordon Morrell that traces a new "higher stage" of imperialism through the Trusteeship Council and the struggle over the oversight of colonies.[21] Another important work that shows the ambiguous position of the United States as a non-self-identifying colonial power with clear imperial ambition is the article by Martin Thomas on the case of France and Algeria and the danger of debating colonialism at the UN. More recent works look at the hybrid nature of the UN position as a global stage for both colonizing and colonized groups.[22] The work of Roland Burke is instrumental to understanding the ambiguity of the concept of human rights and its use and complex history in the creation of the postcolonial state.[23] Burke, Marco Duranti, and Dirk Moses have also produced a very recent edited collection that looks at human rights as part of the discourse of anticolonialism and as constitutive of the postcolonial state.[24]

In dialogue with these works, I examine here both the colonial and postcolonial politics of the csw in order to show the passage of women representatives from the dependent territories as they moved from the objects of debates on women's rights to voices that participated in them. The thread that runs through the different parts of the book allows for a history of tensions, alliances, and conceptual variations of the body politics of empire at the UN. These beliefs toward the colonial world must be inscribed in the long history of the relationship between international women's rights and empires and in contemporary inquiries into the meanings and archives of decolonization.

Bodies, Feminisms, and Hegemonic Categories

The methodology applied here deals with body politics, a concept that may often appear elusive or esoteric. The use of the body as a category to interpret the past has had intermittent success from the 1980s to today. The *politics* part of *body politics* concerns power and, specifically, the way in which the representation of bodies has served (and still serves) to reinforce asymmetries of power, and with what outcomes and consequences. I provide here a conceptual and historiographic map that proceeds from general discussions of the body in history to the more specific case underpinned in this study.

The politics of the body are by definition multidisciplinary, as the body has been the focus of inquiry in fields from biology and medicine to the social sciences and humanities. In terms of the history of the category itself, multiple intellectual "moments" shed light on the body as a term of analysis. The main shifts are connected to religion, philosophy, feminist theory, postmodernism, and contemporary responses to canonical texts, as well as responses to the politics of oppression. The Christian duality of body and soul, Cartesian rationalism, the social contract, feminism from an early liberal understanding to the notion of "the personal is political," the cyborg, and gender performativity are all theoretical constructs that have contributed to the understanding of the body.

Periodically, scholars have written state-of-the-field surveys of the history of the body. Catherine Gallagher and Thomas Laqueur (1983), Roy Porter (1991), and Kathleen Canning (1999) have made assessments of whether the body has functioned effectively in historiography.[25] These scholars treat the issue of race and empire as separated from a general understanding of the epistemological possibilities of the history of the body. It seems that once the option of writing materiality and subjectivity into history can be done, more sophisticated levels of analysis will be possible. Within this realm, the body politics of empires, both in the *métropole* and in the colony, and later, imperial attitudes within the UN can reveal assumptions about power in both the national and international contexts.

Despite centering on different questions, more recent works have buttressed my analysis, among them, the applicability of the body to labor history by Ava Baron and Eileen Boris, and Vrushali Patil's theory of embodiment and disembodiment.[26] Baron and Boris inquire after the usefulness of the body in labor history. In their view, "'The body' allows difference to be incorporated more fully, for it is one of the most powerful and pervasive cultural symbols that define who and what we are."[27] As the authors point out, some social categories are embodied—"they are defined" by their own bodies—because bodies signify relations of power, notably for "women, men of color, and marginalized groups." Baron and Boris's inclusion of the Barthesian "myth" is particularly useful in showing that what might appear as neutral is in truth masculine and, therefore, exclusionary of women's participation, as is the case, for example, of labor unions. They also share with cultural historians of the body an understanding whereby bodies come metaphorically to represent something else. Baron and Boris encourage an analysis in which "bodily discourses are specified, interpreted, and applied in various contexts." They consider labor as embodied both in terms of race and gender and as a "social categorization" drawing on "bodies as a resource" as well as identity. Their article is especially useful because international law universalized "man," and policy provisions of women's rights had to create "woman" as an international legal category.

Also instrumental to this analysis is the work of Vrushali Patil on the United Nations and decolonization. Patil looks at the "modern geopolitical order" of the post-Westphalian system as the architect of identities and differences through "embodiment politics." In her understanding, bodies are metaphors of order and disorder. She observes that in the West, "the body or the bodily" has served to indicate "the uncontrollable, the irrational, the emotional, the uncivilized, the savage and the barbaric in some pervasive and systematic ways." The process of embodiment, in Patil's argument, generated two categories: the "disembodied," representing order, and the "embodied," disorder. The salient point of her analysis is that power "constructs some identities as subjects while simultaneously producing others as less than subjects." Drawing on contemporary commentaries on the contractual philosophers as the group of Enlightenment intellectuals that defined the agreement between the ruling authority and citizens (or subjects), Patil shows how the imaginary citizen of social contracts is a disembodied abstraction. Conversely, this abstraction then created the disorderly "embodied" groups. She observes how debates on decolonization at the UN General Assembly compelled a shift away from an understanding of kinship politics, in which the European colonizer functioned as orderly/ fatherly and the African colonized as disorderly/offspring.

My work is especially concerned with female bodies within colonial narratives. Historically, the female body has been the object of theories, policies, and politics that continue to permeate the present. As Elizabeth Grosz says: "Women are somehow more biological, more corporeal, and more natural than men."[28] In this objectification of the female body, power had and still has a role. In the history of women and empires at the UN, the power component regards commissioners' definitions, collaborations, and eventual extreme challenges to their own assumptions. In a way, those challenges show how the CSW grew along progressive lines from hegemony-dominated into a more diverse entity. Also, in terms of heritage, the same attributes employed to disempower women were used to gender the colonized population abroad and the working class at home.[29] So the history of body politics has a twinned nature: one that is connected to historicism and to how the body became a category of inquiry and another connected to the history of encounters between the West and the rest. Together, these trajectories constitute the body politics with which this monograph engages.

UN policies assumed a specific understanding of the female body. Some international policy provisions aimed to discipline bodily practices as well as limiting the possibilities of female bodies in terms of space, labor, and reproduction. Furthermore, as I show in more detail in the next section, UN visual materials portrayed bodies in specific modalities and arguably with specific intentions, be they reconstituting justice or attracting global compassion. In some other instances, discussions about women indirectly refer to men and their role in society and in the nation-state as assumed and in no need of further justification. Such analyses hold both men and women as two complementary and collaborative categories but render women as bodies whose inclusion in the nation-state is in need of constant justification.

The CSW united and divided the category "woman," and it did so through body politics. Commissioners built two categories of women: the rescuers and the rescued. The rescuers assumed, without questioning, the suffering and limitations of the rescued women's bodies. Commissioners could operate along the lines of disembodied and embodied because race made corporeality evident and vivid and because of the colonial tradition of "humanitarian" and civilizing efforts. The female body can be rescued—in theory—from the constructed-as-male practices that torment it, but it is never rescued from colonial policies of overwork and exploitation. For example, Silvia Federici agrees that postwar family planning policies in the developing world—a topic treated in this book—were based on the fear of revenge of the postcolonial population asking for reparations for colonialism, a bigger population would have asked more forcefully.[30]

When immersed in the framework of human rights, the body functions also as the border of universalism, as its ultimate test—which it constantly fails. Allowing for the self-determination of the female body collided with the designs of the new nation-state. In nation-building understandings, men could contribute through autonomy, but women were required to contribute through limitations, sacrifices, and bodily modifications. The other constraint on universalism was Western interference which recalled the colonial period and which was then seen as bringing gender disruption. Commissioners from the former colonial territories and then from the developing world had to grasp and negotiate the tension between rights and cultural relativism.

While this study acknowledges the actual and possible dichotomy between representation and lived experience, international policies had and have a real impact on everyday life, so the ways in which bodies are framed have serious consequences. For example, the shift from a cultural to a medical approach to "female genital cutting" generated a series of local programs and wider discussions both to fight the practice and, at the other extreme, to welcome it as the ultimate anticolonial resistance and anti-Western interference. Some of the bodily dimensions that I analyze here are indirect and objective, as in the case of knowledge that relegated women to be safe only within their communities and deemed the binomial of education and urban setting as a danger for women's lives and dignity. I also engage with more direct bodily implications expressed in violence, trafficking, pain, and reproduction. The defining authorities of all these bodily manifestations are the various entities of the UN that debated and deliberated on women's issues.

The theme of trafficking runs throughout the stories of this book. While the League of Nations and the UN later dealt with prostitution and trafficking, what I mean here is something slightly different. I define trafficking as the violence of dragging female bodies from one place to another one. In general, while I do not dismiss the individual or nonanonymous experience, viewing bodies in this way represents a critique of a male universalizing category in internationalism and more indirectly to the international women's activism which is often based on comparisons and hierarchies.

I also engage here with different types of feminism that coexist and simultaneously represent a progression in the history of feminisms. Depending on the setting and the inquiry, liberal, imperial, and transnational feminisms can represent both a continuum and a coexistence. These theories can be seen as following the ontological path of the relationship between women and nations. Liberal feminism relies on the rule of law to establish gender equality and to insert women within the social contract. Imperial feminism can be part of the same project, but with the additional elements of exploiting the universal category of womanhood and subsuming difference within a Western model, without considering socially based categories and without challenging the empire. Meanwhile, transnational feminism represents the awareness that the nation-state itself is based on and reinforced through exclusions.[31] In this study, I use these approaches to categorize the relationships between the commissioners and the types of changes they aimed to implement in women's lives.

These different conceptions of advancing women's rights are based on a diverse range of assumptions. General scholarly agreement identifies the commission's politics as "liberal" and devoted to formal equality.[32] Indeed, the goal of changing the status of women through states' laws encouraged commissioners to embrace the nation-state and to overlook it as an agent of discrimination in women's lives. Commissioners believed in the law without considering the structural and cultural exclusionary forces that nations created and reproduced. Furthermore, along with the focus on the law, some commissioners also produced exclusionary mechanisms by defining themselves against a set of "others."[33]

Within the Cold War setting, such self-reflective operations occurred with both Western and Eastern (Soviet Bloc) commissioners. The difference between these two groups, which also represented fluid alliances, was that the Soviet Bloc delegates identified capitalism and racism as interlocking forces that caused discrimination against women. Historians have shown how the Soviet Bloc used the Jim Crow system as an example of American hypocrisy—promoting democracy abroad and simultaneously perpetuating racial segregation at home.[34] Because of the coincidence of Soviet commissioners' opinions with typical Cold War attacks against American racial politics, their interventions at the CSW on this topic were often dismissed as propaganda. A less cynical approach can show how, in contrast to the reinforcement of U.S. empire, the USSR and its allies actually supported the anticolonial struggle—even if in problematic terms. As I mentioned earlier, Soviet Bloc women delegates assumed the role of defenders of the colonial cause. In light of my previous analysis of feminisms, looking at the "other" as a category in need of protection generated political strategies that aligned with imperial feminism.

The scholarship on imperial feminism mostly draws on Edward Said's *Orientalism*.[35] In Said's analysis, East and West have become metaphors to signify power relations. The West defined the East as backward in order to define itself as modern. British feminist activists Valerie Amos and Pratibha Parmar's influential article, "Challenging Imperial Feminism," has been the inspiration for many other works which look at the racist genealogy of white feminism. Along these lines, for example, Antoinette Burton illustrates how Victorian feminists defined themselves against the colonized female population of India.[36]

In the context of the CSW, this approach helps to highlight imperial feminist attitudes emerging from different locales, and not exclusively from the so-called West. If Said and Burton are useful for my understanding of the intersection between colonialism and Cold War rivalries, the work of Chandra Mohanty on imperial feminism has been instrumental for my recognition of feminist-based tensions and geopolitical issues within the commission.[37] Mohanty criticizes feminist movements that focus on the assumption that the Western model of womanhood is the only one. Such direction is highly problematic, she says, because it erases differences among women. This is especially true when hegemonic forces of assumed superiority construct an "other" woman within the general group "women." Therefore, Mohanty is critical of the category of "global sisterhood" because it hides the oppression of women of color by both Western men and women.[38] In a colonial and postcolonial analysis of UN gender politics, Mohanty's theory helps shed critical light on the commission-based category of "women of the world." This macro category was just rhetorical pretense; from the very beginning, commissioners themselves fragmented the group by creating and isolating the category of "woman in the dependent territories."

My last methodological insight on feminisms identifies transnational feminism as an alternative category and political project transcending the separations that imperial feminisms help generate. Transnational feminism is anachronistic for the twentieth-century CSW, but the category can serve as a lens through which to test the findings of the project. In their popular book *Scattered Hegemonies*, Inderpal Grewal and Caren Kaplan discuss the possibilities of linking feminisms around the world without reproducing "cultural and economic hegemony."[39] The commissioners were not self-consciously transnational feminists in contemporary terms. However, this category is helpful for looking at the restored balance of voices within the CSW as well as at the actual "scattered hegemonies" in the formulation of women's rights.

Imperial feminist attitudes changed when delegates from former colonies joined the UN in general and the commission in particular. The symbol of transnational feminist politics as a challenge to hegemony was the category of backwardness. Widely used by first- and second-world commissioners, the label served to define one's own "equality" in oppositional terms with women in the colonies and developing countries. There was also an unexpected twist in the use of backwardness: delegates from imperial powers denied that backwardness was a problem specific to women in the colonies. This argument served to absolve colonial administrations from responsibility for the lack of modernization in the colonies. Within a transnational feminist framework, delegates from the Arab world reacted to the label of backwardness, often used by European and Latin American commissioners, and claimed a political impasse unless the interlocutors believed in the equality of all the participants. They specified in clear terms that, as long as they were called "backward," it would be impossible to establish a dialogue on matters of equality (see chapter 6). The consequence of such reactions pushed all commissioners to realize that inequality existed everywhere and was not confined to the Global South.

Ideas and conceptions of women's rights and historical contexts (national and international) emerged from UN debates. The format of the book therefore revolves around debates, the close reading of international law, and other instruments such as petitions, reports from the UN and its agencies, and exchanges between delegates. Each chapter includes photos from the UN collection to show how the UN represented itself, its programs, and in general what depictions it wanted to leave for posterity. These images reinforce the main findings of the book and serve as a remarkable source of their own for the style and narratives they convey.

A Note on Images

Each chapter of the book includes an image from the UN Photo Archive. Since body politics is a component of this story, images of people depicted in specific contexts are instrumental to this analysis. The visual materials provide a parallel configuration that, through a livelier format, shows how the UN chose to represent itself, through which narratives, and the alleged roles these photos had for the larger public. They are in fact part of a longer story about the relationship between this specific type of photo and its audience. Arguably, the UN photos are restorative of justice and aim to prove the universality of that restored justice. Furthermore, from an organizational point of view, the photos are a celebration, tangible evidence of the UN success. However, as Tina Campt argues, photos have a "quiet" part; in the case of the selected photo, the quiet is the history of gender and empires in multiple modalities of formal and informal control.[40] The first traceable historical layer is certainly connected to the documentary photo, but the quiet part is about hegemonic relationships.

The history of this type of photo, one that aims at humanity and restorative justice, is tied to a specific trajectory that appeared through photographic stories during the Great Depression and continued with World War II with the need to document the battlefield. Both events constitute a conceptual map to understand the role of UN photos. The two layers—the evident and the quiet—met in the Cold War renditions in which claims of universality turned into claims of neo-Western superiority, far from traditional nineteenth-century empires but still with a specific suggestive hierarchy.

Before the Great Depression and its photographic success, European leftist activists had already used images to denounce the mistreatment of the working class.[41] This type of photo clearly identified victims and perpetrators of the capitalist system. Deriving from this tradition, the documentary photo emerged more strongly in 1930s United States with the role of "educating the public about the experience of hardship and injustice."[42] As will be so later for the UN photos, pictures as witnesses of injustice do not attribute responsibility but instead create a specific set of emotions for the receiver of the image.

Within this context, New Deal agencies promoted the production of visual materials. Some of them are iconic, like Dorothea Lange's photo of a mother with her children.[43] Arguably, the photo was successful because the mother recalled Christian narratives of motherhood and sacrifice. It generated specific emotions such as compassion, and it was representative of the hardship people sustained under the Great Depression. This tradition of photos as testimony of suffering continued during World War II; both traditions turned photos into the representation of moments of national pride. Furthermore, Lange's photo inaugurated the gendered politics of pity that contemporary feminist scholars detect in images of women as icons of pain.

As compared to images of the Depression, World War II photos also showed the desire of the public to follow events on the battlefields. Innovations in technology and travel allowed photographers to visit the different fronts scattered around the globe and provide their pictorial point of view.[44] Photographers such as John Morris saw their work as "a glorification of war," showing that the perspective of the photo taker could determine a specific narrative.[45] Eventually, photographing the war also became a matter of showing justice or injustice. Images had emotional power depending on the conflict. Photos of World War II served to reinforce the bright line between good and evil in that conflict. Photos of the Vietnam War blurred that line.

One tradition became consolidated: documentary photos showed the horrors of war but also a universal humanity. If one looks closer, the presumption of universality became fragmented immediately after World War II. In the context of the Cold War, photos served to document the assumed superiority of capitalist countries. As Eric Sandeen claims, "The eye of the photographer and the layout of the editor reinforced the deceptively simple ideology of the victors. Finally, these pictures became a part of an American project abroad that included both marketing and foreign-policy objectives, the two often intertwined."[46] Arguably, Cold War photos were also derivative of nineteenth-century colonial photos, which through orientalist images, reinforced the constructed superiority of the West and the image of the Orient as a sensual and backward place.[47] The difference was in the rhetoric: while colonialism used differences to reinforce dominance, Cold War photos were more subtle; they were aspirational and depicted the benefits of capitalism as adaptable to all humanity. It was in fact in the context of the Cold War, and with the intentions of reconstructing a universal humanity, that the 1955 Museum of Modern Art (MOMA) exhibition *The Family of Man* used photography to ease the tension of the Cold War and emphasize the commonalities of human beings.[48]

The UN itself was part of the exhibition. The photos aimed to show one humanity along with the danger of nuclear war: a danger without culprits. The heteronormative family represented a nonpolitical entity, a common way for humanity to organize that transcended (in theory) the polarization of the Cold War. Moreover, the photos, confirmed constructed notions of the superiority of the West. Through a selective use of anthropological views, the MOMA exhibition showed how societies functioned and how there was "a presumably common sentiment." The sentiment was a Western one that irradiated universally.[49] At the exhibition the UN offered a nonpartisan understanding of peace and justice, one connected to the Universal Declaration of Human Rights.[50]

The photos in this work are part of the tradition of the documentary photo to restore justice. From these images the viewer can extract the specific direction of the UN at a specific moment. However, the UN was (and still is) an organization, and as such had to show the success of its enterprise— which incidentally and rhetorically aimed at justice.

Little is said of the creators of these photos, as they were often the work of freelancers. One popular UN photographer, however, was Todd Webb, who depicted the hope of decolonization and development under the form of Western-style infrastructures and fashion in the new postcolonial states.[51] After the heyday of development and common (yet hierarchized) humanity, images had to translate a more complex moment in which some colonial tropes reemerged along with photos of war and a sense of restorative justice that simplified victims and perpetrators. While the scope of this work ends with 1975, specific discussions of specific photos shed light on the politics of visible and invisible bodies and hegemonic international politics.

Feminist scholars of human rights such as Wendy Hesford and Wendy Kozol have analyzed the popular image, the "Afghan girl," on the 1985 cover of National Geographic.[52] The photo, by Magnum photographer Steven McCurry, became to Western audiences the immediately recognizable icon of the refugee. The specific history of Afghanistan, the last vestige of Cold War imperialism and, later, the terrain of the controversial war on terror (ended only recently in more tragedy), allowed for more layers of interpretation. Specifically, the image of the female refugee served to construct Afghanistan as "female" and in need of Western help through the politics of pity the image inspires.

Hesford and Kozol argue that this young woman became the symbol of "Afghans in need of rescue." Their commentary on this image is to me representative of all the historical trajectories described here in which Western consumption, able photographers of exotic locales, and rigid hierarchies of "the West and the rest" allowed for this photo to became a symbol and the embodiment of the gendered understanding of sympathy and the "aesthetization of suffering."[53] As the authors claim, photos like this "facilitate voyeuristic First World perspectives on Third World subjects, namely women, as passive victims and depict them as 'authentic insiders.'" The photo became even more popular when a second photo of the portrayed Afghan woman, Sharbat Gula, appeared years later with a documentary about the quest for *the lost* Afghan girl. For whom, Hesford and Kozol asked, was she lost? They connect this story to the *Family of Man* exhibition: "Rhetorically, the documentary creates a sympathetic gaze of identification by enabling Western viewers to see themselves. The use of images of family to establish legitimacy and boundaries of the nation abound in American culture from the famous Family of Man exhibition to Laura Bush's use of familial discourse to define the bombings in Afghanistan."[54] The Bush administration made ample use and showed the still powerful scale of imperial feminist rhetoric, rescuing Afghan women by moving a war "of terror" toward the country.

With all these directions in mind, I chose photos that portray the events described in the chapters. I provide an interpretation of the photos that connect them with the major tropes described above and the specific themes of the chapters. The images are also representative of change over time in the UN world. They depict specific UN meetings or initiatives sponsored by the UN. Most photos portray the constructed "other," whether in glorifying terms or in terms hungry for Western pity. Portraying women within and beyond the colonial context has a long history that served to reinforce colonial asymmetries of power, and in more recent times, the multilayered meanings that range from postcolonial settings to contemporary modalities of informal control.

A Note on UN Delegates, Voices, and Archives

This monograph centers on the debates among commissioners, the assumptions of commissioners, and the specific politics that emerged at the CSW. The main focus is the CSW meeting records with references that came from the ECOSOC, the Trusteeship Council, the General Assembly, the ILO, UNESCO, and the WHO. The ECOSOC's plenary meetings sometimes reinforced the same Cold War conflicts that were played out within the CSW, but the space dedicated to the commission's reports was not central.

Commissioners themselves appealed to the ILO and UNESCO, as these agencies were more aligned with the CSW's work.[55] UNESCO and ILO, for their parts, spoke of commissioners as friendly but always pointed out how the expertise lay with the agencies and not with governmental representatives. UNESCO even claimed that John Humphrey, the director of the HRC, looked forward to demonstrating that the agency did not support the UN, a statement that highlighted organizational tensions.[56] While other agencies such as FAO and UNICEF played a role later on, they are seldom mentioned in the CSW's records between 1946 and 1975.

In some instances, the chapters focus on events indirectly related to the CSW, such as the "scandal" of the Fon of Bikom, the issue of female genital modification, and the seminars sponsored by the Human Rights Advisory Program. Some issues, like female circumcision, called for concerted action in which multiple UN parties participated. Overall, the UN system involves multiple sources and responses to issues. The driving narratives here come from the voices of the commissioners.

When writing on the UN, the historian is confronted with the challenge of whether to include the background of the delegates. Some of them were well-known politicians and left a substantial record; others were just occasional state representatives. Providing each delegate's intervention with a biography would disrupt the main narrative and would suggest that the background of the debater always had a deterministic relationship to her/his intervention.

Noticeably, historical accounts in which male delegates are central to a specific event do not even mention the person in question but equate the representative with the country; so "France said" rather than name and background of the speaker. Diplomatic historians often mention the country as the main agent of policies with the intended understanding that a delegate voiced the position of a specific nation-state. These works are usually about male representatives and suggest that men do not need to be mentioned as they are fully associated with the nation-state. This issue presents a challenge for the history of women's delegates, as if they needed a background check in order to justify their historical role. Nuances are necessary here.

Some delegates were known in international activism even before joining the United Nations, and their pre-UN experience was relevant to their UN work. A good example is Minerva Bernardino who, even as a state delegate, always made clear her own history of internationalism and human rights advocacy. Others became recognizable for their consistent records within the UN. For example, sources show that the Soviet representative Elizaveta Popova and the Iraqi delegate Bedia Afnan were voices that distinguished themselves for their coherent and strong positions through the years.[57] The general assumption is that all delegates were instructed by their governments on specific positions to assume vis-à-vis a specific issues. However, even within this rigid rule of diplomacy, some representatives claimed special attention for women's issues. I tried to highlight what I deemed as useful to the narrative flow of chapters, but I do not follow a rigid model regarding who is mentioned and who is provided with a detailed background.

I consciously attempt, however, to give space to delegates from the Global South when the record is available—even by simply providing the names of seminar participants. When necessary to the efficacy of a debate, I add more background information to make the connection between words and experience more obvious. U.S. commissioners' records are the most available including their contribution to national politics, but I tend not to engage with them because the imbalance of background information would reproduce the same hegemonic thrust that I am attempting to disrupt. I include more background on Dorothy Kenyon, as she symbolized an exceptional case of an early commissioner.

Arguably, documented remarks represent a combination of speaker's background, bloc politics (First, Second, or Third world), governmental instructions, and even religious attitudes. Sometimes political and religious positions overlapped; at other times, one can trace a unique derailing from the expected alliance of her or his country. These were never blatant statements but rather attitudes to be traced in speeches such as agreements, congratulations, and other formal gestures. Women's issues presented more fluid bloc politics; for example, there was a clear imperial West (France, the UK, and Belgium) that fiercely argued in favor of empires until the late 1950s, even if those countries disagreed on other issues. Countries such as Denmark and the Dominican Republic often agreed on women's issues primarily because their representatives had a long and strong international record on women's rights that existed before the UN. The new postcolonial nations sometimes had to defend Christianity, equality, and women's rights at the same time, a challenging position that showed the admirable diplomatic powers of the specific representative.

In the case of women, issues of epistemic authority generated even more tensions. In the passage to full commission, the CSW lost the expertise it was able to enjoy as a subcommission. With its new full status, the commission was to be populated by states' delegates. These were not always experts but merely elected representatives. The voices of the UN belonged mostly to nation-states or to alternative international realms under the form of nongovernmental politics, which gave these exchanges national and international dimensions. Furthermore, ideas and tropes belonging to a specific historical context circulated within the UN, and representatives often translated them into international lobbying.

Certainly, sources present the Cold War and decolonization as "expected" conflicts. To the socialist bloc, the United States, France, and the UK were all part of the same capitalist imperial project. Nationalist China always clashed with Soviet delegates over issues of who represented the "real" China. However, even the predictable exchanges, if read closely, can reveal original positions vis-à-vis contemporary theoretical interpretations. Socialist countries' commissioners often agreed; American commissioners promoted their own antisocialist stance while supporting freedom and progress. Christianity was prominent, as exemplified by the Catholic NGO St. Joan's International Alliance's bringing to the UN a series of contested issues on the status of women in Africa. Religion constituted another way of building alliances. Muslim representatives, such as Afnan in the 1950s and the Egyptian commissioner Aziza Hussein from the 1960s, produced fierce defenses of human rights and locally born feminism while presenting a positive understanding of Islam.

One last note regards the question of assessing whether in the time period underpinned here, the UN was an effective organization or not. While tempting, given the constant critique of the organization, this type of framework hides historical nuances. Exploring delegates' assumptions, tensions, and concerns does contribute to a more multilayered scenario that emphasizes the complexities of the postwar moment and the long history of tensions between universalism and difference.

This monograph follows the official UN periodization of the commission's efforts to create international policy provisions in favor of women. The sources on this time period (1946–1975) reveal a change in the tone and rhythm of the commission's work in 1960, with the emergence of delegates from newly formed states. During the period from 1946 to 1960, the CSW advocated sex equality from a legal perspective, resuming the agenda of the League of Nations and adjusting it to the new human rights framework.[58]

Chapters 1 and 2 examine the path that brought gender politics to the UN setting. I show here how different, competing voices justified the inclusion of women in the work of the UN. Two main dimensions developed: women's rights as a legacy of the League of Nations and women's rights as a new component of the UN system. The path to the drafting of the Convention on the Political Rights of Women (1952) included the collection of data, the writing of a convention or declaration, and its submission for approval. These three steps generated debates on the tension between the objectivity of data and propaganda, the principles and values to be included in the convention, and member states' differing and problematic views of women's rights. The convention introduced the question of women in dependent territories, inaugurating the debate that led to challenging formal equality.

Chapters 3, 4, and 5 focus on other sites of UN related women's rights work, far from New York City and Geneva. A seminar in Moscow in 1956 was held to highlight the benefit of communist systems for women, and a seminar in Bangkok a year later debated women's participation in the public sphere. The UN did not sponsor the first seminar, although its theme was framed and discussed within the commission. The second seminar, which presented itself as more "objective" given its UN sponsorship, demonstrated a set of equally rigid ideological bases for assessing the status of women. Chapter 4 ends with the scandal of the Fon of Bikom, which introduces the theme of trafficking. Chapter 5 explores the topic of female circumcision and how different UN parts became involved with a definition and a possible solution.

Chapters 6 and 7 analyze the economic development politics of the commission in terms of tensions over gender equality. As stated earlier, development had a longer history within the UN setting; its story intertwined with Cold War dynamics in the postcolonial era. This part addresses the politics of development and the conflicting definitions of discrimination against women. It constitutes the final stage in the relationship between universalism and differences inaugurated by the founding of the CSW. The commissioners wanted both to maintain women's "power" within families and to question the family as the main locus of discrimination against women.

The chapters follow a chronological order, but themes and events do not fit neatly into these frameworks. For example, I use the Beirut CSW Session (1949) to make arguments on issues that were hotly debated in the 1950s and 1960s. I also use the Human Rights Advisory Program to define the politics of aid in the 1950s and as part of the history of economic development in the 1960s. Issues of colonialism also show up in multiple formulations since they run parallel to other debates. At every session, the commissioners debated different topics that followed varied routes, conflicts, and efforts to constantly insert women in a constructed universalism.

1. Minerva Bernardino signs the UN Charter, San Francisco Conference, 1945.
© United Nations, reprinted with permission of the United Nations.

1

Women of the World

Visible and Invisible Bodies

Depicted here, the president of the Inter-American Commission on Women, Dominican Republic delegate Minerva Bernardino, signs the UN Charter at the San Francisco Conference on June 26, 1945 (see figure 1). The image includes three different levels: flags symbolizing nation-states and, collectively, international cooperation; three men (unidentified in the UN's description of the photo) watching over Bernardino as gendered guardians of this solemn act; and ultimately, Bernardino signing the UN Charter as a gesture symbolic of UN women's participation from the early foundations of the organization. Certainly, this photo is restorative of justice in the sense that women were included in international politics, but the larger context suggests a deeper reading.

On multiple occasions, Bernardino took a strong stance in defense of correct data about her country, her reaction was often unexpected and generated a series of close and intense correspondence, unusual in diplomacy.[1] Furthermore, she clearly told delegates of countries opposed to women's rights that their arguments were flawed. These occasions could have made her seem unruly, and following this interpretation, the three men in the photo could be seen as referees of her signing. From a more contemporary point of view, Bernardino represented the Global South even if her speeches never suggested a commonality with the so-called Third World but rather with the Latin American world and, in larger terms, the Americas. She was popular for her fashion choices, and her photographic record at the UN clearly shows a distinctive style in contrast with other representatives' more sober one. As historians Ellen Dubois and Lauren Derby claim, "The large, dramatic hats in which she frequently appeared, and which drew visual and political attention to her were a millinery strategy of the period."[2] Bernardino was multilayered: she was a symbol of U.S. influence through her patronage by the suffragist Doris Stevens, a symbol of complicated alliances between women's rights and dictatorship, and eventually, a representation of the complex racial policies of the Dominican Republic.[3]

At a more metaphorical level, this photo tells the story of the insertion of women as a group and as a concept within the UN and the fragmentation of the universal category "woman" through the creation of the group "women in dependent territories" which Bernardino helped to construct. This chapter shows the UN's rhetorical and institutional steps for the inclusion and division of the category *woman* within international human rights politics. At every step between the signing of the UN charter in San Francisco, the creation of the Commission on the Status of Women, and the later conventions and declaration, women had to lobby and be linguistically and politically creative because of the hegemonic category of men in international governance and everyday life. Parallel to these processes, there was a crescendo of imperial feminist politics at the UN—from orientalist attitudes toward the East to the creation of protoimperial categories with modern names to the singling out of women in the colonial world as an especially oppressed category. It was apparent since early days that who defined and who talked—and from which location—had a specific valence given the complexity of the postwar world.

The title of this chapter suggests that references to women's bodies and bodily differences between men and women were often implied in these early UN days. More evident was the history of women in the public sphere and the gendered understanding of women and war. Following the differentiation by Patil explained in the introduction, this chapter highlights how women were embodied and, as such, needed solid rhetorical tools to be included in the world of men, who represented the disembodied category.

At San Francisco, the history of women intertwined with the history of empires as both changed within and because of the foundation of the United Nations. Simply speaking, women lived in colonies too, and the new organization—at least rhetorically—aimed for a universal application of its progressive principles. While the preamble of the UN Charter clearly specifies the "nation" as the object and subject of the new international principles, other parts of the charter mention "all," suggesting a universal application of the principles and an intention of setting standards beyond the nation-state. Along with universalism, the charter includes a rule on nonintervention in national sovereignty.[4] Such rule became contested later in the mutual verbal attacks of countries involved in the Cold War and in the context of colonialism.

The immediate postwar period allowed for the foundation of new rights based on the assumption that the nation-state could and did abuse its citizens. The atrocities of World War II created a terrain in which the ruling authority was called into question. War appeared as the primary reason to reaffirm human dignity. The UN Charter's preamble states the UN's intentions to "save succeeding generations from the scourge of war, which twice in our lifetime has brought untold sorrow to mankind, and to reaffirm faith in fundamental human rights, in the dignity and worth of the human person, in the equal rights of men and women and of nations large and small." Confirming the principles of the preamble, the first chapter declares some of the UN's goals: "To maintain international peace and security; To achieve international co-operation in solving international problems of an economic, social, cultural, or humanitarian character, and in promoting and encouraging respect for human rights and for fundamental freedoms for all without distinction as to race, sex, language, or religion."[5]

These words were the result of different encounters, political moves, and dynamics that developed at the San Francisco Conference in 1945; the UN foundational meeting, an initiative of the United States, represented a brief hybrid moment between the end of World War II and the beginning of the Cold War. All the parties involved in the antifascist struggle, including the Soviet republics, were invited to San Francisco.[6] This specific context created the conditions for international provisions that encouraged the inclusion of women and other minorities within civic life. Different groups and individuals attended the conference with a specific lobbying intent in mind. International women's groups hoped for the inclusion of sex equality in writing. The same did anticolonial groups which wanted the new organization to be sensitive to the plight of the colonized peoples. However, traditional colonial powers defended their claims over dependent territories, helped also by the sovereignty clause, which led to the tandem UN attitude toward the colonial world—promoting universal human rights from one side and supporting the interests of colonial powers on the other.[7]

At the conference, the creation of the United Nations Security Council, the last stages of World War II, and the voting games unveiled immediately that geopolitics had a central role in the work of the UN. Small countries had a hard time in being heard, and protoimperial organizations like the Commonwealth allowed Britain to have more voting power; the socialist bloc in Eastern Europe had a similar policy.

Within this context, the South African delegation, under the leadership of Jan Smuts, presented a proposal for the preamble that made the empire more visible and more contradictory. Smuts, although the designer of rigid politics of racial segregation in South Africa, wanted his UN contribution to represent his legacy in the new intergovernmental organization dedicated to human rights and self-determination. Historian Mark Mazower claims that Smuts did not see his support of equality in the charter and his racist policies as opposite. Mazower says, "In Smuts's mind, the UN Charter contained little that was incompatible with this view of the world; there was no commitment to granting independence to the colonies at all, and the United Nations could emerge, as he intended, as a force for world order, under whose umbrella the British Empire—with South Africa as its principle dynamic agent on the continent—could continue to carry out its civilizing work."[8] Arguably, he thought that his support for equality could not affect imperial equilibrium, but it gave him a foundational role in the establishment of UN principles. In the words of an American woman delegate (from the National Woman's Party) attending the San Francisco Conference, "You will never really know what a hard fight was waged by the women in the committees to win these provisions—but the Declaration of Equality in the Preamble you owe to the vision of Field Marshal Smuts."[9] Therefore, Smuts was responsible for the written inclusion of sexual and racial equality in the UN Charter.

Clearer and more unambiguously pro- and anticolonial voices were also present at the conference. The traditional European empires were at San Francisco, both as a continuation of the mandate system (part of the League of Nations) and as actual colonial agglomerates that had survived the war. But the issue of the colonies of vanquished countries presented itself. In contrast with the old paternalistic attitude of previous organizations, the delegation from the Philippines promoted the creation of an overseeing organization—one, however, that did not replicate colonialism itself.[10]

It was in that moment that the American diplomat Ralph Bunche pushed for the creation of a supervising body that carried responsibility and accountability for the colonial powers. Because of him, the soon-to-be-created Trusteeship Council included mandatory reports from the trustees and frequent visits to the territories.[11] Along with the council, under Chapter IX of the charter, at the first General Assembly (GA) meeting (1946), countries with colonies agreed to provide regular reports on their territories about the "political, social and educational advancement of the peoples of non-self-governing territories as well as their just treatment and protections against abuses."[12] The UN began to test its long-term tension between the universalism of its principles and the specific case of the colonial world. The language in favor of the rights of the colonized people (both men and women) carried this intrinsic contradiction that isolated the categories of people (and women) in the dependent territories.

Away from the written principles, San Francisco also inaugurated a series of orientalist attitudes that singled out non-Western delegates. For example, the U.S. delegate Virginia Gildersleeve described Prince Faisal of Saudi Arabia in "Arabian Nights" terms in which he floated around the conference rooms with his white robe and noble sword while other discussed important matters. Conceptions of civilization and backwardness dominated these encounters.[13] Within this context, women's politics simultaneously promoted equality and inequality.

The Brazilian delegation, specifically the representative Bertha Lutz, suggested the creation of an entity to study the national political participation of women from a global perspective.[14] Lutz was a complex activist. She was an experienced international feminist, a member of the Inter-American Commission of Women (an extremely active organization), and a renowned scientist and political activist in Brazil, but she was also an anglophone and later revealed problematic notions of civilization.[15] Her career flourished in the midst of "the second wave international," the activism for women's rights, which was reinforced by twentieth-century internationalism.[16] Her intervention in San Francisco resulted from the synergy between the second wave international, past experimentations at the League of Nations, and the favorable legal provisions of the UN Charter, which allowed for a treaty system on the status of women. Other popular delegates who supported Lutz's proposal included the Australian Jessie Street, the Danish Bodil Begtrup, and the already mentioned Minerva Bernardino.

International women's organizations had been active at the League of Nations (LN) through a reformist agenda that included both national and colonial contexts. At the LN, created at the Paris Peace Conference in 1919, women's organizations—among them, the International Council of Women and the International Alliance of Women for Suffrage and Equal Citizenship—promoted the status of women as an international matter.[17] The LN women's organizations worked for the resolution of social problems affecting women—for example, harsh working conditions and prostitution. These policies, however, did not challenge gender orders, but they represented the heritage of the older social question and the legacy of the social and equal feminist divide. For example, women's organizations, aided by the LN-based creation of the International Labour Organization, intervened to denounce the harsh conditions to which women were subjected and to propose protective measures for women workers.[18] The short life of the LN (1919–1946) did not give women's organizations the opportunity to implement more ambitious politics of gender equality; women representatives only succeeded in establishing politics that aimed to solve isolated issues rather than a treaty system for the status of women that could challenge the status quo.

The successful motion of the Brazilian delegation contributed to the genealogy of women's politics at the UN. This history can be viewed from both ideological and institutional perspectives. From an ideological standpoint, the creation of the CSW extended the main feminist trajectory that originated in the mid- and late nineteenth century at an international level (the antislavery, antiprostitution, and temperance movements) that was subsequently subsumed into governmental organizations.[19] The quest for universality of the female experience justified international collaboration, the measurement of national progress compared to other countries where women had reached a higher status, and a tradition of rescuing less fortunate "sisters."

From an institutional perspective, feminist lobbying at the San Francisco Conference consolidated the social and humanitarian agenda of the LN, "the engendering" of an intergovernmental organization, and ultimately, the institutionalization of women's rights and legal provisions dedicated to women.[20] Although women's rights activists had found a distinct space within the LN system, their participation at the foundational meetings of the UN created a new and more central role for women. The U.S. observer from the *Equal Rights Magazine*, who was in attendance at San Francisco enthusiastically claimed that the UN had not only "treated the rights and freedoms of women differently from the rights and freedoms for all" but it had also "implied these rights . . . [and] stated them."[21] With the UN, women's activism inherited some of the objectives of the LN, representing a temporal continuum in efforts to achieve the most urgent goals for women's lives with a series of challenges to insert women into a false universality that centered on men.

The UN road to consolidate women's participation at both an international and national levels was far from smooth. In San Francisco, politics in favor of women remained contentious. Claiming rights on the basis of bodily differences appeared confrontational given the climate of universality that transpired from the conference. Prior to San Francisco, the Soviet delegation had communicated a proposal for the charter's preamble that included sex differences among the categories to be protected by the new organization. Smuts and the Latin American delegations supported this principle; in Lutz's words, "It was advocated also by the sponsoring powers, which thus facilitated the adoption of this principle of equality." She mentioned Smuts, who "included the equality of men and women in the Preamble." In her opinion, "the magnificent support that . . . Latin American women" received from male representatives in all delegations demonstrated that that "the world" was "thinking along these lines of elementary justice."[22] It was Lutz's powerful speech at the conference, however, that created the actual foundation for women's rights at the UN: "The delegation of Brazil recommends that the Economic and Social Council should set up a special commission of women to study conditions and prepare reports on the political, civil and economic status and opportunity of women with special reference to discrimination and limitations placed upon them on account of their sex."[23] Her insistence on looking at discrimination against women resulted in the nickname "Lutzwaffe," which highlights the contemptuous attitude toward claiming women's rights.[24] The Sub-Commission on the Status of Women was born under these auspices that simultaneously promoted equality and inequality, and it developed along these lines with expected and unexpected results in terms of the politics of universalities and differences.

Delegates who participated in this phase of the women's movement were well-known in international feminist arenas. They brought to the UN meetings their distinct national perspectives as well as the feminist values of the gender politics-oriented NGOs with which they had worked. For example, Jessie Street's experience was symbolic of the multiple women's networks born between the late nineteenth and early twentieth centuries. Street participated in different women's struggles, became an active member of the International Council of Women, and was a feminist activist in the LN.[25] At the conference, Street carried around a volume of cables from 1,200 Commonwealth women's organizations that supported equal rights but whose members could not attend the San Francisco conference; among the organizations was St. Joan's International Alliance, a religious NGO active in sub-Saharan Africa.[26] Other renowned international feminists at the conference were Begtrup, who had a similar institutional history, and Bernardino. Begtrup was a member of the Danish National Women's Council and the International Council of Women and served as the Danish government's representative at the LN.[27] Bernardino was not only an experienced women's activist but also an able politician.[28] She was active at both the national and international levels. Her problematic political alliances with Dominican dictator Rafael Trujillo contributed to the promotion of women's rights in the Dominican Republic and secured her a brilliant diplomatic career.[29] Despite the authoritarian measurements of her government, Bernardino used her agency to promote human rights at a global level, albeit—as I show in the next section—with somewhat controversial and yet expected ideas about race.

These female delegates brought their experience to the UN and to the Sub-Commission on the Status of Women in particular. Moreover, they were the pioneers of women's activism in the context of the new international human rights framework and the UN machinery. Their groundbreaking role induced UN delegates to frame "old" rights within a new structure that was both ideological and institutional in a national and international context.

Laboring Bodies of the Nation

At the first plenary meeting of the newly created United Nations Organization (London, 1946), the U.S. representative and human rights activist Eleanor Roosevelt, along with other women delegates, delivered an influential speech to promote women's participation in the work of the UN.[30] The speech, also known as the "letter to the women of the world," along with the reactions that it generated offer a vivid picture of how the UN came to terms with the novel international principle of sex equality, as established in the preamble of the UN Charter.

The title "women of the world" suggests that London was a podium where Roosevelt and other UN representatives declared their intentions for a global female audience. As presented by the women delegates, the scope of UN politics was supposed to encompass all women. Such assumed totality suggests a set of consequences in terms of representation and speaking of behalf of the invisible "other" both physically and conceptually. For example, the only actively participating delegate from a country with a somewhat colonial past was Minerva Bernardino from the Dominican Republic; colonizer countries were instead heavily present. Furthermore, the letter as a top-down account depicts a Western sacrifice for a Western-guided conception of rights and its relations to the nation-state. In the rhetoric of the letter, women are outside the nation-state, and their peace contribution appeared so extraordinary that it deserved a reward.[31] Such position of outsiders also erased differences between women delegates and their audience—as all women were outside the nation-state—and in more general terms, it erased social categories as connected to war's participation and reconstruction, as the letter did not describe specific ways.

The letter—read by Roosevelt herself—shows that the UN followed an ambivalent direction on the issue of women's rights. In the UN rhetoric, the nation-state was responsible for enlarging the scope of rights to women because of their civic contributions in times of war. As Simone de Beauvoir asserted in her popular manifesto for women, "It is not in giving life but in risking life that man is raised above the animal: that is why superiority has accorded in humanity not to the sex that brings forth but that which kills."[32] Arguably, women were included in the UN because they "killed" too, or at least they derived their civic importance from supporting the killing. Simultaneously, the nation-state was the guarantor of citizens' rights, regardless of their "proof" of civic value. Roosevelt's letter declared that the women delegates' legitimacy to take part in the UN inaugural meeting in London was a reward for their war participation: "In view of the variety of tasks which women performed so notably and valiantly during the war, we are gratified that seventeen women representatives and advisers, representatives of the eleven Member States, are taking part at the beginning of this new phase of international effort."[33] Roosevelt expands this concept to women in general (beyond those at the assembly); she continued with a call for governments to reward women's war efforts and for women to become involved in the public sphere.

Moreover, the letter explains both the role of states and of women within the participation-as-a-reward plan. The rationale for both of them contributing was the war: "To this end we call on the Governments of the world to encourage women everywhere to take a more active part in national and international affairs, and on women who are conscious of their opportunities to come forward and share in the work of peace and reconstruction as they did in war and resistance."[34] This part of the speech clearly indicates that women's search for civic suitability, achieved through the war effort, assured their qualifications to help establish peace. The letter to the women of the world indicated that governments were obliged to "recognize the progress women have made during the war," that recent history had shown that women "deserved" to participate in politics, and that women had proved to be loyal and capable.

The following intervention by the representative of Norway, Mrs. Dalen, signee of the letter, encompassed all the rhetorical elements of the recognition of the value and consequent inclusion of women; she stated, "When the nation was in danger the women were called upon and they came, did their jobs, sacrificed and suffered. Now, when the war is over and the United Nations are trying to build a new world, trying to lay the foundations of peace and freedom for humanity, the world cannot afford to do so without using the rich resources . . . women's experience and capacity for work . . .

for the various nations of the world."[35] Her statement indicates that when the nation called, women responded. In peacetime, Dalen claimed, the nation was "to recognize the progress women have made during the war and to participate actively in the effort to improve the standards of life in their own countries and in the pressing work of reconstruction, so that there will be qualified women ready to accept responsibility when new opportunities arise."[36] State delegates therefore considered women's participation in the war effort as appropriate training for rebuilding their own countries in peacetime.

Other responses to Roosevelt's letter highlight more specific ideas about the relationship between women, wars, and societies. For example, the UN French representative, Mr. Paul-Boncour, associated women's participation in the war effort, (specifically in the French antifascist Resistance), with the force that uniquely contributed to the "honor" of the nation.[37] He therefore added a stronger dimension to why women deserved rights for participating in the war: defending national honor. Paul-Boncour noted the specifically gendered aspect of the Resistance: the association of women and honor in times of war suggests problematic representations that relegate women to male-derived roles.[38] His statement unavoidably divided the female population into those who "resisted" and honored France and those who collaborated and dishonored the country.

Focusing instead on peace, the Dominican representative Bernardino offered a more complex scenario. She called on different categories of women to participate in politics, among them "the wife; the mother in the home; the teacher in the school; the church-worker; the missionary; the social service worker."[39] In her example, women appeared as individuals dedicated to a life of service inside and outside the domestic sphere. These were the women who, in Bernardino's words, "turned their minds and hearts to the problems of humanity, and to the even more formidable undertaking of re-educating, readjusting and enlightening the recalcitrant people of the conquered countries."[40] Therefore, she focused on women as civilizing agents and unapologetically embraced colonialism and war occupations, a position not unexpected for the time period.[41] Ultimately, her wording of women as "mothers of the race" confirmed their traditional roles in wartime and nation building.[42] Such references to racial motherhood represented the Dominican politics of the time. As mentioned earlier, Bernardino herself embodied a problematic aspect of women's activism. She navigated between women's rights involvement and support of General Trujillo, who, unpopular for his racial and oppressive politics, had allied himself with women's groups to showcase his embrace of "democracy."[43] Trujillo's strategy was part of the tendency of despotic regimes to defend the rights of women in order to provide the appearance of a benevolent dictatorship. In this way, the state appeared as the defender of women's rights while invisibly engineering inequality. In the context of the gender politics of the UN, the reaction of Paul-Boncour and Bernardino are relevant because they show the persistence of women's roles as linked to men under the form of honor and service. Roosevelt's letter provided the background for such a framework since it assumed that women had to do something— some sort of laboring—to obtain rights.

The 1946 debate transcended the institutional destiny of women's status (Lutz's proposal of an organization in favor of women's rights) and focused on the reasons why it had become necessary for women to participate in the work of the UN and, consequently, in its new global agenda. The 1946 plenary meeting, which garnered attention due to Roosevelt's letter, evoked the rhetoric on the relationship between women and the nation—one that did not develop through a critique of the nation and its mechanisms of exclusion but rather through discursive negotiations between gender and civic participation.[44] The context allowed for a somewhat original position at the UN: an intergovernmental body as the entity that defined the conditions and politics behind gender and civic participation at a national level. Moreover, *woman* emerged as the hybrid category that required definition within the larger context of peace and reconstruction. Ultimately, the gendered language of the letter inaugurated an imaginary relationship between the UN and "the women of the world," terminology that UN women's rights activists later used widely in their policies.

At the inaugural UN assembly, both female and male UN representatives discussed women's "inclusion" and accepted the private-public divide that allowed for a discourse of the insertion of women in the public sphere. The invisibility of the state's gender-discriminatory mechanisms reinforced the state's role as a mediator between the UN and women as well as it encouraged state representatives to discuss the status of women in terms of moral concepts, such as duties in times of war and peace for the nation. This sentiment was the product of the general UN atmosphere of correcting the horrors of World War II coupled with the liberal awareness that oppressive mechanisms—gender inequality among them—were the product of "irrational bias."[45] This argument suggested that if inequality was the product of irrationality, reason could lead to equality. Therefore, the women delegates believed that the best way to counteract biases was to measure efforts when the state called citizens to action.

Within this context, the war functioned as a gender equalizer, at least from the perspective of common efforts and sacrifices. Whether these efforts were gendered and worked to maintain existing structures was not in question. The French ambassador claimed that "the horrors of war have put women on equal foot with men" everywhere and therefore, women deserved equality for their contributions to the war.[46] The narrative of war sacrifice and struggle against fascism became a lively part of the early phases of women's activism at the UN. European representatives—whether self-consciously or not—dominated this portion of the debate given their greater war casualties and the wide European dominance in the early stages of the UN. The so-called formal equality aimed to equalize the positions of men and women within societies from a legal point of view.[47] According to this political goal, women had to reach men along societal hierarchies based on full citizenship.

Using the war as the ontological place of definition for womanhood did not question men's roles within the state.[48] The GA's positioning of women as helpers solidified their social role as such and defined the receiver of women's services while it reconfirmed that men did not need a justification to participate in the public sphere.[49] Men were silently positioned as the primary irradiating force of a state's ideology, the primary stipulators of the social contract. War proved that women were capable of contributing to the nation, although through strictly gendered models as nurturers and "mothers of the race" and as belonging to the "social" rather than the political realm. Additionally, the war argument suggested that civic participation and suffrage could crystallize women's roles within the national and international orders. Indeed, both orders in Roosevelt's letter reciprocally reinforced the logic of the effort and sacrifice required of women to become a part of the polity. Whereas civic participation was expected of men, women had to fight to participate.

The letter to the women of the world epitomizes the chronological continuation of Lutz's proposal in San Francisco. The creation of the CSW symbolized instead its ideological continuation. Commissioners resumed the issues of war and peace, but they connected them to the UN legal principles in favor of women's equality. Ultimately, they adjusted and appropriated the category of the "women of the world" as the main constituency of their policies, which allowed them to be politically visible and useful to the causes of the UN, including extending its principles to the colonial world.

Tensions of Universalism and Difference

The Economic and Social Council (ECOSOC), the part of the UN responsible for economic and social issues, welcomed Lutz's suggestion and oversaw the creation of a new entity dedicated to women, a subcommission dependent on the HRC. Article 68 of the UN Charter establishes all the ECOSOC's commissions for "economic and social fields and for the promotion of human rights." Creating a body dedicated to human rights was therefore not in question as clearly expressed in the charter. Indeed, it is the only commission mentioned in the charter.[50] The Sub-Commission on the Status of Women was therefore established with the purpose of acting on those aspects of human rights pertinent to women and with an institutional role of presenting "proposals, recommendations, and reports" to the HRC. Through the HRC, the subcommission, also called the *nuclear commission*, could present suggestions to the ECOSOC.[51]

The nuclear commission's first task was to produce an agenda for the UN status of women to be submitted to the HRC in May 1946. Begtrup was nominated chairperson and Bernardino vice chairperson. To them the most pressing items were equal political and civil rights in state and marriage matters, equal pay for equal work, and equal access to education. Along with these goals, and from this very early stage, Begtrup's words were directed to women in the dependent territories, even before the Trusteeship Council took over with international tutelage: "In the area which may be placed under trusteeship there were six-hundred million people and a great work was to be done for their sake and that of mankind."[52] Consciously or not, Begtrup isolated the category of woman in the colonial world "to recommend that the United Nations Trusteeship Council, when it comes into being, bears in mind the special need to raise the status of women in the non-self-governing territories placed under its care and to that end to consult the Sub-Commission."[53] The French delegate to the subcommission was against the fragmentation of the category "woman" because, arguably, a debate on dependent territories could highlight the responsibility of colonial powers.

At the oral presentation of the subcommission's goals, the results were not what the international feminists expected. Roosevelt and other representatives considered the subcommission's demands to be too advanced.[54] After this episode, Begtrup wanted independence from the HRC. Possibly, her goal of wanting an independent commission, derived from a decades-long experience with women's activism, encouraged her and the San Francisco group to lobby for an independent commission.

The human rights framework provided further support for Begtrup's plan for an independent commission. The episode at the HRC demonstrated that the theory of universalism as the basis for human rights, as described in the UN Charter, and women's inclusion were two different things. Therefore, Begtrup pushed for the creation of an independent entity because she had tested the terrain in favor of or against women's rights within the HRC. She feared that women's issues would be ignored within the larger human rights framework. In her autobiography, Street stated that the main concern of feminists was that "most human rights had been enjoyed exclusively by men and denied to women and that a single body [the Human Rights Commission] would not address this."[55] Roosevelt voiced her concern that the two human rights entities would duplicate each other.[56] Begtrup secured Roosevelt's support—or tolerance—for the creation of a full commission mostly because the ECOSOC, which guaranteed the making of the CSW, was higher in the UN hierarchy in respect to the HRC and Roosevelt.

This tandem history was shaped both by Roosevelt, who led a larger debate on the position of women in the postwar order and was a prestigious exponent of prewar and postwar American politics, and by Begtrup and the San Francisco group's adjustment of traditionally liberal feminist agendas to the new human rights framework. The human rights system therefore contributed to a stronger internationalization of women's rights and to a major global exposure for the "woman question," thereafter referred to as *women's rights*.

After the critiques on the nuclear commission's report in May 1946 and together with other women's rights experts, Begtrup submitted a request for a full commission.[57] She maintained a commitment to peace but also introduced the human rights dimension, opening the path to contesting the universal claims of the human rights system. The measurement of women's political participation was not compensation—like the participants to the 1946 inaugural meetings had proposed—but inclusion within the human group. In the request for full institutional independence, the subcommission proposed that the "world opinion be stimulated in favor of raising the status of women as an instrument to further human rights and peace."[58] The new entity was supposed to be in charge of "half of the population of the world," and this required it to be independent from other commissions.[59] Begtrup's presentation convinced the members of the ECOSOC who in June 21, 1946, agreed to the creation of a full and independent commission for the status of women.[60] The CSW inaugurated the tandem path of women's rights: from one side, the claim of rights as part of the human group, and from the other side, the claim of rights as contributors to war and peace. Because women were "embodied" (as per Patil's differentiation), they needed justification to participate. Commissioners incorporated both directions in a unified political line that focused on women's participation in rebuilding the postwar order—given the urgent matters the postwar presented—as well as claiming the fundamental importance of gender equality in modern societies.

The Women of the World

Many rules limited the newly born full commission. For example, the commission could not "take action in regard to any complaints concerning the status of women."[61] This clause indicated that commissioners could not engage with specific and individual violations of women's rights like, for example, NGOs could and can do. The UN dealt with states and NGOs rather than directly with individual claims of abuse. This situation changed only for the HRC in 1967 but stayed the same for the CSW, and this is why NGOs had such a central role for the commissioners' activities. Moreover, many delegates had professional links to NGOs and knew how their local activism could bring important data to the commission, which was otherwise dependent on the more statistical records by the Secretariat for information on individual countries and the status of women.[62] The Secretariat was also supposed to provide commissioners with some level of guidance on the possibility of specific data and on the different competencies of other UN bodies. However, it was often ineffective and provided commissioners with little to no guidance.[63]

The CSW operated along two different institutional paths. According to the first path, commissioners requested that the Secretariat research a matter concerning women at the global level. As I will show later, the Secretariat's knowledge production was often contentious. The Secretariat had a Section on the Status of Women dedicated to the collection of data and mediation between the CSW and the secretary-general. When the Secretariat presented the data (usually gathered through surveys or questionnaires), commissioners debated, deliberated, and presented their resolutions on specific topics to the ECOSOC.[64] If the council agreed to promote the commission's proposal, it would pass the proposal to the GA for further debates, possible amendments, and voting by member states' UN delegates. The second path derived instead from the GA's initiative, which could ask the CSW to draft a piece of international legislation or deliberate on an issue. For a complete chart to understand the 1946 institutional hierarchies and the place of commission within the UN (see figure 2).

The CSW, as a unified entity, had to express its goals through a language that resembled the UN institutional chart. The rigid structure only allowed for horizontal instructions and vertical proposals. This meant that in the reports, commissioners could only "desire, hope" that the ECOSOC and other superior entities consider a specific matter. Expressions such as "instruct" could be used only when the CSW referred to the Secretariat's Section on the Status of Women.[65] The main interlocutors of the commission, ECOSOC, and GA were member states. Yet the universal language of the UN, and the CSW in particular, served as a standard for global women's rights that transcended specific national situations. Commissioners clearly participated in

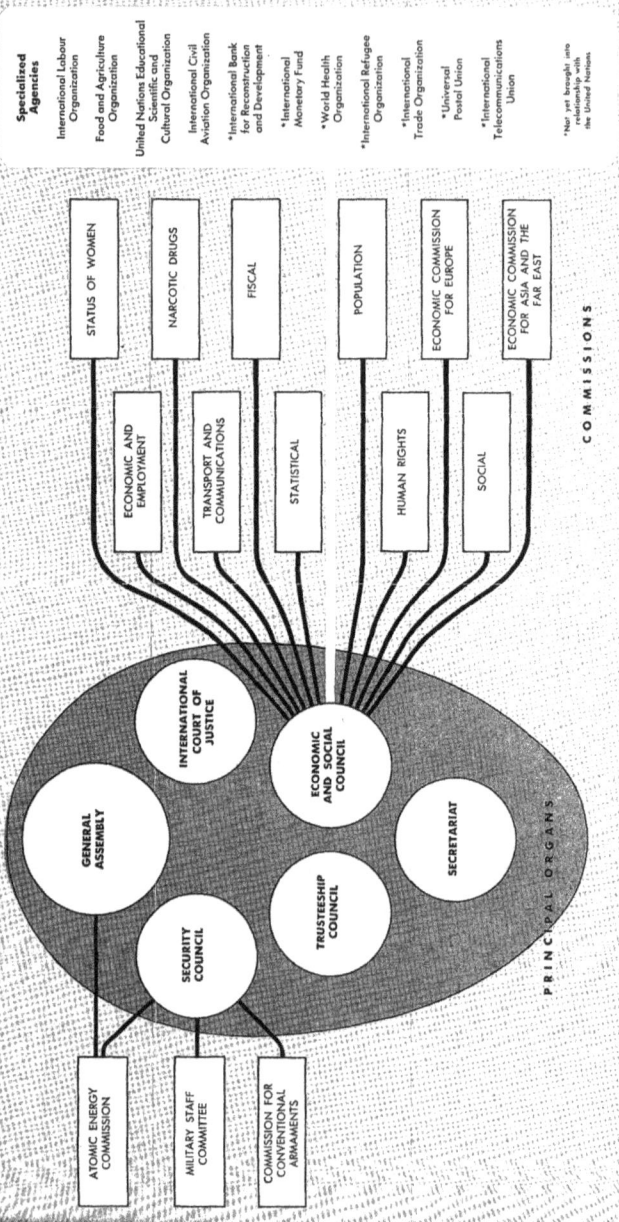

ORGANS OF THE UNITED NATIONS

Specialized Agencies

International Labour Organization

Food and Agriculture Organization

United Nations Educational Scientific and Cultural Organization

International Civil Aviation Organization

*International Bank for Reconstruction and Development

*International Monetary Fund

*World Health Organization

*International Refugee Organization

*International Trade Organization

*Universal Postal Union

*International Telecommunications Union

*Not yet brought into relationship with the United Nations

UN Presentation 468.2

COMMISSIONS

STATUS OF WOMEN

NARCOTIC DRUGS

FISCAL

POPULATION

ECONOMIC COMMISSION FOR EUROPE

ECONOMIC COMMISSION FOR ASIA AND THE FAR EAST

ECONOMIC AND EMPLOYMENT

TRANSPORT AND COMMUNICATIONS

STATISTICAL

HUMAN RIGHTS

SOCIAL

PRINCIPAL ORGANS

INTERNATIONAL COURT OF JUSTICE

ECONOMIC AND SOCIAL COUNCIL

GENERAL ASSEMBLY

SECRETARIAT

SECURITY COUNCIL

TRUSTEESHIP COUNCIL

ATOMIC ENERGY COMMISSION

MILITARY STAFF COMMITTEE

COMMISSION FOR CONVENTIONAL ARMAMENTS

2. The organizational chart of the United Nations, 1946. *United Nations Yearbook 1946.* © United Nations, reprinted with permission of the United Nations.

this operation and did not limit their debates and deliberations to women from their own countries.

The ECOSOC nominated government-selected commissioners on the basis of geographic distribution and for a period of three years. There were initially fifteen members representing the countries of Australia, Byelorussia SSR, China, Costa Rica, Denmark, France, Guatemala, India, Mexico, Syria, Turkey, the USSR, the UK, the U.S.A., and Venezuela. Begtrup was aware that in the passage from subcommission to full commission, the danger was that states' representatives could focus only on national interests. In the early stages, expert international feminists constituted the commission's membership. The delegates' past expertise in both national and international organizations contributed to politics that went beyond single countries' interests.[66] The membership of newly postcolonial nation-states, along with traditional pro- and anticolonialism ones, allowed for the colonial question to have a prominent place in CSW's debates and deliberations.

Once the commission was established, the members defined their terms of reference. Different conceptions of equality reflected different experiences, but eventually commissioners agreed on a common ground. During the commission's first session (Lake Success, 1947), the Indian representative Begum Hamid Ali highlighted the tension between the relational aspect of formal equality and the new human rights system. Hamid Ali, founder of the All India Women's Conference and an anticolonial activist, presented the scenario of those countries where men did not have rights, and the ways relating the rights of women to the rights of men could be problematic.[67] Her argument can be interpreted through the specific Indian scenario: India was in the process of gaining independence from Britain, and a general lack of rights for the colonized population, both men and women, was arguably prevalent under colonial rule. Hamid Ali thus advocated for the use of the term *women's rights*, as in some areas of the world, "even the status of men was such that to grant women equality of status would amount to practically nothing."[68] Along similar lines, Dorothy Kenyon, the U.S. representative, claimed that setting the standards to the rights of men could also be "an equality of slavery."[69] Kenyon, an expert jurist and women's activist, showed that those who included the word *rights* in the commission's terms of reference promoted the tool of an absolute category independent of the particularities of a context and linked to international standards. At that moment, the UN counted only fifty-eight member states, but the language included global expressions, such as "universal," to indicate that the organization was both setting standards and hoping to enlarge its membership.

From the early stages of the commission's work, Begtrup insisted on referring to the "women of the world" as opposed to the "women of the UN member states." Begtrup's political strategy suggested that by detaching rights from specific national contexts, UN women's instruments could be applicable at a global level and create standards for all states, independent from their UN membership and status of nation-state. The commissioners followed her lead and agreed on the following call: "We the representatives of fifteen countries gathered in the Status of Women Commission of the United Nations to safeguard the interests of all women, appeal to the many millions of women throughout the world to work in every possible way for peace and prosperity of peoples everywhere."[70] They simultaneously created an imaginary dialogue with "the women of the world," claiming that it was their duty to "express the desires of women throughout the world."[71] This function was ambitious and established an unprecedented relationship between an intergovernmental body and women as a group. The issue, of course, was representing the desires and goals of absent groups.

Once commissioners defined their audience and their politics, Begtrup created rhetorical devices to insert women into the human rights framework. After she was confirmed as chair of the CSW, she persisted in promoting women from the status of civic warriors (Roosevelt's main line) to that of "human beings." She confirmed her stand against wars and her encouragement of dialogue for solving "material or mental conflict" that she identified as the cause of women's discrimination. "Women are more than half of the population of the world," Begtrup stated.[72] She strategically focused on numbers, claiming, as she did in her previous speech to the ECOSOC, that demographics reinforced the notion that women were relevant not only for their war effort but also because they constituted over half of the world's population. While reinforcing the concept of women as a numeric force, Begtrup also reintroduced the connection between women and peace.

During this early phase to define the main direction of the CSW, Begtrup claimed, "Peace throughout the world is the ardent dream of all women."[73] In the commissioners' world, peace and womanhood were inextricably linked. Not only were women predisposed to peace—as men were to war—but in Begtrup's words, "the growing influence of women in public life" was "an influence for peace." Ultimately, she established the role of the commissioners as connected to peace building by declaring "let women play an historical part in the prevention and removal of present and future threats of war, so that it can realize the deepest aspirations of women everywhere for a world of peace and freedom for their children and generations yet to come." Her appeal is revealing of the larger context outside the UN "palace" for the establishment of the women's rights agenda.[74] In this case, the right to civic participation was connected to the emergencies of the postwar period (reconstruction), the importance of women as a group (their numeric force), and women's traditional devotion to service. While Begtrup's view included some elements of the 1946 UN inaugural debates, other commissioners contributed to expanding that scenario.

To the Soviet representative Elizavieta Alekseevna Popova, the appeal was effective in principle but failed to call on women "to fight for peace." In Popova's opinion, "the appeal should go further, and [include a] call for propaganda against a new war." Kenyon aligned with Popova and stated "that the Commission itself was a practical demonstration of peace and peace-mongering."[75] This seeming alliance was unexpected, as Kenyon and Popova represented the two opposing Cold War blocs. In the early stages of women's rights activism at the UN, however, these episodes were not uncommon. At the first meeting of the subcommission, for example, Fryderyka Kalinowska (the Polish delegate) "thought, and the members agreed, that the Sub-Commission should pay special homage to Mrs. Roosevelt, one of the greatest personalities of her country, who was a living example of what women could do."[76] The agreement of Kenyon and Popova is notable given the contested status of the word *peace* in later debates, a tool mostly used to indirectly criticize member states involved in Cold War containment conflicts.[77] Kenyon also symbolized a unique type of U.S. delegate, soon substituted by a range of "Cold War warriors."

Begtrup welcomed Kenyon and Popova's ideas and consolidated her own position with a more specific resolution that connected the postwar context and the rights of women. She declared that "woman has thus a definite role to play in the building of a free, healthy, prosperous and moral society, and she can fulfill that obligation only as a free and responsible member of that society. Women must take an active part in the struggle for the total elimination of the fascist ideology and for international cooperation directed towards the establishment of a democratic peace among the peoples of the world and the prevention of further aggression."[78] Freedom and responsibility went hand in hand in Begtrup's resolution. Women could participate in reconstruction as free individuals, and thus their rights were crucial to the general welfare of a state. Rights made sense if coupled with civic participation. Begtrup and the other commissioners had to negotiate categories that rendered women's rights possible and useful for the greater good. Such reformulations were only the beginning of commissioners' struggle to insert and consolidate an agenda for women's rights within and beyond the UN system. Another challenge to the space of women's politics was the Universal Declaration of Human Rights (UDHR).

At the CSW's second session at Lake Success in 1948, the commissioners debated possible amendments to the UDHR. Resolution 48 (IV) of the ECOSOC indicated that the HRC circulated the draft of the international bill of human rights to the CSW.[79] The commissioners then reviewed the draft and proposed verbal guarantees against women's discrimination. The possibility of expressing their official opinion on the UDHR represented the opportunity to encourage higher UN bodies to inscribe women in the declaration without accepting "man" as the universal human category. This type of politics expanded the later actions of the CSW because the declaration provided equal gender rights without the need for extra definitions linked to the historical context, as in cases of war and peace.

Australian representative Jessie Street wanted a provision in article 1 of the declaration that stated, "wherever the word 'man' is used the Commission on Human Rights implied both men and women."[80] Street's concern was that the sole use of the masculine grammatical form had historically excluded women from legal provisions. Alongside Street's concern was

Kenyon's proposal of substituting "men" with "people or persons." Kenyon believed in a simple and direct declaration; she argued that a gender specification in article 1 risked rendering the text less direct. What Kenyon meant was that, especially in the English version, including *his/her* in any article would have made the text less immediate. Commissioners therefore proposed to include one general amendment that indicated that masculine terms included women too. The linguistic result of this proposal generated verbal contradictions and showed the limitations of having a simple text while including exceptions to the hegemonic masculine language.

The representatives from Nationalist China and India advanced other proposals on the use of gendered language. Cecilia Zung (China), a Columbia University graduate and expert in Chinese theater, spoke against a gendered familial language; in her opinion, the term "brotherhood" excluded "sisterhood."[81] Zung claimed that the expression "members of the same family" enlarged the applicability of the article. Similarly, Begum Ali suggested adding "brotherhood and sisterhood."[82] Eventually the CSW reached a compromise and found an expression that did not exclude women but was still gendered, voting in favor of "in a spirit of brotherhood." They thus proposed the following article: "All people are born free and equal in dignity and rights. They are endowed by nature with reason and conscience, and should act towards one another in the spirit of brotherhood." Begtrup's position on this issue did not focus on semantics but rather on a more positive statement directed toward reaffirming women's political equality, saying "everyone has an <u>equal</u> right to take an effective part in the government of *his* country."[83] This is an example of linguistic tension. The commissioners did not propose "his/her country" but decided to add "without discrimination." The struggle over a gender-inclusive language revealed the unproblematic use of "man" as a universal category despite the affirmation of gender equality in both the UN Charter and the UDHR. Moreover, this issue demonstrated how commissioners had to negotiate the insertion of women within the language of international law. A direct and lean text was easier to approve than a confusing one, but it was also problematic for women.

Conclusion

This chapter illustrates the difficult early stages for the inclusion of women within the UN, both as working delegates representing member states and as individuals deserving rights. The San Francisco Conference highlighted the geopolitical interests intrinsic in the establishment of the United Nations. The status of women seemed unimportant in the great schemes of keeping the world free from fascisms, but the UN Charter and UN women delegates claimed otherwise. The call arrived from experienced international feminists: Lutz, Begtrup, Street, and Bernardino pushed for the creation of an experts' group in charge of assessing the status of women at a global level. Right after their proposal, Roosevelt's letter to the women of the world confirmed the role of women in postwar reconstruction, although with problematic and rigid assumptions.

The genealogies of gender politics at the UN passed through different conflictual levels that showed from the early stages the challenges of inserting women within the universal language of human rights. Along with such issues, the UN presented itself both as geopolitical and imperial through the power of the Security Council and as in favor of universal equality and self-determination through the language of its charter. Commissioners engaged with this duality when they discussed the first actual formal equality international convention.

3. Palestinian refugee camp, Damascus, Syria, 1948. © United
Nations, reprinted with permission of the United Nations.

2

Imperial Encounters and Occupied Bodies

The photograph on the left portrays two Palestinian refugees.[1] With Resolution 181 of 1947, the General Assembly (GA) voted for the partition of Palestine into two different states.[2] The CSW was involved in the events post resolution and, specifically, in an attempt to show official support for the Palestinian refugees in Syria. The anonymity of the people in the photo renders them archetypical representations of the woman refugee. The apparent age difference between the two women and their proximity could possibly indicate that they were mother and daughter in a camp. The mother has a resigned expression and does not look at the camera; the daughter instead looks over the camera with an almost defiant expression. The proximity of the photographer does not allow for an understanding of the surroundings but seems to focus on capturing the women's facial expressions. As will be discussed later, it was actually a Catholic NGO which, at the CSW meeting, brought the attention to the pain of "women and children" of Palestinian refugee camps, creating the possibility of a religious reading of this photo. Arguably, such images attracted international sympathy and symbolized a warning against the displacement caused by wars. Commissioners were exposed to these facts through their first meeting outside the Global North (Lebanon, 1949). From that moment, women delegates had a series of other encounters, both physical and rhetorical, with women under colonial and postwar occupation.

At the general meeting of the ECOSOC in 1948, the Lebanese delegate offered Beirut as the location for the 1949 CSW session; in his words, "Lebanon would be a meeting-place for men and women from Asia and Africa who would thus be kept in touch with the commission's work and be able to make known the results when they returned to their own countries."[3] The events of this chapter start with this proposal and end with the complex voting sessions of the 1952 Convention on the Political Rights of Women. After Beirut, commissioners worked for the formulation of the first instrument for the political rights of women, an agenda item that they inherited from the League of Nations. The drafting of the Convention and the debates around it showed a clear goal of isolating the category of woman in dependent territories. This operation, however, was not based on a coherent and consistent attitude but rather on different relations to territories under formal and informal control.

This chapter introduces the politics on who, according to commissioners, needed women's rights and how the quest for these rights intersected with macrohistorical processes such as colonialism, the Cold War, and the multiple conflicts that emerged in the immediate postwar. The category of imperial feminism is here useful to read the commissioners' words and their assumptions within the logic of rescuing "the other." The nature of such a rescue varied from delegate to delegate, and the differences revealed larger cultural tensions among the delegations, not to mention drawing attention to the colonialist nature of this apparently philanthropic and progressive endeavor.

What is original in this UN women's rights mosaic is that the so-called "other" was different depending on the circumstances and discussed through different political tools useful to the country of the debating delegate. Imperial feminism, however, gave a space to commissioners to be present in the international podium—even if it was through problematic constructions of hierarchies of women—and grapple with the divergent opinions of countries in regard to the status of women. Certainly, commissioners discussed "the other" as women to be rescued; the "other," however, changed depending on the debater. To Soviet Russia, the other was both the African American woman in the Jim Crow American South and the woman in European colonies. To the British and French delegates, the colonial other was to be rescued but was also somewhat unrescuable. To the U.S. representatives, the other was the woman of occupied Japan who could learn democracy from the West. While most countries differed little in terms of women delegates and main governmental lines, the U.S. represented a unique case. The delegation ran the gamut from Dorothy Kenyon, a feminist lawyer who, as shown in chapter 1, sometimes even agreed with the Soviets, to women who did not veer from typical Cold War positions.[4]

This chapter maps the events that led to the voting session of the 1952 Convention on the Political Rights of Women. This was the first legal instrument based on the principle of sex equality included in both the UN Charter and the Universal Declaration of Human Rights. The voting session of the convention showed the different geopolitical tensions as well as visions that countries had for women's rights. In some instances, carefully designed arguments claimed that women were not to have political rights, at least not at that moment.

On Identifying and Rescuing the Other

At the commission's second session in 1948, the representatives of India and the USSR wanted a clear reference to the non-self-governing and trust territories in the commission's resolutions on the political rights of women. India had just acquired independence and arguably had an interest in advocating for dependent territories since its own independence had been based on the principle of self-determination; the USSR had a more complex position, one grounded in the condemnation of imperialism as connected to capitalism and exploitation. The Soviets portrayed their own society as one in which racial and gender discrimination did not occur.[5] This position, of course, never included the Soviet interventions and control over other countries; specifically, the case of Uzbekistan which—as I show later—could be equated to a colonial formation under the Soviet Union.[6] This Soviet effort went beyond the CSW. At the ECOSOC debates on women in colonial territories and political rights, the Soviet delegation presented a statement in which it condemned the colonial world where women were "not better than slaves" and where the argument that women were unready for political rights would exist as long as the "colonial system" existed.[7] At the commission, the Indian and Soviet representatives pushed for a clear reference because in substance, these territories had a different status than trust territories in which the transition to self-rule and the necessary UN-based preparations for such steps were planned and overseen by the Trusteeship Council. As mentioned earlier, the non-self-governing territories were instead de facto colonies under European rule. "Writing" colonies into what later became the 1952 Convention on the Political Rights of Women meant that in theory, colonial powers were to expand rights to countries in which their rule was predicated on denying them.

In this instance, Begum Ali (India) supported the idea of international tutelage for all colonies. She praised the trusteeship system and its administration, multistate in nature and delegated by the UN. Therefore, she was not directly criticizing colonial powers; she even mentioned (ironically or not) a "tribute to the British administration in India." She nevertheless insisted on a specific mention of all dependent territories in the CSW's proposals.[8] For the USSR, a written provision meant a clear confrontation with Western colonial powers and their reluctance in conceding rights to the colonized people.[9] Moreover, on the basis of the commission's frame of reference, the specification of women in the colonial world created a subcategory to the macro category of women of the world. For Kenyon, the commission was not sufficiently aware of the condition of women in dependent territories to be "singling them out in such strong terms."[10] The representative of Mexico spoke in favor of a specific mention of women in dependent territories and also supported the inclusion of a detailed list of the territories, rather than exclusively referring to "certain" territories.[11]

From a UN structure point of view, the rigid rule of not interfering and criticizing other countries allowed space for discussions of nonmember countries, specifically, dependent territories. Commissioners, however, were not entirely responsible for the tropes through which women in colonies were described. The knowledge/data on which commissioners based their provisions came from different sources. NGOs active in the colonies presented reports on the status of women in sensational details and contributed to a specific modality in which commissioners described and debated the status of women in these countries. Sensationalism had also a practical purpose as the CSW, per definition, operated to implement women's rights where those rights did not yet exist. Even if highly problematic, the process of "othering" looked like a convenient element of the commission's politics.

Comparisons were a rhetorical tool to establish guidelines for the commissioners to debate and obtain a clear picture of the blurry and distant colonial world and, especially, to demonstrate the strength of their initiatives. The specificities of the debate reveal how early commissioners pioneered the linguistic tension, so prominent in the context of imperial feminism. The most contested expression was "backwardness." Commissioners often used this expression to denounce the conditions of women in dependent territories, with a few exceptions from those delegates aware of how the expression was myopic and problematic.[12] For example, the Venezuelan commissioner responded that backwardness was specific not only to dependent territories but also to other areas of the world.[13] The newly elected CSW's chairperson, the French Marie Helene Lefaucheux, regarded the Venezuelan statement as an opportunity to rescue her own country from direct accusations of having contributed to gender inequalities in the colonial territories.

Lefaucheux, who chaired the commission for the following six years, had been a member of the antifascist Resistance and an active political participant in postwar France. The UNESCO delegate at the CSW defined her as "a feminist and an Africanist."[14] These terms were meant negatively, as someone who was politicized as opposed to an apolitical expert. Her interventions on the subject of colonialism were no different in substance from Charles de Gaulle's plan to include the colonies into "modernization."[15] In the immediate postwar period, Britain and France were weighing the costs and benefits of maintaining their respective empires; they were considering a fruitful, post-independence future collaboration with native elites.[16] This plan was short-lived; it was part of the rhetoric of acknowledging the colonies for the war effort. The postwar period was characterized instead by turbulent and violent wars of decolonization through which both women and men in the colonies demanded rights.

In the case of the status of women in the dependent territories, Lefaucheux also aligned with Mary Sutherland, the representative of the UK who occupied different positions in Labour Party ministries through the years.[17] They both claimed that the French and British initiatives in the colonized territories raised "the level of women's education."[18] Sutherland, in accordance with the chairperson, declared that in the colonies, the UK promoted initiatives for women's education in conjunction with a commitment to eliminate "old-established [local] prejudices" against the advancement of women.[19] Sutherland was therefore transferring the responsibility for success from the colonizer to the colonized. Both Sutherland and Lefaucheux faced a struggle of definition and differentiation to make "backwardness" a global problem rather than a specifically colonial one. By making backwardness a problem for women internationally, they absolved traditional European colonial powers from any responsibility for the status of colonial women and actually reconfirmed the old humanitarian argument of the colonizer who, in this case, attempted to and failed to, rescue "brown women from brown men."[20] The category of backwardness is symptomatic of the binary system that imperial feminism constructs and reinforces with different nuances dependent on the national or international actor in charge of creating the dominant narratives of women's rights.[21]

Including the colonial and trusteeship worlds in the convention for women's political rights presented further challenges. Since its first session, the CSW promoted the same fact-collecting process in the form of questionnaires on the status of women's political rights for all member states and dependent territories. When discussing whether to clearly mention the colonies in the draft convention, Kenyon spoke in opposition to the production of a double resolution, encouraging all states responsible for the dependent territories to be transparent. For Kenyon, the question was not merely political but social: in the trust and dependent territories, women as a group were victims of discrimination. She therefore argued that, according to Sutherland's legal differentiation, European imperial nations were required to communicate information concerning groups that were discriminated against.[22] The representative of India, claimed that if the government responsible for a country did not denounce the discrimination affecting a group, the government itself was responsible for discriminating against said group.[23] In this context, the government's role was ambiguous, since the colonial system was actually constructed on discrimination.

In defending British rule in the colonies, Sutherland provided a set of contradictions on the work of the commission itself. She did not agree with Kenyon's claims on the association between absence of political rights and group discrimination. For Sutherland, "women could be debarred from voting without there being discrimination." She presented the example of "certain territories . . . for which the UK had been made responsible" where political institutions did not align with the "Western democratic procedure" and did not allow voting for anyone.[24] Sutherland supports here a sort of paternalistic utopian system where equality was guaranteed from above. Lefaucheux, on the contrary, wanted to show how France expanded republican ideals rather than compressing them. She claimed that in territories under French rule (she provided the example of Ubandi-Chari in central Africa, where a member of the *Conseil de La Republique* was a woman), women were eligible for both local bodies and the parliament.[25] She supported a dual resolution, one for the trust territories and one for the non-self-governing territories.[26] Eventually, the convention text did not include any specific reference to women in dependent territories. What appeared as a political failure revealed important aspects concerning the limitations of the UN and tensions between the postwar human rights framework and the heritage of the old order. Also, a new dimension emerged from colonial powers' contribution, the tension between liberal institutions such as voting and the colonial context: the question was how these two could coexist.

The 1949 Beirut Session and Challenging Hegemonizing Categories

In an effort to spread the CSW's initiatives in the non-Western world, some sessions were held outside Europe and the United States (Lebanon 1949 and Argentina 1960). The first of these attempts was the 1949 session in Beirut, an initiative that the Lebanese representative and national minister Charles Malik widely supported.[27] At the Beirut meeting, the representative of the USSR, Elizavieta Popova, denounced the tension between the false promise of equality in liberal democracies and the actual equality in the socialist countries. She argued that, although the GA adopted the 1946 Danish resolution to promote equal rights for women, many countries, among them self-proclaimed democracies, did not allow political equality for women. Popova provided a list which included Spain, Greece, Switzerland, India, and the United States. In the American case, she stated that African American women could not vote freely. Similarly, in colonial territories "belonging" to self-defined democracies, Popova highlighted, women were not free to vote.[28] The Chinese delegate Zung harshly responded to Popova, generating the first in a long series of attacks between Nationalist China and the Soviet Bloc.

For the Chinese representative, the CSW, given its commitment to "true" facts, should refrain from any recognition of women's political rights in the Soviet Socialist Republics, as such information was not available. For Zung, the commission could not declare itself satisfied with the way in which the Soviet Union implemented the principle of equality of rights between men and women, as it was not in a position to judge the extent to which sex equality had been achieved in the Soviet Union.[29] The status of women, therefore, became a contested locus to differentiate "objective" facts from nationalistic propaganda. Nonetheless, the emphasis on establishing the reliability of data on women revealed how women's rights became the measure of good governance, at least rhetorically. Two presentations from two different NGOs graphically illustrated the point, revealing different reactions to the matter of facts and propaganda.

The intervention of members of the Women's International Democratic Federation (WIDF) in Beirut gave commissioners the opportunity to challenge the relationship between facts and propaganda. The organization had communist ties, but it also had a strong global membership.[30] Commissioners were concerned with the authenticity of the WIDF's work vis-à-vis Soviet-like propaganda. During the commission's plenary meetings in Beirut, the Lebanese representative of the WIDF took the floor to denounce the forced termination of the Organization of Democratic Women, affiliated with WIDF, and the arrest of several members. She also illustrated the abysmal conditions faced by Iranian women, specifically, the lack of universal suffrage, the limitation of women's civil rights, and the lack of protections in labor legislation. In Iran, she claimed, bigamy and the forced domiciling of a woman under her husband's name "could prevent her from exercising a profession." She added that mothers had no possibility of legal guardianship over their children and that women were not allowed to seek divorce, but men could. She also illustrated the conditions under which Iranian women sought a discussion and analysis of "women's democratic rights." Ultimately, she expressed gratitude to the representatives of the SSRs and the World Federation of Trade Unions for their support.[31] The WIDF's speech generated strong reactions that focused more on the presumed communist ties than on the conditions of women in Iran. Also, the WIDF representative was taking into consideration the plight of women in Iran, which created another conflict of representation, another instance of voicing the concerns of absent women.

The Indian commissioner reacted in strong terms; in her view, the WIDF had "seized the opportunity" to bitterly criticize another country, one of the member states, rather than to publicize women's activities in her own country, Lebanon. The Indian commissioner added that the WIDF had already shown in the Indian context that it had dubious ways of collecting facts.[32] Sutherland, the British commissioner, took the floor to say that the commission simply lacked the instruments necessary to confirm the WIDF's facts on Iran; she herself contended that these "accusations" were "in no way objective."[33] Therefore, in this instance, the commissioners lamented the use of propaganda as opposed to true facts given the challenge of verifying local realities.

Contrary to the rejection of the "subjective" presentation of women in Iran, the commissioners listened with great attention to another issue afflicting the region. At the same meeting, the International Union of Catholic Women's League presented the case of the Palestinian refugees, displaced after the 1948 conflict with Israel. This NGO advocated for the rights of the women and children in the Palestinian refugee camps in Syria. The Syrian delegate supported the request of the league that "the present Commission would be able to do something to alleviate their deplorable situation." She proposed a resolution to request "the Secretary General to express to the competent organs of the UN, the desire of this Commission that all possible measures be taken to facilitate the repatriation of Palestine refugees at the earliest possible moment."[34] In complex cases such as the dispersion of Palestinians after the creation of the State of Israel, the commission could do nothing more than extending its sympathies during a plenary meeting and in its report to the ECOSOC. The risk of having a resolution on this topic, especially the text that the Syrian commissioner proposed, would have forced the commission to take a stance on a matter concerning a soon-to-become member state (Israel joined the UN in November 1949). Furthermore, the GA had adopted Resolution 194 and created a conciliation commission on the matter.[35] The Indian delegate noted how repatriation as expressed in the proposed resolution was not within the scope of humanitarian issues. Repatriation, she pointed out, could only occur through negotiation with the Israeli government. She, like the other commissioners, could only express sympathy, as her government did not instruct her on this intricate political issue.[36]

The Palestinian case reveals how the commissioners selectively embraced other states' causes. In the case of the testimony of the representative of WIDF, the commissioners dismissed her intervention as "propaganda." In the case of the presentation of the Catholic Union regarding Palestinian refugees, the commissioners felt compelled to engage with the issue, albeit within the limitations of their governments' instructions, but without questioning the facts the Union presented. As historian Francisca de Haan points out, the position of socialist countries was often dismissed as "political" contrary to first world's positions which were deemed neutral;[37] in this case the Catholic concern for refugees was a moment of collective pity even if challenged by the rigid UN rules. Furthermore, if this instance might represent a clear act of commissioners' compassion in the context of an armed conflict, the Korean War largely complicated this scenario.

The submission for approval of the Convention on the Political Rights of Women took place in the midst of the Korean War and encouraged the Soviet Bloc commissioners to press for the urgent matter of peace as a precursor for political rights. As shown in chapter 1, peace was a common element in the early CSW declaration (Begtrup adamantly mentioned peace in her speeches) and of the UN at large. The Korean War turned "peace" into another contested term. Popova claimed that peace was the necessary element for rights to flourish.[38] Because of the war, the fifth session of the CSW (1951) opened "in an atmosphere that was definitely more politically-charged than ever before."[39] The Soviet Bloc delegations pressed the commission to revamp its order of references and priorities in order to produce a declaration on peace. In this instance, the commissioners did not even comment on this issue, as they had in the case of the Palestinian conflict. The Polish commissioner stated, "the armament race and the maintenance of peace were of immediate concern to women, as was shown by resolutions adopted by women's organizations throughout the world. The Commission should resist the tendency to avoid discussion on this cardinal point by laying down a procedural mock screen."[40] The representative from Byelorussia, continued the Soviet Bloc line of defending peace, however, with a more direct attack on certain member states. She stated, "The hysterical preparations for war now being made in the United States of America and in other countries of the North Atlantic Treaty Organizations were worrying millions of women, who demanded that the United Nations avert that new threat and lift the heavy burden from the already sadly oppressed workers and women."[41] The commissioners' level of engagement in matters of geopolitical importance reveals how propaganda was present in different and complex ways.

What constituted "fact" and "propaganda" changed depending on the setting and alliances beyond the status of women. While peace and war were foundational of the gender genealogy within the UN, at higher stages of the Cold War, commissioners dismissed Soviet connections between women, war, and peace.[42] When debating these issues at the plenary meeting of the ECOSOC, the delegate from Chile clearly accused the Soviet Bloc of using "peace" as a strategy, "the word 'peace' had not the same meaning for the free as for the Eastern countries of Europe. When the representatives of the Soviet *bloc* [italics in the original] spoke of peace, it was easy to see that it was a mere matter of propaganda with the aim of leaving countries undefended against breaches of peace by certain countries." The Polish delegate at ECOSOC responded, "In reply to the Chilean representative, it should be pointed out that their conception of peace was simple and unequivocal. As for the charge of propaganda, the Polish delegation was not ashamed of being accused of spreading propaganda in favor of peace; in fact, it was ready to do so on all occasions."[43]

From outside the CSW, these conflicts appeared as damaging the work on women's rights. The delegates of special agencies, such as the UNESCO and ILO, often noticed and reported on Cold War conflicts. For example, to the ILO delegate Mildred Fairchild, the back and forth compromised "the technical competence" of the commission and of the UN in general.[44] In this constant hierarchy creation, even commissioners themselves were not considered very efficient because of the relentless attacks and counterattacks on propaganda.

In the context of the Korean War, the UN Security Council had voted to "repel the armed attack and to restore international peace and security in the area."[45] Commissioners were limited by the UN rules (the CSW was institutionally lower than the Security Council). The Korean War forced them to face the dualist nature of the UN system, in favor of both human rights and geopolitical power. From the commission's perspective, this war appeared highly problematic. The UN-led operations in Korea were designed to "bring peace." This formula produced a hybrid and ambivalent conception of peace.[46] World War II had revealed a fertile ground to include women in civic duties, but as Popova argued, armed conflicts affected the exercise of rights. While the Palestinian struggle generated reactions of solidarity for dispersed people, the Korean War appeared as truly out of the commissioners' limited actions, even if women's rights were in danger in all war zones. This was another instance where the Soviet Bloc commissioners made valid points that unfortunately not only corresponded with Cold War propaganda's themes but, in this specific instance, challenged the commissioners' range of movements vis-à-vis the UN hierarchy.

All these debates happened as background to the drafting of the 1952 Convention on the Political Rights of Women which, besides rules for member states in terms of allowing women to vote, integrated women's responsibilities of preparing themselves for civic duties.

Turning Women into Citizens

Included in the preparation of the 1952 Convention on the Political Rights of Women was the preparation of women as active citizens. In an effort to decentralize the UN activities on women's rights, the CSW asked for authorization to create informative materials to prepare women for voting for the first time.[47] The commissioners were therefore concerned with the specifics of political participation and sought to maintain close ties with local women's groups. This debate highlighted the complexities of inserting a new group into the national political fabric, the tension in differentiating between groups of women, and the difficulties of local/global interventions. The decision to provide specific political education to women had conceptual repercussions. As the following debate shows, at stake was the persistence of discrimination against women, the practice that the commission itself was attempting to challenge and eliminate. A delegation of Japanese women visiting the UN showed the intricacies of advertising the right to vote in occupied territories as well as the variations of imperial formal and informal control.

For the commission's chairperson, Lefaucheux, women were supposed to participate as citizens and any "special [political] education" seemed inappropriate.[48] The U.S. position on this topic shifted with a change in personnel. Kenyon had claimed that persons voting for the first time constituted a gender-neutral category.[49] The new American commissioner, instead, indicated that women's political education was necessary to fight discrimination in the public sphere.[50] The Lebanese delegate advised on possibly discriminating against women in the process of "liberating" them. She claimed that it was unfair to require that women receive special training for voting. In the case of male suffrage, no further education was requested for men to exercise their rights. Women, therefore, the Lebanese delegate claimed, did not need to learn how to be citizens, and instructing them seemed biased. In a sense, if political rights were to contribute to eliminating discrimination, providing political education for women, instead, discriminated against them.[51]

This debate reveals the tensions regarding equality in the commissioners' politics. The struggle derived from the insertion of a new group into the nation-state electoral politics; that same group that in Eleanor Roosevelt's understanding, deserved rights because it demonstrated its civic duties during the war. In theory, educating women to exercise their right to vote meant treating them differently from their male counterparts. In practice, the commissioners focused on education, political and not, as a right connected to civic participation: the right of education depended on political rights, and hence women were not educated *because* they did not hold political rights.[52]

The commissioner from India promoted the creation of an educational program for those women who had recently gained the right to vote. She believed that the commission had to cooperate with locally active NGOs in the creation of political education programs for women. She also called for the participation of the UNESCO in those areas in which women had recently acquired the right to vote; in her opinion, the UNESCO could "undertake a study of effective programs of education in citizenship" and collaborate with local women's groups devoted to preparing women for voting.[53] The UNESCO, however, resisted calls for programs *exclusively* for women, claiming that the scope of the agency was to create and improve educational opportunities for all, with the aim of improving the human rights of both men and women.[54] As an alternative, the UNESCO representative proposed a wider distribution of the UDHR, "which in itself was one way of spreading the concepts of democracy and equality." She also declared that the UNESCO was already involved with the commission as far as general education was concerned and could not be involved in another program.[55] She proposed a general instrument, the UDHR, as opposed to a more concrete and direct action to promote women's political rights in local settings. A few years later the UNESCO did indeed promote women's political education showing how from a hard line of not isolating women, the agency eventually created a specific gendered instrument.[56] Similarly gendered was the teaching of democracy to women in occupied territories as the example of the United States and Japan shows.

At the CSW's fourth session (1950), two women observers from Japan attended the commission's meetings to showcase the country's achievements in the political education of women. The American commissioner introduced the observers and stated that despite the inheritance of a feudal regime in Japan, new programs contributed to women's participation in the public sphere.[57] One program, specifically, targeted all categories of Japanese women, who worked both inside and outside the home. It was intended to create a direct connection between the status of women and the harsh conditions of Japan: greater women's participation could help the country. The program's instructors explained to housewives that the vote would help increase their rations of food for the household. They also claimed that for women workers, voting could have changed wage discrimination and the obligation to sleep in factory dormitories. Ultimately, the instructors argued that, for peasant women, voting could increase the number of available resources that was required for effective farming.[58] This case represented an example of three different aspects: first, the local implementation of programs to encourage women to participate, second, the nonmember's adoption of UN-based principles, and third, advocating rights within an occupied country. From the perspective of the debate in the commission, the Japanese example was also representative of the necessity of educating women politically. Arguably, the observers were part of a U.S. plan to promote the benefits of occupation and a "democratic" reorientation of Japan.

The Japanese observers aligned themselves with those commissioners who favored political educations for women who had recently acquired the right to vote. For the American delegate, the CSW should broadcast the success of such programs to a wider public. The Japanese observers, she proudly claimed, certainly derived substantial benefits from the work they had witnessed at the commission; they then presented evidence that these initiatives could be successfully implemented. She confirmed that methods to increase women's political awareness were instrumental to properly exercise the right to vote.[59]

Programs, such as the Japanese one, were supported and encouraged by the United States and aligned with General MacArthur's declared intention for occupied Japan, which was to "reorient" and "rehabilitate" the defeated country.[60] Although these narratives evoked imperial history, MacArthur's rhetoric aimed to differentiate between two types of intervention in foreign countries; while European colonialism was "exploitative and oppressive," a higher, "humanitarian" purpose guided U.S. operations abroad. Women's rights and democracy were part of the U.S. mission in Japan; however, the humanitarian rhetoric employed the same tropes of the civilizing mission of imperial memory. American women participated substantially in this mission, from the complex collaboration of Beate Sirota Gordon and the writing of women's rights into the Japanese Constitution, to parading the participation of Japanese women at the United Nations.[61]

From the commission's perspective this case represented a concrete instance of women's involvement in reconstruction, although this example occurred in a contested geopolitical context. Countries without a traditional colonial stance such as the United States (colonialist but mostly self-claimed as noncolonizer) and the Soviet Union showcased here aspects of their democratic exports; if the United States brought the case of Japan, later the Soviet Union presented the case of Uzbekistan. Clearly, the colonial ambitions of the postwar superpowers differed from traditional European colonialism. While Europeans reinforced hierarchies even when they embraced a colonialism of welfare, the United States and Soviet Union, paradoxically, adopted a similar line of wanting the occupied people to become similar to American and Soviet citizens.[62] Mutual attacks of imperial and oppressive attitudes were unleashed at the voting session for the Convention on the

Political Rights of Women. A moment that beyond the expected conflict confirmed some small countries as progressive, anticolonial, and in favor of women's rights.

The "World" Responds: Supporting Women, Supporting Rights

When the CSW sent its report to ECOSOC in May 1952, the delegates discussed the convention. Cold War based attacks dominated the discussion with Czechoslovakia directly referencing the discrimination of women of color in the United States. Along with American racial politics, the Czech delegation introduced an important critique of political rights, an issue that emerged later but that was salient especially for countries that were struggling with poverty. In the delegate's words, "It was useless to guarantee equality between men and women in cases where men's political rights existed only in theory. It was difficult to see what advantages the draft convention could bring to an Indian or Negro woman in the Union of South Africa, considering the position of men of those races in that country."[63] Cold War-based conflicts dominated both the ECOSOC and CSW meetings; state representatives protected their own agenda and narrative across different levels of the UN. The 1952 ECOSOC plenary meeting was in fact just the dress rehearsal for the GA debates which involved multiple opinions on whether women should have political rights and the locations of these rights.

At the GA voting session on the Convention on Political Rights of Women (December 1952), the community of member states addressed, for the first time, women's rights as proposed by the CSW and approved by the ECOSOC. The Third Committee was, and still is, the portion of the GA in charge of human rights and social affairs. During the debate over the convention, multiple narratives developed, and delegations with strong stances in favor or against women's rights sought to persuade the audience of the legitimacy of their position. The exchange that happened at the GA is not only important for the larger framework on gender political equality but also because this same scenario produced a set of arguments on how countries perceived themselves vis-à-vis the status of women within the contested postwar geopolitical order.

The Soviet Bloc ambassadors at the UN did not abandon the line adopted during the commission's sessions. However, by bestowing the case of a benevolent Soviet introduction of rights to other countries, they presented a similar example of American policies in Japan and distanced themselves from European imperialism. The GA delegate from the SSR offered, in fact, a positive example of the inclusion of women from a different ethnic group, of expanding rights from the center to the periphery. Specifically, she promoted the "great improvement" of the condition of women in Uzbekistan. She proudly declared that prior to becoming part of the Soviet system, Uzbek women "were denied the most elementary rights" and "their lives had been made intolerable by religious laws and usages."[64] Now, she continued, the women of Uzbekistan enjoyed the same rights as other Soviet women. Uzbekistan had been a contentious issue since the early discussions by the ECOSOC on the CSW's reports. The British, especially, claimed that the Soviets denounced the lack of rights in European colonies, but they did not consider the rights of women in countries such as Uzbekistan. At the ECOSOC, the British delegate said that "a Tajikistan Communist newspaper . . . had recently reported that only a small proportion of Tajiks and Uzbeks reached the higher classes in the public schools and that only a small percentage of girls attended those schools."[65]

In the Soviet logic and wording, the composition of the Soviet system did not suggest imperial narratives but only humanitarian ones, in the sense of spreading the good values of Soviet Russia to multiple ethnic "others." She concluded by saying that the USSR, contrary to Czarist Russia, which perpetuated horrible conditions for women, had "granted and guaranteed political rights," as "demonstrated in the case of Uzbekistan."[66] As I show in chapter 3, Soviet women delegates always looked at their own condition in oppositional terms not only with women in other parts of the world (Soviet women believed to be the most advanced in terms of equality) but also with women in Czarist Russia, whom they considered victims of an oppressive system. In this context, however, the Soviet ambassador had the clear goal of referring to other countries' treatment of women and minorities.

At the Third Committee, delegates from the Soviet Bloc assumed "racism" as the dominant category of "Western imperialism" and the cause of discrimination in the United States and Europe. The Soviets aligned European powers with the United States and rendered capitalism the main discriminating force. In capitalist countries, the Ukrainian ambassador stated, women were "impatiently awaiting" an international law that "would free them from their position of political inferiority to men."[67] She pointed out how while the American delegate—Roosevelt—had declared complete gender equality in the USA, women of color—in the Ukrainian delegate's words "Negresses"—could not freely exercise their right to vote. She also added that in South Africa, Black women could not vote. Moreover, she claimed that the CSW and the Trusteeship Council Administering Authorities had remained silent in the face of the inhumane practices in the trust territories, as denounced by multiple NGOs. The SSR reinforced the Ukrainian point by stating, "The Administering Authorities always took shelter behind local tradition and custom to justify their policy of perpetuating slavery in the dependent territories."[68] She highlighted how even if the Trusteeship Council represented a new institution, its problematic composition (which included colonial powers) did not allow for an innovative transition to self-rule.

Soviet attacks based on race and gender discrimination did not pass uncontested. First, the South African ambassador claimed that women's rights could not be abruptly inserted into the fabric of society because of their potential interference with local customs.[69] Second, the British representative consistently advanced the same argument in favor of a smooth transition and missionary education as a bridge between local tradition and enlightened Western culture. Noticeably and yet aligned with settler colonialism, South Africa (an independent state) used the same benevolent colonial language Britain used for its colonies when discussing the status of its own citizens, Black women in South Africa. Ultimately, Roosevelt dismissed the Soviet assessment of the status of Black American women by arguing that the contested data were not recent. She focused on how federal law promoted equality both in the north and south of the country.[70] These three interventions epitomized the main arguments in favor of the status quo: moderation, smooth transitions, and a focus on education as opposed to progressive laws or the enforcement of such laws.

Other delegations, such as the one from Czechoslovakia, pushed for an explicit inclusion of discrimination in the convention. For the Czech delegation, the draft convention only represented a declaration, as it did not specify guidelines for states. The text was therefore not helpful for women. The Czech ambassador stated that the convention only reaffirmed the equality of men and women as "identical groups," without mentioning "race, color, ethnic origin, and property status." For him, "all progressive peoples" were relying on the UN to abolish discrimination. The capitalist system produced discrimination, he claimed, not only in the dependent territories but also in Western countries. The Czech delegation supported a convention that included written provisions against discrimination on "the grounds of race, color, property status, language or religion." According to the delegation, equality on the basis of gender would be useless in those cases in which men did not enjoy full rights.[71] The Czech position challenged the language that framed women's equality as a male-derivative goal; being on equal footing with men did not always correspond to having rights, as the case of African American history demonstrates.[72]

France and the UK voiced their support for women's progress, although they were also critical of the convention. The main issue, as I mention earlier in the chapter, was the so-called colonial clause: the inclusion of persons from the colonies in the UN international provisions.[73] The French delegate declared that in the French territories, the "Government prided itself precisely on not resorting to violence for the purpose of changing deeply rooted customs."[74] Education represented the best means of introducing women's equality. This is another instance of praising a smooth transition through the argument that local customs were against women's equality.

The British ambassador reproposed the women/war binomial foundational to the insertion of gender politics within the UN: women had to share the burden of both war and peace with men. In her speech she pointed out how it was unfair for men to hold "the whole responsibility of great political decisions alone." Wanting political rights, she claimed, was the product of "angry militant women demanding power," rather than "an offer of true companionship" to address difficult matters together with men. Reforms, the British delegate said, were much more effective than "revolutionary methods," and a legal "convention was not a good substitute for . . . social education." She added that instead of supporting gradual reforms (as opposed to the "revolutionary convention"), a provision on the political rights of women would have "weakened rather than strengthened their case."[75] Ultimately, she declared that the UK abstained from voting rather that openly dissenting with the principles that supported the convention.

The UK presented the hybrid combination of supporting women without international activism in favor of their rights.[76] This case was not unique as other states claimed the centrality of women's rights for a modern state without supporting women's advocacy for their own rights.

Another way of discouraging women's activism for their own rights came from the Egyptian representative who argued that the political rights of women should be addressed by a general human rights covenant.[77] He approved for this strategy because, he argued, it would be a more effective tool as opposed to the convention. As in the case of the UDHR, an inclusive instrument would, the Egyptian delegate stated, persuade "public opinion to accept a covenant dealing with all 'members of the human family'— men and women alike—[more] than a convention which would grant to women alone, political rights still denied to millions of men." He identified positive prowomen initiatives that emerged in the national context; for example, that his own countrywomen "had discarded the veils" through their own nationalistic endeavors. However, he claimed, even if women had fought next to men, "their astounding and indeed revolutionary progress had taken place quietly and naturally."[78] His speech is important for two reasons; first he introduced the contentious issue of the Islamic veil, which other delegates mentioned at different times and in different modalities; second, he highlighted how gender cooperation for nationalist purposes was to be praised as opposed to activisms for the sole purpose of advocating for the rights of women. The Egyptian motion suggested that men—and not women—were to be the primary receivers of rights and this order was not to be inverted.

Ultimately, the most progressive conception of women's rights came from another part of the Muslim world. Muslim women ambassadors were instead concerned with the association between Islam and discrimination against women. The UN representative for Iraq, Bedia Afnan, for example, applauded the convention. As I show in multiple chapters, Afnan distinguished herself in multiple occasions for a progressive global understanding of human rights. In her opinion, the fact that Iraq welcomed the convention disproved with the general idea that the Muslim world discriminated against women. Afnan discussed the role of smaller countries in the GA voting dynamics. For her, these countries should carry a weight equal to that of the militarily and economically powerful ones. Small countries, Afnan said, could offer "the benefit of their culture and . . . unspoiled idealism in the services of the common cause."[79] This was the rationale behind her support for the convention, even if she claimed that her government might not agree with it. According to her, her support "was perfectly consistent with her responsibility as a Moslem." Islam, she argued, was not responsible for women's discrimination, as historically, Muslims were more politically open than their Western counterparts and with more progressive ideas as compared to the West. In the contemporary world, Afnan claimed, discrimination against women lay in their reproductive ability and hence in men's desire to protect them.[80] However, Afnan said, the cause of discrimination against Muslim women was not Islam but Muslims themselves. She did not differentiate among national Muslim communities but advanced a common Islamic identity beyond national borders. Ultimately, she added that the Convention was not contrary to Islamic law.

Afnan's intervention was salient for multiple reasons. She disentangled Islam as a theory from its practitioners who, in her contention, had misinterpreted the religion and claimed that discrimination against women was an Islamic practice. She hints at patriarchy as the force that damaged women. She noted that women in Asian and Arab countries were already fighting to alter discriminatory institutions, specifying therefore that contrary to general accusations of political inactivity, women were reacting to forces that discriminated against them. Second, she argued that in the Arab countries, there was not a "feminist movement as such," and "complete emancipation had been the joint aim of both sexes." Women's suffrage, she claimed, was already established in the West, but Arab countries were implementing tools to improve the lives of the overall population. Afnan found in the UN Charter the means to conflate all these elements. She trusted that the majority of states would vote in favor of the convention because even the charter codified women's equality.[81]

While Afnan made a case for an Islamic identity while supporting the convention, a third representatives from the Muslim world proposed different interpretations connected to both Islam and the local specificities. The Pakistani delegate, Begum Liaquat Ali Kahn, disconnected women's discrimination from Islam, but she also presented a special case for Pakistan. She argued that Islamic law "had recognized woman as a person under the law in her own right, independent of her parents or husband."[82] In the case of Pakistani women, she continued, the struggle for independence from Britain and the guidance of Mohammed Ali Jinnah contributed "to denounce the seclusion of women as a crime against humanity." Interestingly, Khan used the charged language of crimes against humanity to highlight how the newly born Pakistan fiercely supported women. Arguably, this type of language served as propaganda in the partition struggle.[83] She also stated that the separation from India caused women to readily intervene to aid the newly arrived population fleeing from India. These circumstances, Khan noted, were instrumental to the creation of the All Pakistan Women's Association.[84] Moreover, while Afnan embraced suffrage as an emancipatory tool for women in the Arab world, Khan argued that the equality of women, even under private and public law in almost all spheres of activity, could be achieved without advocating for suffrage. The future constitution of Pakistan, Khan claimed, included "the principle of freedom and equality as enunciated by Islam," therefore no "suffragette agitation" was necessary for women to achieve equality.[85] Her intervention confirmed Afnan's vision of a prowomen Islam but simultaneously discouraged advocacy for women like the Egyptian and British ambassadors did in the same context. The three speeches of delegates from the Muslim world show the coexistence of a diversified opinion on the modalities to adopt in order to secure women's rights, whether through a specific women's political tool or within a larger legal framework, Islamic law or a human rights covenant. At stake in the case of Pakistan was the "agitation" that women's advocacy would have caused.

At the end of debate, Minerva Bernardino presented a speech that responded to those member states that did not support the convention. She spoke in favor of international legal instruments as representing a "more modern concept" to fight "social injustice" detrimental to "all human groups."[86] She provided an accurate summary of the debate to promote or reject the convention: there are states that were, in Bernardino's words "feudal" and resisted the concept of women's rights. Countries that did not support the convention, she claimed, fabricated arguments to justify their lack of support. Specifically, she referred to states that refused to support an international tool that confirmed the already existing principles of equality at a national level. She denounced their argument on the convention as a potential harm to the "normal development" of women and their progression to full equality.[87] Other states, referring to Egypt without doing so specifically, called for women's rights to be inserted in the larger human rights initiative. For Bernardino, this type of critique did not legitimize the commission's efforts as a promoter of rights but implied the superiority of the Human Rights Commission. To states such as Egypt, she responded: "Admittedly, women ought to benefit from the proclamation of human rights, but it was nevertheless true that, in some countries, they could not hope to derive any advantage from it because they were not regarded as human beings." She concluded by stating that the old "antifeminist" formulas, such as depicting women as the "'weaker sex,'" justified discrimination against women on the basis of their bodily abilities. However, she brought back the discourse of women and the war effort claiming that the Second World War showed that women were as capable as men.[88] Bernardino's speech to support the convention at the Third Committee reconfirmed the principles that justified the creation of the commission for the sake of the rights of women. Rights, if left to the larger human rights framework, would have not changed the position of women in societies.

Conclusion

This chapter has shown how the work for an international instrument for the political rights of women led commissioners to isolate the group of women in need of political rights, how these women were to become active citizens, and how the UN member states looked at women's rights in general. In the midst of this work, the Palestinian partition and the Korean War served as a tool to question peace, propaganda, and the possibility of criticizing a member state, directly or indirectly.

The meaning of "peace" shifted from postwar reconstruction in which there was a general agreement emerging from antifascism. To the Soviets, peace meant social justice at a national and international level—at least in the case of capitalist and imperialist countries—to self-defined democracies, reconstruction turned into "development" as the Korean war—sanctioned by the UN—complicated the meaning of peace.[89]

The Japanese case illustrates, instead, a sort of imported and forced gender equality from another country. The United States encouraged voting rights for Japanese women but not for African American Women in Jim Crow South. The showcase of the two Japanese observers, still in the context of Cold War politics, proved how self-assumed humanitarianism was part of the U.S. strategy of expanding its sphere of influence.

The Palestinian case highlighted the limitations of CSW when it came to discuss other member states in their resolutions. At a debate level, commissioners released a series of attacks, but the ECOSOC received a lean and unified message. Both Palestinian and Japanese lands were occupied according to different international law provisions; both cases served to reinforce American alliances in geopolitical complex areas such as Asia and the Middle East.

This chapter also shows how woman still represented a contentious category. Claiming rights meant agitation, disharmony with men, and subverting the natural order of things that saw men as the primary claimers of rights. Postcolonial states, with the exception of India, were at that moment mostly self-claimed Muslim countries which related to Islam in various ways showing a pronounced diversity between North Africa, the Middle East, and South Asia. The decolonized state had to grasp with questioning Western imports of progressive concepts and looking at the UN principles as universally applicable to their own local realities. Within these contexts, religion emerged as a central category; the Catholic motion in favor of Palestinian refugees and the Muslim support of political rights appeared as an unequivocal presence of religion in the UN work. The Islamic veil started to appear as both the symbol of tradition as well as of anticolonial modernity.

The issue of backwardness appeared in discussion of women to rescue, mostly located in the dependent territories but also in the occupied ones. While commissioners' prejudices and rigid hierarchies can be interpreted through an imperial feminist understanding it was also accurate that the only meter of comparison outside the direct Cold War polemics was the colonial sphere or war zones.

The following chapter illustrates how in the background of the passage from political to economic rights, colonialism became an attack that provoked stern defenses from the West. At the CSW's seventh session (1953), the Byelorussian delegate argued that by considering rights separately, the commission could not forecast how a lack of economic and social rights might affect women even if they held political rights. As she stated, "political, economic and social rights" were supposed to be a "single subject."[90] Her argument was consistent with the early GA's 1948 declaration on the indivisibility of human rights.[91] Through voting sessions and debates, however, state delegates agreed on two covenants that separated rights into political, economic, and social rights.[92] The CSW had already moved toward such a separation through the creation of the Convention on the Political Rights of Women. The convention's separation of political rights represents historical continuity with traditional liberal feminism, yet in the larger history of human rights, commissioners served as the pioneers who divided rights and produced a legal provision for a specific group. The rationale behind the Convention on Political Rights was to bring women to an equal footing with men in the area of civic participation first and foremost.

4. UN Technical Assistance Program, Indonesia, May 1956. © United Nations, reprinted with permission of the United Nations.

3

Cold War, Competing Womanhood, and Bodies in the Microcosm

The photograph at left portrays people involved in a UN technical assistance program in Indonesia. This type of visual material belonged to the UN's own promotion of involvement in different countries; work and training symbolized a universal dimension and created a unifying narrative that allegedly transcended Cold War divisions or rather created a sense of exportable knowhow. The depicted event is possibly related to carpet making, an activity that attracted a wide audience. Such initiatives represented the early stages of what later became the full-blown development era. The UN, along with the main agencies such as the ILO, the UNESCO, and the WHO created programs to train women in traditionally female tasks, including home economics. In the context of the status of women and dependent territories, these programs highlighted the need for international aid in the post-colony as well as the rigid gendered aspect of these enterprises. The image is also representative of how the Asian context became prominent because of international aid experimentations and, consequently, Cold War politics in which, for some Asian countries, a clear stand against First and Second World spheres of influences developed.

The Bandung Conference of 1955 showed how the nonaligned movement was advancing independent from the pressure of allying with one bloc or the other. Close to Bandung were two events that signaled the Cold War options for women's rights: the Moscow Seminar of 1956 and the Bangkok Seminar of 1957. These two events show two competing models for postcolonial women, one formulated and showcased in the Soviet Union and the other one supported by the United States and its interest in Asian countries for containment as well as a blend of capitalist aid and reinforcement of local traditions. By the late 1950s, it was clear that European empires were in crisis, lingering in the international scene through a series of rhetorical devices. An example was an article presented at the CSW as a reputable source to discredit the Soviet Union along the lines of colonialism of conquests and colonialism of welfare. Paradoxically, the hostile attitude of the Soviet Bloc commissioners helped the cause of the West. The Americans and British feared that a discussion on economic rights would have showed the flaws of capitalism,[1] but their defense of the "colonial" attack did not leave space for a solid engagement and clear comparison of the two systems: capitalism and socialism.

More broadly, assistance programs revealed the centrality of economic rights in both the dependent territories and the newly created nation-states. The shift to economic rights opened a new set of limitations and assumptions of women's roles in society. Historically, women's work saw two competing narratives in which women bodies were central, protection versus legal equality. The protectionist rationale restricted women's access to jobs that were deemed dangerous in light of reproductive functions and familial duties.[2] The legal equality position argued that protective measures unfairly restricted women's access to jobs.

Since its first session in 1947, the CSW included in its long-term agenda the fight against discrimination of women in private law. An examination of private law allowed also for competing understandings of political versus economic rights. Chapter 2 shows how civic duties and women's insertion into the public sphere provoked contentious responses. Economic rights were both public and private: public in the sense of paid work outside the home and private in the sense of how working outside the home could affect the unpaid domestic duties, an expectation that commissioners did not dismantle. Just as the issue of education had created conflict with the UNESCO, economics rights along with the Cold War formations reinforced tensions of expertise with the ILO. Although the CSW leaned against protective measures, eventually, as I will show in chapter 6, commissioners repositioned mothers as a central category of their policies.[3]

In their own unique way, the two seminars—Moscow and Bangkok—created the postcolonial subcategory of the woman to be trained in either socialist or capitalist model. The former colonies in Asia represented a new terrain onto which to test modernization, in either a planned or market economy. First and Second World commissioners aimed to show that agency could be exported, assuming of course their own position of fully emancipated women. Their efforts, however, were not undisturbed. While attending a 1950s CSW session, the ILO chief of the Women and Young Workers Division, Mildred Fairchild, noticed that "the preference of the majority for the Western position was marked, but the abstaining votes of the members from Burma, Iran, Lebanon, Pakistan . . . were equally evident."[4] The criticism through abstention could also reveal that the postcolonial Asian countries were suspended in between the need for international aid and their possible disdain for any type of Western influence.

This chapter shows how, in the formulation of an oppositional conception of the status of women, the two Cold War forces dominated the debate, and through a series of activities sponsored by or designed within the UN and the emerging thrust of international aid, they were able to propose the application of their understanding of women's rights abroad. In their own terms, the Soviet Bloc and U.S. representatives discarded the colonial world where the Europeans had failed to bring equality; they both proposed a new and improved civilizing mission; the Soviet one aimed at economic and political equality with men. The U.S.-supported seminar instead formulated that women had a specific responsibility within the Cold War-led civilization; they had to sacrifice their own individuality for the community away from the urban setting, a place of danger and corruption. In this view, the countryside offered solid ties and possibilities to use women's education for the greater good. Within this scheme, an important tool to promote women's rights in the developing microcosm was the UN-sponsored seminar which became a successful formula and lens onto the status of local women and an attempt to solve issues of voicing the needs of absent women. Furthermore, the seminars, born as a human rights initiative in 1953, officially embraced technocracy as a tool for promoting human rights.[5] The CSW participated in these human rights initiatives which, at least under the specific form of the international seminar, unified the category of women's and human rights.

Beyond the attacks of propaganda that I discussed in chapter 2, the Cold War plot developed at the CSW through more subtle politics. The activities for the political rights of women led to two different results. First, the subsequent work on the nationality of married women led the United States to push for a less invasive CSW, one with a purely fact-finding role. Second, the activism for suffrage encouraged the Soviet bloc to highlight how political rights without the economic ones meant little for women's lives.

During the background work for the 1952 Convention on the Political Rights of Women, the Secretariat issued a questionnaire to member states covering both public and private laws related to nationality, family law, and property rights.[6] The Secretariat's report on private law as well as the NGO's testimonies encouraged commissioners to center primarily on marriage, first on the nationality of married women and later on customs affecting the status of women in marriage.[7] Focusing on marital unions and marriage practices created the trajectory that led the CSW to look into forced marriage, equality within the family, and (later) into reproductive rights.

Traditionally, the man as head of the family, father or husband, determined the nationality of the family as a group; legally the family members had the same nationality of the father.[8] With the emergence of voting rights for women, those who married a foreigner lost their political rights because they were forced to acquire the nationality of the husband, possibly from a country that did not allow women to vote. Nationality in this case showed the different access to citizenship for nationals and the gender hierarchy within the family. Symbolically, the loss of political rights appeared also as a patriarchal punishment for women who chose to marry a foreigner and (in the case of xenophobic politics and countries with migrants) it could be seen as a punishment to marry outside of one's race and/or ethnicity.

Commissioners fought against the idea that women should lose their own nationality upon marrying a foreigner, which was the common rule globally. The decision to work on the Convention on the Nationality of Married Women therefore represented a challenge to this contested norm and questioned the patriarchal authority of both the husband and the state. Compared to the Convention on the Political Rights of Women, this new international instrument ruled over both private matters such as marriage and public ones such as nationality. It did not propose a narrative of "deserving rights for having contributed to the nation," but it was rather a corrective tool to the loss of nationality. Ultimately, a broader focus on marriage led to the exploration of women's everyday lives and, consequently, to cultural practices as the discriminating agent in women's lives.

As discussed in chapter 1, the commission was born under a contested view of the relationship between the universalism of human rights and the specificities of women's rights.[9] The UN efforts to pass the 1957 Convention on the Nationality of Married Women once again defined the rights of women as existing in a dichotomy between the universal and the bodily specific. During the background exploration for a possible international instrument to protect women's nationality, the representative of the United States proposed a resolution in favor of the inclusion of the question of the citizenship of married women within the larger issue of stateless people.[10] At that time, the UN was preparing a convention on this emergency because the postwar geographical order had created the problem of displaced people without citizenship. However, the issue of married women differed greatly from the general problem of statelessness.

The U.S. resolution on inserting women's nationality within the general framework of stateless people aligned with the delegation's expressed desire for the commission to be a pedagogic organization opposed to a more influencing mediator of international affairs.[11] The American proposal was consistent with the government's goal of protecting the commission from strong statements that could threaten the United States' self-assumed leadership over the First World and future postcolonial allies. A weak and informative commission could not question dubious U.S. policies at the national and international levels and could also affect the strong role of the Soviet Bloc commissioners. Relegating the CSW's work to a non-gender-specific framework—the issue of stateless people—could limit the commission's work on deliberating (or proposing deliberations) and aligned with the politics of the U.S. State Department which aimed to limit international interference in national matters.[12]

During the debates at the CSW's seventh session (1953), the Soviet commissioner, Popova, brought attention to the discrepancy between legal and actual equality for women. The promotion of economic rights, a tangible measurement of equality with men, was the way to assess actual progress for women, in Popova's opinion.[13] She argued that the data that the commission used as the base for its provisions was "misleading," because women were often legally allowed to participate but could not fully use their political rights. The data were especially distorted for women in the dependent territories, as a focus on the law obscured the colony's racial practices in everyday life. Even on this occasion, the commission's chairperson and French delegate, Lefaucheux, highlighted women's progress in the métropole as a general measure of women's progress in the entire French Empire.[14] The entanglements between the Cold War and colonialism complicated even traditional empires which, by the late 1950s, started to crumble.

The Soviet delegation also supported a more specific language that attributed the responsibility to enforce women's rights to individual states. However, voting procedures and states' concerns for their own sovereignty diminished the chances of approving more specific guidelines. The Byelorussian delegate advocated for a more practical role for the commission: providing a clear direction to states both for the implementation and enforcement of women's rights. This role meant collecting information on each member state's enforcement mechanism to ensure "practical guarantees for the enjoyment of equal rights in all spheres."[15] In their criticism of formal equality, the Soviet Bloc pushed for procedures that appeared impossible to achieve but were effective from a rhetorical point of view. Their support for a more effective and intrusive commission appeared ambiguous, since historically the Soviet Union aimed to limit UN interference in national matters.[16] The call for a stronger role for the commission vis-à-vis the reluctance toward international interference in national matters suggests that the Soviets used the narratives of women's rights within the traditional Cold War drama. Whereas the United States advocated for a mere research role for the commission, the Soviets pushed for a forceful, albeit impractical, role for the commission as a mediator between women and states—but elsewhere, rather than within the Soviet setting where illustrating the status of women was part of a state-sponsored curated mechanism.

Reading the support or rejection of legal equality in tandem with the Cold War drama reveals the complexity of American and Soviet politics, which were centered on a competition over which Cold War ideology best represented democracy. In the case of the Soviet Union, rejecting formal equality served to connect women's rights to economic rights. Under this rationale, the ability to work and earn money was an indicator of emancipation beyond suffrage that, if isolated from economic rights, did not improve women's lives.

The Soviet Woman as an Exportable Model

At the commission's meetings, the main Soviet diplomatic tactic for women's rights was comparison and showcase: they glorified their own progress to demonstrate the benefits of Soviet-based sex equality and, simultaneously, denounced those countries where state-sponsored sex discrimination threatened policies promoting women's rights.[17] Soviet criticism of the UN, the United States, and the so-called West produced unintended international political processes that benefited women or at least reinforced the direct relationship between UN principles and national progress transcending the post-WORLD WAR II logic of deserving rights because of war sacrifices. As showed in chapter 2, the Soviet delegation accused the European colonial powers, the United States, and South Africa of perpetuating racist and discriminatory policies against women. By contrast, this critique suggested a story of progress for the Soviet woman and promoted Soviet claims of jurisdiction over the status of women in the dependent territories. If the West was colonialist, the Soviets were liberators; this narrative was far from linear, and rhetoric played a prominent role in constructing Soviet progress.

The UN Soviet delegates presented themselves as communist success stories even if the history of exporting the Soviet model of womanhood had been problematic. The case of the 1920s forced public unveiling of Muslim women had demonstrated how women's bodies were central to the Soviet colonial designs in central Asia.[18] The presumed Soviet liberation and intervention, however, relegated even more Uzbek women into the home. The Islamic veil came to represent (as it did later in other colonial conflicts) a symbol of resistance. By the 1950s, the earlier unveiling fiasco gave space to a model central Asian Soviet Republic. As discussed in chapter 2, the Soviet mentioned Uzbekistan as a success case; as I illustrate later in this chapter, the British, instead, listed Uzbekistan as an example of aggressive Soviet imperialism.

Soviet commissioners turned the post-revolutionary women's experience into a transnational model to be followed globally. Russian women of the Khrushchev era (1953–1964) portrayed themselves "less as individuals than as representative of a collective experience."[19] Their model was exportable also because under Khrushchev a major interest in international development and the end of colonialism emerged.[20] The Soviet delegation's framework of human rights and its eagerness to promote the communist model of everyday life produced an account that, though national at its base, became transnational, making the Soviet *testimonio* a part of the history of international women's rights. It was also the desire of the global applicability of communism that made the model exportable. However, there were striking differences between rhetoric and reality.

The Soviet state was patriarchal, but it did not reinforce patriarchy in the public realm.[21] Within this framework, Soviet women delegates depicted the transnational woman worker as independent from her husband and in full control of her civic duty. The glorification of labor as a form of political participation led commissioners to question the divisibility of rights that the Convention on Political Rights of Women had pioneered in the UN system of human rights.[22] The Soviet attitude toward women and modernization and the separation of rights represented the theoretical background for the Moscow Seminar a meeting—designed within the UN—in which Soviet women's activists could illustrate their home progresses. The 1956 Moscow Seminar provided the Soviets with the opportunity to exhibit the new Soviet woman and her special relationship with the state as an example that could irradiate from the Soviet Union to the rest of the world.

The planning of the Moscow Seminar started during the Beirut meeting when the commissioners agreed on the necessity of advertising their UN activism within local settings. In 1953, the CSW proposed to ECOSOC a more concrete promotion of women's rights through technical assistance and seminars at the local level. At the eleventh session (1955), the Polish delegate proposed a conference on women's rights in which female members of parliament could meet with NGO representatives. The American commissioner favored smaller seminars over a larger conference because the commission could financially support the former but not the latter.[23] Soviet Bloc delegates aimed to emphasize women's political leadership rather than mere "pedagogy" as deployed in smaller settings. The Soviet women delegates succeeded in designing a meeting which was not directly sponsored by the UN but aligned with the CSW principles. UN delegates did participate in the seminar as invited guests.

The 1956 Moscow Seminar represented a hybrid between a conference and a seminar; its purpose was to show off women's rights in the Soviet Union, where policies in favor of women were supposed to appear as an internationally adaptable model for the attendees. Ninety-eight delegations from thirty-seven countries participated in the seminar. NGOs, UN special agencies, the Secretariat representative, and national women's organizations were present. The representatives of the Secretariat's Section on the Status of Women attended in their "personal capacity," as the UN did not officially support this seminar.[24] The event was paid for by the Russian government, and so it was not one of the UN-sponsored seminars under the Human Rights Advisory Program which later founded the Bangkok Seminar, the Addis Ababa Seminar, and the Lomé Seminar, just to mention the most prominent ones.

At the 1956 plenary meeting of the ECOSOC, the Soviet delegate detailed the program of the seminar, stating that "the purpose of the seminar" was "to make known the experience acquired by the Soviet Union in giving effect to equality of rights of men and women in all spheres." The agenda included the "participation of women in government in the Soviet Union; equality of rights of men and women; women of the Soviet Union and equality of rights in the economic field; social insurance in the Soviet Union and state maternity and child protection; rights of women of the Soviet Union in education; and cultural and scientific activities of women of the Soviet Union."[25] The planning contemplated postsession discussions and also the possibility of a conversation with Soviet political representatives. The seminar included trips to different Soviet areas. This type of organizing arguably aimed for a unilateral participation rather than a conversation. The UNESCO delegate at the seminar claimed that the extremely busy calendar did not really allow for actual discussions. Along those same lines, experts in specific areas of women's lives were not paired with the Soviet counterparts in their fields.[26] The seminar, therefore, was an exhibition that did not allow for a direct dialogue.

Included in the Moscow programs were visits to collective farms, factories, hospitals, educational establishments, and maternity and childcare facilities.[27] The underlying narrative of the seminar revolved around the "before" and "after" of the Bolshevik Revolution; in contrast to Czarist Russia, the status of women in Soviet Russia appeared as proof of the success of the communist model.[28] Likewise, for the other socialist republics, the seminar's rhetoric emphasized the backwardness of their previous societies as compared to the modern Soviet model. A night plane trip took the participants to Uzbekistan. The two stops the plane made before reaching the country showed the vastness of the Soviet area. Once they arrived, participants visited a dacha along with cotton fields to show the Soviet aesthetics and the development of the area.[29] The days of public unveiling were long gone and left space for what was presented as a modern and efficient Soviet state.

Modernity assumed a different representation depending on the area. In a way Moscow illustrated the splendor of a métropole as an example to follow for dependent territories. The host delegation brought the participants to film screenings, ballet performances, and concerts, as well as to tractor plants and textile factories to show how Soviet women could be both graceful and strong.[30] Central Asia was a good case of the already successful export of the Soviet model. The glorification of the Soviet woman went hand in hand with the advocacy of women's economic rights—the workingwoman, the seminar proceeding suggested, performed her civic duty through labor inside and outside the home.[31] Soviet women epitomized the same laboring bodies contributing to the nation-state that Roosevelt praised in her letter to the women of the world. Showcasing women's tasks across the gender border served to illustrate a similar mechanism of deserving rights.

The UNESCO delegate highlighted how, at the Moscow Seminar, the construction of Soviet women's everyday life was effective to foreign eyes and rhetorically blended with the commission's support of women's rights as civic participation. The seminar allowed for a close observation of a local setting where—according to Soviet rhetoric—an efficient and successful state led to an advanced status for women.[32] Nonetheless, displaying the model of the Soviet woman in connection with the commission's focus constituted a protoimperial feminist performance of communist propaganda in which global comparisons and the promotion of women's advancement imposed an alternative to local typologies of womanhood, while pushing national propaganda—especially to the newly decolonized countries. This positive model of women in the Soviet Bloc contrasted with the depiction of an oppressive and expansionist Soviet state raised by other voices within the commission. Whereas these dynamics were specific to local settings, the discourses surrounding them revolved around the commission's politics. The performance of the Soviet Bloc states and the reaction described below were byproducts of the commission's operations and reflected also colonial Cold War dynamics.

Colonialism of Conquest vs. Colonialism of Welfare

On March 13, 1956, the *Times of London* published a lengthy article titled "Russian Colonialism in Perspective: New Twist to an Old Tradition."[33] The article came to assume a central role at one of the commission's meetings. The unnamed British special correspondent in Russia claimed, "The Soviet empire is the outcome of a policy of colonial expansion steadily pursued over the past 300 years." The author argued for a long history of Russian colonialism dating from Ivan the Terrible and continuing into Soviet Russia and claimed that traditional strategies such as "gaining a window in Europe" explained early "colonialism," whereas a more complex system of postwar abusive land attribution explained the more recent colonial conquests.

The article was a direct response to Soviet propaganda against British imperialism as it stated, "In the light of this record, Russian propaganda about British 'colonialism' cannot expect to go unchallenged." Within this intention of redeeming British colonialism, the author harshly criticized the Soviet modes of conquest and the "mass enslavement" of the conquered population. The horror of the discovery of the Stalin-era massacres gave the author the opportunity to piece together the terror of the Stalin era and geographical expansion. Furthermore, the author's use of dates as well as names of places and communist representatives provided an aura of authenticity. As the author put it, "It is in the ideological field that Soviet colonialism differs radically from all other types of colonialism. Boundaries, nationality, national aspirations, ancient cultures—all must give way to Soviet Communism." The British imagined themselves as "respectful" colonizers, contrary to the Romanov or the Soviet ones (the author depicted continuity between both colonizing agents) who imposed their "ideology." During an intense debate between the British and Soviets on women in the dependent territories at the commission's tenth session (1956), the British delegate quoted this *Times* article as "evidence" of Soviet "hypocrisy."

The search for evidence—as opposed to ideology—to support the Eastern or Western Bloc was one of the outcomes of the centrality of ideology during the Cold War; for the West ideology was a synonym for communism, condemned as lies opposed to the plain truth. The British commissioner's use of written "evidence," as embodied in a news article, represented Western "truth" in contrast to ideological Soviet propaganda.

As the British article suggested, during the first decades of the commission's activity, the word *colonialism* became an international insult; the British found a way to describe their colonialism as more noble and aimed at modernization and the welfare of the people. Whereas the French were eager to show the extension of French civic traditions in their colonies, the British argued for a moderate transition that did not impact local customs throughout the British Empire. Women's rights, as the British delegate claimed at the voting session for the Convention on the Political Rights of Women (see chapter 2), were too revolutionary. The Soviets, as noted earlier, conflated Western colonial practices and U.S. racial segregation. The Chinese delegate followed the British model and declared mainland China as a "trust territory" under the Soviet Union.[34] As stated earlier, the UN Trusteeship Council was created to substitute the League of Nations mandate system. Mainland China was under the rule of Mao's communist regime, which was allied with the Soviet Union until the late 1960s. This accusation was problematic particularly because it involved the official Chinese delegate indirectly criticizing the UN trusteeship system as a colonial-like administration and the Soviet of meddling into another country's sovereignty.

Within this animated context, the reverse side of the "colonial insult" was the word *democracy*—a term that in postwar politics became a symbol for the struggle against totalitarian regimes as well as a self-assigned label of the leading world superpowers. Because commissioners conceived of the nation-state as a guarantor of women's equality through the law, delegates used a spectrum from colonialism to democracy to define states and their relationship to the status of women. Through such differentiations, they reinforced a system of comparing states based on women's rights. While these dynamics contributed to a tense climate, they did not directly affect the commission's operations.

Arguably, when human rights entered the realm of propaganda, they lost their chances of concrete implementation; they became part of the façade of democracy.[35] Exploring the role of gender in these Cold War debates and following the commission's local policies can provide an alternative interpretation. Three main dynamics developed around the topic of colonialism, race, and women's rights. First was the confrontation between the Soviets and European colonial powers, the second involved the emergence of a contested meaning of tradition, and the third highlighted the gendered role of the U.S. commissioner in her work promoting the self-reflective American idea of democracy.

The representatives from Russia, Byelorussia, and Poland used figures to reinforce their arguments about Western powers, race, and the rights of women. The British, American, and Chinese commissioners disqualified Soviet statements as "ideology" and propaganda, and in so doing they suggested that imperialism and capitalism were not ideologies but "natural" processes. Furthermore, the British self-detachment from a colonialism of conquest created a new version of British colonialism in which the West brought modernization in cooperation with the UN. By the mid-1950s, the French and British delegations spoke about colonies in terms of modernization and the welfare of the people. The UN Charter included an article on colonial powers' voluntary reports on their territories. Through these reports, the French and British delegations shared with other commissioners the "progress" that their colonies had made on the basis of UN-based principles.[36]

Connected to this new version of colonialism was also the testimony of representatives from former colonies who needed international aid. For example, the delegate from Pakistan was interested in creating international legal provisions to correct traditional practices detrimental to the status of women. Tradition became a contested term within the commission's debates. Western colonial powers (Britain, France, and Belgium) claimed that they respected local traditions; however, allowing women's rights in a context of colonial hierarchy arguably would have challenged European power.

The U.S. case was different, but as stated above, the Soviet Bloc commissioners included the United States in the list of colonial-like powers; they considered the United States to practice colonialism within its boundaries (racial segregation) as well as abroad. The American commissioner replied to attacks on U.S. racial politics by saying that the CSW's role only concerned discrimination against women. In her opinion, "discrimination on other grounds . . . was adequately dealt with by the Sub-Commission on Prevention of Discrimination and Protection of Minorities and by the Commission on Human Rights."[37] She felt obliged to respond to the criticism of the Soviet Union representative and hence produced an account of American efforts to solve the racial problem at home. She discussed equality under the law and legal instruments for integration.

The U.S. delegate reproduced the institutional story, which neglected the impact of the dominant mentality that favored racism. She concluded by saying that "she regretted the unfair reference made to the position in the United States of America by the representative of the Soviet Union, where grave breeches of human rights and freedoms occurred. That country was scarcely in a position to criticize another." Her reference to "breeches of human rights" in Soviet countries was difficult to bring to the table, as evidence of such breeches was not discussed in the commission.[38] She did not address issues related to U.S. policies directly but rather used a different diplomatic strategy, which, however, was representative of one of the multiple images of Cold War women's politics on display at the commission.

Different models of 1950s American women dedicated to women's politics and/or reinforcing rigid models of traditional womanhood existed.[39] Women anticolonial activists were part of the political scenario, but their activities were weakened by the anticommunist crusades.[40] In the context of the divergence between women's equal and social rights in the United States, legal equality appeared as more aligned with Cold War thinking in which everything "social" became equated with socialism. Within this framework, the commission presented yet another model of American woman: the gendered diplomat who represented a government that struggled to "keep the dirty laundry in the family." The commissioner from the United

States rarely responded directly to racial accusations made against her country, and when she did, she only discussed the law instead of describing the actual practices that reinforced and perpetuated inequality. At a time when the CSW was transitioning to a focus on individual behavior as the main agent of discrimination, the United States pushed for a renewed focus on legal equality and, consequently, called for a research-like role for the commission (collecting information on the law as opposed to providing standard settings on the status of women to member states).

At a national level, the U.S. government showed an interest in civil rights mostly as a reaction to Soviet attacks on American racism, so that, as historian Mary Dubziak argues, "the story of race in America, used to compare democracy and communism, became an important Cold War narrative."[41] However, national women's activism pioneered some of the integration policies of the civil rights era.[42] Within the international setting of the commission, the State Department's logic of washing dirty clothes at home (the UN was not home, but a platform of exposure) prevailed, and American female delegates were entrusted with protecting their racially vulnerable country against the Soviet enemy. Interestingly, the familial metaphor prevailed both nationally and transnationally. The logic of Cold War "containment" promoted the family as a "psychological fortress" at a national level, while the American diplomatic protection within the CSW reinforced women delegates' gendered role at a transnational level.[43] In the context of searching for the true causes of discrimination against women, this attitude aimed to slow the commission's work as the association of discrimination and practice were ideologically dangerous for the United States within the global context.

Women and Postcolonial Development in Asia

At its 1956 session, the commission expressed its intention to explore "the possibility of holding regional seminars to assist women who . . . acquired political rights" in order to help them "in developing their understanding of civic responsibilities and increasing their participation in the public life of their countries."[44] As discussed in chapter 2, in the early 1950s the CSW proposed programs to assist women in their transition to full citizenship. The General Assembly embraced this project and included the planning of seminars on women's rights under the Human Rights Commission Advisory Services. Therefore, the csw started its local activities through technical assistance programs (see figure 4) and international seminars for women's rights.

The csw's transition to a closer observation of local societies was consistent with the un's new initiative to instruct populations on human rights through advisory services. These un-sponsored programs aimed to collaborate with local organizations to increase women's participation in public life. Under this new un initiative, the performative politics that were on display at the Moscow Seminar gave way to more collaborative efforts, which nonetheless presented at times problematic solutions for women.

All commissioners were enthusiastic about offering un-sponsored technical assistance to those countries that needed it.[45] The United States greatly supported these programs; this type of aid connected U.S. imperial-like practices with modernity.[46] Situating the early stages of un-based aid within postcolonial relationships aligned with the csw's emphasis on the unified category of "women of the world." The Soviets believed it was possible to export the modern standard of Soviet womanhood as well. The United States, Pakistan, and Indonesia advocated for the international modeling of the csw's principles in conjunction with Western expertise.

The U.S. commissioner expressed her gratitude to the General Assembly for resolution 729 which allowed the un to offer technical assistance.[47] The first country to request this new type of aid was Pakistan. In the American position, technical assistance was not only beneficial to women but to the general well-being of a country. The U.S. delegate listed the many un outreach programs that, in the mid-1950s, emerged in every corner of the globe. In the Caribbean, a Swedish expert was training local teachers. The Iranian government created a program of technical assistance in cooperation with the United States to train female students in home economics and homemaking. In Liberia, the un helped to create classes on nutrition, childcare, and local governance. In the U.S. view, it was the csw's duty to advertise these projects to the broader public. Among such enthusiastic outreach efforts, the United States was the first country to offer to host a seminar on women's political participation based on un principles.[48] Arguably, by hosting the seminar, the United States could have more control over issuing invitations to participants along Cold War lines.

In the course of the preliminary work for the seminar, the Secretariat and the U.S. State Department engaged in a tense diplomatic exchange on the possible participation of Laos and Cambodia. The seminar was supposed to be for women who had recently acquired the right to vote. At the same time of the debate over whether to invite Laos and Cambodia, Laos had changed its constitution to allow women's suffrage. The State Department presented several arguments that stood in the way of these countries' participation: a lack of women's suffrage, the countries' French affiliation with consequent translation problems, and the governments' ongoing transition from being part of French Indochina to independent rule.[49] Arguably, the "containment" U.S. interests in the newly independent states that resulted from the dissolution of Indochina rendered the international political scenario more intricate. These tensions, moreover, rendered the U.S. aid listed above as a Cold War tool.

Eventually the seminar did not take place in the United States but in Thailand, which was one of the few Global South countries that was never colonized. Yet the UN engagement with this issue is useful to reveal Cold War tensions connected to the politics of aid. The mid-1950s represented a transitional moment for Asian countries, and this much was reflected in the former Asian colonies' requests for technical assistance programs as well as the politics surrounding the seminar's invitation list which anticipated the soon-to-happen Vietnam fiasco.

The role of rights and the language that came with it was complex for the postcolonial arena. Certainly, rights were useful to promote anticolonialism, but they were also a political tool to align with the superpowers in need of providing aid and alliances.[50] As historian Roland Burke asserts, newly formed governments in both Asian and African contexts promoted human rights also as a political tool to attract economic aid.[51] Conversely, the language of development, as connected to human rights, reinforced the rigid imperial mentality that "rights" were for white settlers only and limited to the political realm; the same mentality held that "colonial development" represented the maximum political aspiration for the non-white population.[52]

The 1955 Bandung Conference challenged the idea that "development" was a colonial concession and also emphasized the centrality of economic rights.[53] International cooperation for the sake of development had become a need for both newly formed nations and the Soviet Union. For the Soviets, aid exemplified a way to spread the model of Soviet conceptions of sex equality to counterbalance American values globally. Within this framework, newly formed countries that asked for UN technical assistance programs focused on women's participation.[54]

At the CSW, the Indonesian delegate, for example, claimed that such programs were essential for local development because economic well-being would guarantee "peace and prosperity" in the world. Indonesia had greatly benefited from technical assistance programs, particularly those that focused on aspects of women's lives such as nutrition, domestic economy, nursing care, and the protection of children. Seminars proved to be one of the most effective ways of implementing international-based technical assistance within a local setting.[55] Furthermore, they provided an understanding of human rights connected to modernization and technocracy, far from ideology and principles.[56] But the training aimed at women relegated them into traditional roles turning Cold War modernity into a reactionary goal.

The Pakistani commissioner presented her country as an example of an underdevelopment, as one of the poorest, with a per-capita income of just a few dollars per month. Her description is central to understand early accounts on the meaning of development as connected to the status of women. She stated that Pakistani women worked primarily in agriculture and in textile factories. Female refugees from the Partition conflict experienced reintegration by working in the cottage industry. Whereas war and poverty encouraged rural women to work and take part in national economic projects, tradition and middle-class status affected the chances of urban women.[57] Like other UN delegates from the Muslim world, she spoke favorably of Islam and challenged the idea that religion negatively affected women in the former colonies. She explained that the Koranic verse stating that "men have a degree of advantage over women" meant that men were financially responsible for women who were not obliged to contribute financially to family expenses.[58]

The Pakistani position disentangled the rigid understanding that Islam affected women and explained that discrimination against women was part of national culture rather than the Islamic one. In her opinion, the problem was not Islam, which like any other religion gave "a message of love and understanding, of tolerance and justice," but rather individuals and societies that did not respect the ideals of tolerance and justice.[59] Her position was similar to that of Muslim delegations that had discussed the 1952 Convention for Political Rights of Women. Such testimonies provided the CSW with insights into the local setting where the relationship between women, culture, and development was emerging as a contested terrain.

Bangkok 1957: Women and Communities

As stated above, the UN decided on a series of assistance initiatives to aid newly formed countries. According to the Secretariat, the main goal of these advisory programs was to combine local people's testimony of their experiences with problem solving and international experts' perspectives on the status of women. The motivation behind the 1957 Bangkok Seminar was to find new ways of increasing the political participation of Asian women. The working group consisted of experts speaking in their own professional capacities and not only as representative of countries. Most of this knowledge was somewhat "colonized" and described Asian women in stereotypical apathetic terms.

At the opening speech of the CSW's 11th session (1957), the Chief of the Secretariat Section for Women, the Australian lawyer and women's activist Mary Tennison-Woods promoted a newly formed working group that was exploring the possibility of a seminar for twenty Asian countries on women and political participation, held in collaboration with human rights experts.[60] The Secretariat office asked the CSW to "redouble its efforts in the legal, social, economic and cultural fields until all women throughout the world enjoyed the same rights and assumed the same responsibilities as men." Tennison-Woods announced that the seminar on civic responsibility and increased participation of women in public life would be held in Bangkok in August of 1957.

The working group prepared the seminar program with the help of national and international experts. The secretary-general invited the UN's special agencies to present papers on women's participation in public life. In the past the UNESCO had harshly criticized the commissioners for their unrealistic goals and lack of precision on matters of education and women.[61] Therefore, in the case of the Bangkok Seminar, the working group incorporated issues that the commission had formulated and discussed, including the economic, social, and cultural obstacles to women's advancement. The seminar's working group demonstrated its clear intention to move beyond the law and explore how local culture affected the status of women. The human rights framework of the seminar helped to unveil an early denouncement of cultural factors that affected women's right to participate in public life but often through a binary understanding of urban versus rural.

The delegates and experts in charge of the organization of the Bangkok Seminar identified educational, economic, and health factors that limited women's participation in the public sphere. They understood that the definition of "civic rights and responsibility" had to move beyond suffrage to include other factors in women's lives; in turn, this definition would be used in the implementation and execution of government programs for communities. The experts paid special attention to communities and to the strong role of women within them. They also argued that the strength of a community was contingent on the justice within it; discrimination against women weakened communities and, consequently, the nation-state.[62] The UN was moving toward a conception that saw progress and the status of women as directly related.

Suffrage appeared to be the only sticking point. The presenters at the seminar agreed that a certain degree of political apathy existed for women in Asia who, in certain countries, already had the right to vote. The keys to women's advancement, they argued, were civic responsibility and full citizenship. However, the seminar also conceived of a narrow role for women and expectedly did not resolve the double burden of working inside and outside the home. Many presentations actually advocated that an important role for women was to raise future citizens within the home.[63] This late nineteenth-century logic still persisted.

At the Bangkok Seminar participants viewed education as an advantage for women and, simultaneously, as a disadvantage for the community. They observed how educated women tended to leave their communities of origin, which were mostly rural areas, to live in urban spaces. The discussion revolved around strategies to bring these women back to the countryside to share the benefits of their education with uneducated women.[64] The well-being of the community, therefore, served as an argument against the mobility of educated women. The language of sisterhood was used to reinforce the notion that educated women bore the responsibility for bridging the gap between themselves and their uneducated "sisters."[65]

The urban setting was represented in nineteenth-century terms as a place of both pleasure and danger. Moreover, the assumed lack of community within urban space was considered detrimental to women's lives. According to the seminar's proceedings, discrimination affected women's chances of finding secure employment and decent, comfortable lodging. Participants focused primarily on the single woman as the object of urban danger. In their view, education for these women was both a privilege and a curse. One of the seminar papers claimed, "Modern girls in particular need a type of education which will not only provide academic skills but will assist in molding the whole personality of the individual through community. . . . They must be made aware of the responsibilities attached to their newly won rights, and in particular of their responsibilities to women who have not had the advantage of education."[66] Academic knowledge, the paper argued, produced isolation, "dissatisfaction," and the dangerous tendency to criticize society.

Contrary to the Soviet model, the "working girl" envisioned by the Bangkok Seminar participants was in continuous danger of exploitation and faced the hardship of adjusting to a life far from home.[67] The discussants claimed that as long as women asked for maternity leave, the principle of equal pay for equal work was in danger because women would emphasize the bodily differences between the sexes rather than equality.[68] Protection appeared as a difficult concept to define: women were to be protected from urban dangers, but in the labor context protection meant disrupting universalism. This debate, which was already taking place at the UN and CSW, reflected the traditional positions of egalitarian and socialist feminists. Those in favor of complete equality saw protective measures based on bodily differences as a limitation to gender equality. Socialist feminists, in contrast, favored the protection of women's bodies *because* they were biologically different. At

Bangkok unrealistic demands faced by the working woman emerged almost as a punishment for women who worked outside the private sphere. The seminar for public participation seemed, in fact, to discourage the same principles that had justified its existence.

Ultimately, the seminar proceedings produced a unified voice condemning ancient laws, customs, and traditions that affected women's participation in public life.[69] The working papers generated from the seminar advocated laws "which would effectively implement the principle of equality between men and women." Women's demands for equality, however, were also met with criticism. Some accused the women participants of "continually demanding rights" and "antagonizing men." This problematic critique relegated the feminist agenda to a bothersome disruption of the status quo. In contrast, the topics of training, moderation, and reforms acquired a central role in the seminar's promotion of women's citizenship.[70]

The Bangkok Seminar was the commission's first attempt of a UN-sponsored pedagogic experience in a local setting. The transnational encounters between experts on women's issues and national delegates represented a strong stance toward enhancing women's participation in public life. However, the seminar produced reports that served to create new hierarchies and sustain old ones. The community emerged as a type of new, enlarged family in which women had even stricter roles. Patriarchy was not questioned, and as with Roosevelt's letter to the women of the world, women were required to prove their worthiness for participation in civic life.

Conclusion

This chapter has followed the applications of CSW-based principles outside of the UN headquarters of New York and Geneva in order to explore the formulation of international women's rights in different locations. Topics such as development and modernization were emerging, and the Cold War context rendered this setting more complex and prone to new geopolitical hierarchies.

The discourse of development carried a set of assumptions and strict images about which countries were worthy of aid. Within this framework, the CSW started to grapple with economic rights as human rights. Conversely, the UN embraced modernizing theories seen as necessary to create global equality; modernization appeared to be the perfect solution, one that combined international cooperation and economic rights. The relationship between perceptions of women's roles and Cold War tensions revealed how, in the midst of modernization, the notion of sex equality was still blurry in a legal sense, and the fear of a feminist disruption of the status quo was ever present.

The Moscow and Bangkok Seminars were public performances of equality, both with strong political connections to a specific Cold War understanding of gender politics and hiding the authentic plights of women in the private sphere. From the Moscow Seminar emerged a model of woman whose strong ties to the state manifested in working at home and in the factory. Ultimately, from the Bangkok Seminar (supported by the United States), the family and the community embodied the private and the public spheres of the modern state along with the dilemma of an unquestioned patriarchy. At Bangkok, the city appeared as a dangerous factor in women's lives; it represented the possibility of education and the ability for independent thought as well as the danger of structural discrimination and the anonymity of noncommunal life.

These new models of womanhood, with old gender-based restrictions, arose in the midst of the Bandung era in which women's organizations from the Global South worked in conjunction with their male counterparts in order to combine recognition of their anticolonial efforts with new demands for developmental measures. The commission's shift to policies linked to culture, customs, and ultimately, economic rights contributed to a stronger focus on the Global South as well as a shift from the legal to the cultural aspects of women's lives.

5. 1949 visiting mission in West Africa. © United Nations,
reprinted with permission of the United Nations.

4

The Sacred Trust and
the Body in Pain

The photograph at left portrays a meeting on education, held in 1949 during the Trusteeship Council Visiting Mission in West Africa.[1] These trips were part of the new instruments the UN used to measure in loco progress toward self-rule. The meeting depicted here suggests that the participants were measuring and assessing. In the late 1950s the United Nations commissioned the American photographer Todd Webb with the task of depicting modern Africa. While the photo included here is not by Webb, it epitomizes Webb's characteristic ethos of showing the benefit of modernization on the continent. Webb did portray some of the trust territories in transition, producing visual accounts that today appear more like a warning of the interaction between Western interests and African lands.[2] A recent collection of Webb's photos does show African women from the postwar period, but in the final brochure that he produced for the UN, they are invisible, as if the UN imagined modernization as a purely male process.[3]

The audience for this type of technocratic material (see figure 5) can see in full view the representatives of the Trusteeship Council (TC); the representatives of local institutions, are instead visible only from the back. Women are unseen in this photo, even if the council, according to the charter rules, had the role of implementing sex equality in the trust territories. Because of the council's guidelines and the CSW's focus on women in dependent territories, commissioners pushed for a participation in the council's activities, but the only thing they obtained was the inclusion of data on local women in the reports of the council. Yet the invisibility of African women is here symptomatic of a tendency to connect their experiences to sensational emotions, hidden rituals, and an aura of international investigative push. This chapter traces the 1949–1952 entanglements between the CSW and the Trusteeship Council. In order to provide a clear understanding of how the council worked, the chapter starts from the end of the story to then trace all the elements that brought to the centrality of the female "native" body in pain.

Even before commissioning the American photographer Webb, the UN promoted the Trusteeship Council through visual materials in different formats. The 1953 UN advertising pamphlet titled, *A Sacred Trust: The Work of the UN for Dependent People* expressed in clear terms how the UN was contributing to independence and modernization across the colonial world under international tutelage.[4] Much like Webb's photos, the pamphlet aimed to illustrate a "better" Africa and a generally better post-colonial global context. A more in-depth analysis of its content demonstrates what and how the UN wanted to advertise its own version of the African continent.

The title immediately suggests a religious tone; words such as "sacred" and "fate" recalled the same narratives of the nineteenth-century civilizing mission. The beginning of the booklet includes a solemn, almost moving, account of "the voice of Africa": a man travelled lands and oceans to declare in front of the then community of sixty countries that "Africa" needed independence and development. In his own words, "The independence which we desire is a real, not a theoretical one. The independence to which we aspire with all our hearts, and for which we work, requires political maturity, enough staff, technical skill." The speaker, Guillaume Bissek from Cameroons, under French administration, hints at a nonreadiness for independence along with a need for modernization. For the UN author (not mentioned in the pamphlet), Bissek has a "practical mind" as "he goes on to speak of the arts of government, of public health, industry, agriculture, and of the desire of a people to be taught these things." Here, underdevelopment is a "fate" that only the UN could help change. Along with a description of the Trusteeship Council, the brochure includes a photo of Mount Kilimanjaro with the following caption: "Mount Kilimanjaro, highest peak in Africa, dominates the Tanganyika highlands. Although a belief in magic and witchcraft is still common to many of the tribespeople, modern progress has in the past few years gathered moments in Tanganyika, the largest of the Trust

Territories. The particular responsibilities of the administrating authority in this vast territory arise from the important European and Asian minorities which exist alongside the large African majority."

The emphasis on nature, magic, and witchcraft belongs to a prepackaged and ahistorical "Africa." The described contrast between magic/modernity recalls earlier "civilizing" efforts along with the racial hierarchies enforced by imperial powers. The Trusteeship Council administrating authority included also traditional colonial powers such as Britain, France, and Italy because, as colonizers, they were considered experts of the countries in question.[5] Arguably, in those dependent territories, a new collective colonial master substituted the original one. The passage hints at a responsibility that arose from the presence of European and Asian minorities in the territories, which seems at a disconnect with the honorable goals expressed at the beginning of the brochure.

The trusteeship scenario included many challenges; among them, how traditional European colonial powers could play the role of mediators for self-determination when they had based their imperial rule on inequality. The pamphlet specifies, "But in the case of the Trust Territories, although the administrating powers may be the same [as the de-facto colonial ones] their rights are based not on possession or protection, but on agreement with the United Nations."[6] Specifically, the trust regulations included the language of the charter: human rights, dignity, and sex and racial equality. The brochure engages with all these elements, including women in a way that was symptomatic of the gender question in the dependent territories. As I showed in previous chapters, the question of women in dependent territories had been a pressing issue since the early stages of the CSW. The intersection with the work of the trusteeship world produced further challenges to the applicability of international women's rights.

In the pamphlet *A Sacred Trust* women are the invisible "visible." Most images include them without a specific mention but as the symbol of progress: one is a white woman with a sundress and sunglasses standing by a car on a raft carried by a native man in British Cameroons. Another one is a native teacher trainee in Western Samoa. A last photo includes women in a scene from an outdoor market in New Guinea. Interestingly, the only woman represented in the African context is a white woman. The UN propaganda mostly focused on the tractor, which triumphantly closes the pamphlet, as the symbol of 1950s modernized agriculture.

This chapter shows another example of closer intervention in the local setting but this time in territories that were still dependent. As in the case of Asia, the UN, through its multiple actors involved in women's rights in the colonies, claimed to advance women's rights while simultaneously undermining them. Outrage over the presumed ill treatment of native women in the trust territory of British Cameroons widened the space for the realism of the technocratic approach in which pragmatic considerations encouraged the acceptance of the same practices that generated the initial outrage. Along with the closer intervention of the UN the chapter also shows how local women's groups used the Trusteeship Council to manifest dissent against colonialism.

More broadly, I present here a two-way relationship in order to explore how women's rights were used within the dependent territories and how debates on those rights and local cultures, in turn, influenced the UN representatives' conception of rights. With this chapter the theme of pain and trafficking is introduced. However, one differentiation is necessary between the UN's legacy on trafficking—mostly connected to forced prostitution— and the type of forced movement in the case this chapter analyzes.

While at the League of Nations women had been involved with antitrafficking advocacy, in February 1947 the British representative at the ECOSOC clearly opposed the involvement of the CSW in the matter of prostitution since, he argued, it was a problem that single governments and special agencies were tackling, and additionally, the issue was more in the scope of the Social Commission.[7] The first instrument against trafficking was created less than a month later, the 1947 Convention for the Suppression of the Traffic in Persons and of the Exploitation of the Prostitution of Others.[8] Commissioners did not use the word *trafficking*, but they discussed dimensions that involved forced movement from one place to another one, a movement also connected to sexuality; specifically, the selecting of women as future spouses of a local chief through a violent ritual that included "dragging them to the chief's compound," like in the case described later in this chapter.

Delegates debated these topics in sensationalist but always blurry terms. They did so by emphasizing the dignity of women in what they presented when they problematically discussed the far away "other." One premise is necessary here; it is not clear whether these facts happened or not and what the right level of commitment should have been for an international organization; but what emerged from the sources is an intense engagement with the topic that illustrates a clear and direct example of imperial feminist attitudes. Contrary to other issues, this type of ritual suggested that the alleged victim felt physical and psychological pain.

Literary scholar Elaine Scarry declares the usefulness of speaking on behalf of the person in pain who "is ordinarily so bereft of the resources of speech." She also points to the difficulties inherent in specifying the "other" in words that "somehow convey to the reader the aversiveness being experienced inside the body of someone whose country may be far away, whose name can barely be pronounced."[9] These stories, therefore, present the tension between alleviating pain and creating victims emblematic of gender politics. As political scientist Jennifer Suchland demonstrates in her work on human rights and trafficking in Eastern Europe, focusing on the victim the (perceived) abject woman, contributes to a focus "on locating individual rather than structural violence."[10] Even victimhood, however, has its own problematic aspects; an identified victim involves an identifier and the objectification of the "abject body"; a self-claimed victim, on the other hand, implies that the victim tells her own story.

Because of the multiple layers of knowledge from the local to the inter-national setting, 1950s direct personal accounts at the UN would have been difficult to produce. In the case of the Trusteeship Council, petitioning the UN for local matters involved public rituals with obvious social control and no privacy, and so denouncing the so-called rituals that affected women and their bodies was not an option.[11] This chapter inaugurates an engage-ment with the first of two separated bodily events here: trafficking as in the forced movement from a location to another one and the debates on female genital modifications (discussed in chapter 5), which did include the same trope of being forcibly moved to the location of the operation as well as the dimension of the abject body.

I first describe the relationship between the United Nations and the colonial world with more emphasis on the private sphere. While the previ-ous chapters have examined the possibility of public violation of women's rights as the lack of franchise and political education, this part of the book discusses private violations with public implications. In this context, the improvement of the status of women was especially difficult to underpin because of the several layers of rhetoric that had instrumentalized it in the history of traditional empires. As stated earlier, this chapter subverts a traditional chronology; it starts in the 1950s and it ends with a scandal that started in 1949; the background described previous to the scandal is necessary to elucidate the intersections between the CSW and the colonial world, as well as the deployment of the scandal.

Through the Trusteeship Council, the UN presented an idyllic picture of a united international goal toward the freedom of the trust people. However, a focus on the status of women in the trust territories shows the limitations of women's rights and the ambivalent understanding of the UN toward women's rights.

Commissioners' Reactions to the
UN Sanitization of the Colonial World

The commission's involvement with women in dependent territories derived from the UN design for such territories as well as the specific composition of the commission, as some members were particularly attached to the issue.

As stated earlier the UN Charter created a separation between nondependent and trust territories. Chapter XI of the charter defined the UN's aspirations for the dependent territories. Chapters XII and XIII described the trust system, its duties and procedures, and the rights of the population in the trust territories. Although colonies and trust territories had different international legal status, the charter, in its general aspirations, used similar language that assigned to traditional colonizers and to the TC administrative authority (the group of states in charge of the tutelage) the roles of promoter and guarantor of fair practices, nurturer of local cultures, and mediator for democratic procedures.

The authority also included New Zealand, Australia, and the United States. The UN Charter clearly expressed that the trust system was temporary and that the transition to self-rule was to be based on the human rights framework, which prescribed equality of race, sex, language, and religion. As illustrated in chapter 1, in the context of the dependent territories that were not part of the trust system, (de facto colonies or non-self-governing territories), the secretary-general asked member states in charge of these countries to submit information on the overall progress toward independence.[12]

The inscription of the principle of self-determination in the UN provisions served as the legal basis for independence movements, but it also provoked resistance from the colonial powers. For example, countries such as Portugal did not abide by the charter's instructions. Portugal claimed that it did not have colonies and that overseas territories were part of metropolitan Portugal.[13] France and Britain moved along a more hybrid line as they had to support measurements for self-rule in the trust territories under their supervision and simultaneously fought to hold onto their colonies. The Portuguese stance occurred because outside the trust system the communication of progress toward self-rule was on a volunteer and nonbinding basis.

Undoubtedly, the language of the trust system proposed something new and aligned with the postwar movements for decolonization. Specifically, the UN-led concept of the "welfare of the people" consisted of an improvement compared to the LN's mandate system. The league had, instead, used the language of childhood and stages of growth, which reinforced the paternalistic aspect of colonial rhetoric.[14] Therefore, the UN offered a forum to directly discuss the framework of human rights applied to colonized people and to define colonialism in the postwar era.

From the early meetings to outline the competency of the TC, it was clear that smaller countries pushed for a Trust System for the trust people, not to favor old colonialism. For example, in early debates on these issues, the Syrian delegate objected to the assimilation of Togoland and Cameroons into metropolitan France, arguing that if such assimilation happened, these two countries "would lose their cultural heritages." The delegate of New Zealand claimed that European colonial powers such as France aimed to continue in the spirit of the mandate system, which he argued led to a quasi-property of the territory in question. The New Zealand representative went further and proposed that all dependent territories ready for self-rule should be put under the trust system so that "the UN secured for a change in their status."[15] Thus, beyond the Cold War attacks based on this topic, the colonial debate happened at the level of member states and was not limited to the colonizer/colonized confrontation. Member states were aware of how the mandate system had reinforced colonial practices under the auspices of an intergovernmental organization. The UN, at least on paper, aimed to create a new and more efficient system where self-rule was a concrete goal and not a rhetorical one.

The insistence on the preservation of native culture as a tool of the TC aligned with the voice of the anti-colonial elites. Local customs served to "imagine" the national community and to disprove the claim of necessary tutelage by more advanced countries.[16] However, as discussed in the case of women, from the perspective of the colonial powers, local culture, and specifically local customs, demonstrated the impossibility of the so-called civilizing mission. As stated in chapter 2, the two main colonial powers, Britain and France, formulated two hypotheses on native culture. British delegates highlighted how Britain benevolently attempted to civilize local people but failed because of the persistence of native customs. In contrast, French delegates praised the assimilation of the colonized people within the republican model. The status of women was central to the definition and international assessment of local customs.

The instruments to measure progress toward self-rule inscribed in the charter included a questionnaire on political and social issues.[17] At the first session of the CSW, delegates asked for a more inclusive version of the TC questionnaire to officially include questions on women, suffrage, and their general status. For the dependent non-trust territories, commissioners instead "expressed the hope" that women delegates could be included in the conferences of the representatives of these territories.[18] The commissioners' requests created a direct connection between the UDHR and the status of women in the trust and non-self-governing territories.[19] The modifications of the questionnaire aimed to better understand the status of local women in both the public and private spheres with a special concern for the issue of monogamy and freedom of choice in marriage.[20]

The TC and the Secretariat provided the commission with regular reports on the condition of women in both the trust and non-self-governing territories. These reports constitute a valuable source to explore the political imagination of the members of the TC as well as the multiple agents that defined the roles and responsibilities of women and men in the territories. Furthermore, NGOs with close ties to the colonial missionary world provided the CSW with additional data and information that presented common elements with more formal reports but included the language of moral outrage typical of some religious institutions.

Commissioners worked through a unified category of "women in dependent territories" and not on the basis of the UN differentiation of the colonial world. In the reports to the ECOSOC, the two categories appeared individually, but most commissioners verbally agreed that the differences for women living in formal colonies or in trust territories were minimal. Deliberating and discussing on the basis of a unified or separated category also had ideological implications. For example, the Soviet Bloc representatives pushed for a unified category that associated racism with capitalism and colonial oppression.[21]

As I show in chapters 2 and 3, this direction produced multiple outcomes: the disqualification of Soviet assessments of the colonial world as "propaganda" by the United States, China, France, and Britain and the opportunity for the Soviets to praise their "humanitarian" cases of interventions in foreign countries. For the Soviet Bloc delegates, the trust system appeared not as the guarantor of human rights practices but as the perpetuating force of colonial schemes; hence, the dependent territories were to be discussed as a unified category. Although the Soviets considered themselves as the "rescuer" of the colonial world, at the Bandung Conference many participants denounced Soviet interventions and territorial occupations as a "new colonialism."[22] Afro-Asian leaders, specifically John Kotelawala from Ceylon, considered Soviet support of the anticolonial cause a "cynical propaganda exercise."[23]

Within this context, women delegates with previous international feminist experience produced a hybrid of a new imperial feminism coupled with the UN's promotion of modernization. For example, the Brazilian delegate Bertha Lutz, who had been instrumental in the creation of a separate UN entity for the status of women, regretted the lack of direct testimony by women from the dependent territories but identified "native customs" as the main cause of women's subordination. She presented the example of remote areas of Brazil that were not "ready to assume the responsibility of independence." In the case of India, she claimed, anticolonial elites reverted to "barbaric customs" against women, specifically *sati*, once the country attained independence.[24] Lutz did not question colonialism as a contributing force affecting the status of women. Rather, on one hand, she warned against discussing something that was geographically distant without the presence of direct local witnesses; on the other hand, she proposed traditional monolithic images of the colonized woman as a victim of her own culture. More importantly, the discourse of readiness for self-rule and the example of India produced a narrative of a somewhat deceitful pretense of democracy that disappeared once independence was obtained.[25]

In the same discussion of practices that affected local women, the French chair of the commission, Lefaucheux, claimed that the indigenous population of French Africa could choose whether to be under French status or under customary law. Evidence of how French law was to "revolutionize the living conditions for women in Africa" was the establishment of an official emancipatory age (twenty-one years) that allowed women to marry without parental consent. More specifically, this decree allowed couples to marry according to the French code, which prohibited polygamy. Lefaucheux's publicity of the French model aligned with a unique political system where the empire and the nation-state were both sides of republicanism and not a contradictory model. Hence, colonialism coexisted with political rights and the advancement of women.[26]

Both attitudes and data that the commissioners used as the background for debates and the consequent resolutions on dependent territories confirmed elements familiar to imperial feminism, such as the trope of rescuing women from their own culture and the depiction of women in the dependent territories in oppositional terms to their European and American "sisters."[27] At least until the early 1960s, when women from the newly formed states in Africa joined in the commission's work, most voices coming from colonies were from the TC authorities and the colonial powers, both of which used missionary work to define the status of women. In these early stages of work on the colonial world, commissioners adjusted the framework of human rights to issues that missionaries, both Anglican and Catholic, had identified much earlier. And it was a missionary-led scandal that brought to the global spotlight the status of women in the trust territories.

Control and Redemption of Local Women

The early administering states of the TC were the United Kingdom, France, Belgium, Australia, and New Zealand. The council also had four members elected by the General Assembly (GA). Originally there were only two elected members, but after allowing the United States a trusteeship agreement with former Japanese territories, the GA elected two other members to create more balance. The four members were Mexico, Iraq, the Philippines, and Costa Rica.[28] Between 1957 and 1962 the trust territories of Africa acquired independence. In this process, British Cameroon disappeared; the northern part was annexed to Nigeria and the southern portion to French Cameroon, which is contemporary independent Cameroon. The other territories changed in the following ways: British Togoland was annexed to Ghana, French Togoland became independent Togo, Tanganyika became independent Tanzania, Somaliland became independent Somalia, and Ruanda-Urundi became the two independent states of Ruanda and Burundi.

In their reports to the GA , the authorities described the political and social implementations that led to self-rule. Because of the sex equality principle included in the trusteeship agreement as well as the CSW's direct request, the reports included a substantial section on the status of women. From these sources, the condition of native women appeared linked to the long history of gender and colonialism and to UN measures of civilization for the welfare of the people.

Since its early formulations on women in trust territories, the trust authority associated women with wives and highlighted the inescapable destiny of all "trusted" women to go from children to wives. Because coupledom was the "natural category," most if not all problems regarding women were issues surrounding marriage and the status of woman within the family. Administering countries defined marriage in the territories as an affectionless institution and a purely business transaction between two families. Such an exchange happened with compensation to the bride's family of a "bride-price" paid by the groom's family. The price was a guarantor of the stability of the marriage transaction. Brides knew that if they did not abide by the agreement, their family had to return the marital transaction earnings. The TC administering authority saw this as encouragement for the family to create good matches: "Every tribe, primitive or otherwise, must, indeed be given credit for some delicacy of feeling about such matters and for a great deal of natural affection between parents and children."[29]

The TC reports differentiated between Muslims and "pagan" populations, attributing somewhat rigid rules to Muslim communities as well as a more sophisticated level of organization. For example, Islamic customs allowed widows to inherit their husbands' properties. "Pagans," in contrast, included widows within the husband's family and patrimony, where the older brother inherited the deceased's property, wife, and children. This aspect underlined the business aspect of the marriage transaction.

The TC authority described the microcosm of "African" life in which women's progress represented also choosing the right partner. An *incorrect* choice generated danger and the possibility of extramarital affairs for women. The authority therefore described women as disorderly agents and men (fathers and husbands) as rational businessmen who conducted man-to-man business to "sell" women to the most suitable candidate.[30]

Although the TC authority condemned customary practices, it also justified their existence and persistence for an orderly society. This aspect shows a shift from an earlier colonial ideology; colonial rule had traditionally presented the rhetoric of rescuing women as part of the civilizing mission. Later, economic and political realism prevailed in the design of saving them.[31] Specifically, the TC authority claimed that even if women were subordinates to their husbands, they were under their care, which constituted a privilege.

In the case of British Cameroons the TC aligned with the prominent British argument that identified a smooth transition to self-rule through education rather than legislation; the report stated, "It has been suggested that the status of women can be improved by legislative action in the direction of registration of marriage and the limitation or abolition of bride price but it is felt that it is erroneous to believe that inequalities and anomalies will yield to legislation. The moral pressure brought to bear on a girl in her own family, the long tradition of humble acceptance of her position by the African women are things which will yield to education and social contacts, not to legislation."[32]

For the trust authority of British Cameroons, the educational tools for the status of women were to come from missionary teaching, from Christians in general, from "the inclusion of educated wives of Government employees," and from "enlightened" traders. Within this context, the authority assigned female European counterparts a role in the "democratization" of the territories.[33]

Statements on the status of women and customary practices also highlighted the relationship between economic and social progress. In the colonial context, the ruling elite assumed that women's rights depended on economic development and welfare. Polygamy, especially, epitomized a category that locked the status of women within the economic realm. According to the TC authority, "it should be noted that one of the greatest obstacles to the emancipation of native women is the practice of polygamy, which is rooted in antiquity and can only be eliminated with the development of economic life and democratic ideas of equality."[34] The right setting for the flourishing of democratic ideals, the TC delegates believed, was the urban setting as opposed to the rural one.

A cash economy in cities allowed women a certain level of expenditure independence, and contact with alien manners, the TC argued, produced a positive influence. However, the town woman, "contrary to her rural sister," became accustomed to having "all her wants . . . supplied by the efforts of her husband." The authority presented an ambivalent scenario for women in the rural areas: they were the victims of polygamy, yet they were in charge of the main agricultural tasks, which contrary to the town women, allowed for a greater range of self-sufficiency, but they depended on men for their needs.

In the early 1950s, the TC members also identified resistance to change as one cause for the woman question. They stated, "In many tribes it is the women who are the more conservative and the less amenable to change. In some cases, senior women are in effect the guardians of tradition, and they are responsible for seeing that the young women are fully initiated and instructed in the manners and customs of the tribe. It frequently happens that opposition to such new ideas as female education and maternity and child welfare clinics come most strongly from the older women."

Trust policies in effect shifted communal order and simultaneously promoted and disrupted the status of women. Older native women had a stronger agency within traditional practices because they had a prominent role in midwifery and initiation rituals.[35] Missionaries' interventions, which the TC considered with great admiration, enclosed women in the stronger male dependency of the Victorian model according to which public and private spheres were separated and the bourgeois model of the dependent woman was glorified.[36]

In later reports, the TC authority reinforced the relationship between bride-price and communal order. The price, trust authorities argued, was a stabilizer of marriages and a source of moral strength for the community. Its members argued that the bride-price helped couples stay together because women who married for high compensation felt a sense of pride. A woman, the TC delegates claimed, usually avoided leaving her father in debt; hence, the "price" solidified the matrimonial union. Simultaneously, the TC representatives agreed that a "change in public opinion" was necessary to fight the practice of bride-price. While the TC recognized the economic value of this practice, it also encouraged a shift from this custom. The constituencies who were supposed to promote the rejection of bride-price were missionaries, "enlightened" chiefs, and "educated Africans."[37]

The trust reports included the 1951 decree that French commissioner Lefaucheux presented as an example of French measures against polygamy. In its postwar colonial strategies, the French state granted the possibility of living under French or native law. From the TC's point of view, there was a certain level of uncertainty regarding young native girls and their ability to use the French law, created for their "special benefit." The administering countries claimed that the council was trying to "liberate women from the burden of centuries of male domination."[38] They considered themselves the rescuers of women in the trust territories. The council, therefore, intervened in the space between native women and native men by claiming special benefits emerging from European law. However, the option of a legal choice was not enough; the council also claimed that "the status of women will be raised chiefly by means of slow and persevering action."[39] The specificities of such "action" were not mentioned, but in this context the emphasis was on "slow." The council, and therefore the UN, created a hierarchy of countries and native groups that were "more ready" for self-rule. The status of women became a narrative which determined such readiness, or lack thereof.

For the TC authority, the success story of European-led civilization was the territory of Ruanda-Urundi, where "the proud and haughty Mututsi women" did little work and never left the family compound.[40] When the Mututsi woman traveled, she was carried. If she worked in the fields, she shared the tasks with her husband. Mututsi mothers were treated with the highest regard, and as the TC delegates said, "A woman who has borne her husband a number of children is treated by him with special deference." They also added "Whereas in some parts of Central Africa [women] are treated as beasts of burden, in Ruanda-Urundi they are almost on an equality with their husbands."[41] If a wife was not treated well, she could return to her family of origin until the husband proved that he could take good care of her. The model of Ruanda-Urundi centered on women's satisfaction within familial life but not on their ability to have an independent life from both the original and the marriage-based family. Chapter 3 shows how education emerged as the determining force to foster women's independence. Yet in this setting, education and knowledge in general happened through the interaction between colonial and native worlds.

Throughout the 1950s, the trusteeship authority also praised education as the new moderator of gender relationships: education—possibly the missionary one—gave "the Africans the example of real partnership between men and women" and showed the central role of women within the family. Young girls learned gender-specific activities such as knitting and sewing. Families had to make special accommodations to send young girls to school because they were usually instrumental to the running of the house.

In the TC context, therefore, modernity for women meant a European level of gender relationships that saw them as the center of the family, which codified their role within society. This new model existed together with historical customary elements that had given women some levels of influence within communities. The TC recognized that every "tribe," even the most "primitive one," had customary law instruments run by women and for women-related issues. They also claimed that such instruments reflected contact with alien cultures, external influences such as education, and the improved status of women.[42] By recognizing women's authority as derived from "alien culture," the TC sanctioned the positive aspect of the colonial encounter for women.

In the language of the Trusteeship Council, colonialism appeared as a remote parenthesis that created encounters and confirmed the greater value of European compared to native culture. Even when local customs showed a progressive understanding of women's issues, the TC did not recognize such merits, but it explained them through contact with other cultures. In the TC's accounts, trust territories went from "ancient" customs straight to underdevelopment. The discourse of continuity ignored the negative impact of colonial rule on local customs as well as on development.

Colonial administrations had a long-contested history of traditional practices that were harmful to women. Customary traditions represented a useful tool to justify the "humanitarian" aspect of the civilizing mission. The focus on women was not in favor of women per se but in favor of the patriarchal order. Under colonial rule, contempt for local rituals that modified women's bodies coexisted with regulations against women who refused sexual obligations.[43] For example in the case of Africa, British rule first forbade female circumcision in Kenya and later it condoned it as part of colonial pronatalist politics in search of increasing the number of exploited native laborers.[44] The focus on women's bodies had a purely proempire propagandistic rationale to be ignored if the matter in question could not be useful to reinforce imperial practices. Within the context of advancing universal human rights for all women of the world, the commissioners had to face ambiguous politics that aimed to frame women as defenseless victims of both native and colonial cultures. Parallel to the commissioners' efforts, local women in the trust territories had a voice on how colonialism did not advance human rights, and they found in the UN a forum in which to share their dissent.

The Petition Machinery and the Status of Women

Petitions symbolize different aspects of the relationship between an individual (or organization) and the TC. Article 87 of the UN Charter is the fundamental instrument for the petition machinery. It allows reports from the administrating authority, petitions from the population, visiting missions, and the discussion of all these instruments within the GA. Petitioning groups include both colonized people claiming political and social injustices and other groups such as missionaries, workers, and victims of postwar displacements. The petitionary machine was, however, too prolific and too disparate in the search for justice at an international forum. Petitioners presented a variety of topics, from serious violations of human rights to perhaps less pressing matters such as the failed homework of a schoolboy.[45] Ultimately petitioners epitomized the incorporation of the UN language of human rights as well as women's rights within the last stages of colonialism. Communicating dissent to the UN showed the microcosm of local realities and also the coexistence of tradition and modernity in the trust territories.[46]

On February 28, 1950 the women's committee of the Union of the People of the Cameroons presented their petition to the UN Visiting Mission.[47] Their appeal consisted of two parts: the denunciation and analysis of the current conditions of women's lives and demands to the administrating authorities. In the first part, they claim an association with women on a global scale, saying "Women have the same rights as men and can no longer be kept on one side when it is a question of the political, economic, social and cultural interests of their country." Then they presented the specific situation of Cameroonian women: "The Women of Cameroons are the victims of a policy of contempt aimed at keeping them always in a state of inferiority." As such, they recognized that women's rights as intended in the postwar period could contribute to both sex and race equality.

The women's committee identified the main enemy of the politics of contempt in the *Code of Indigenat* and European discrimination, as they stated, "The policy of racial discrimination treats the women of the Cameroons as contemptible creatures who have no rights to get served in butchers' shops in the market, in stores or anywhere else before white women and their servants." Beyond daily instances of racist practices, the committee blamed colonial discriminatory laws for putting in danger the Cameroonian family and contributing to underdevelopment.

The dominant belief and ideology of the European missionaries was that "traditional culture" was detrimental to the stability of the native family and hence to the creation of an independent nation-state. This was a position shared also by the representative of the Vatican in Cameroon. The female

committee instead stated that "forced labour and the *indigenat* [were] caus-
ing the disorganization of family life in the Cameroons."

In the second part of the petition, the female committee presents a list
of requests. The most salient were the "recognition of human and civic
rights for all men and women of the Cameroons" and the "abolition of
racial discrimination in the political, economic and social life of the country." Such statements show how the women representatives of the Union of
the People of the Cameroons were capable of simultaneously supporting
self-governance for Cameroon and women's rights. They identified themselves as both part of the universal category of "women" and as part of the
colonized population. Furthermore, condemning colonial discrimination
as detrimental to women's rights could exemplify the historical forces that
contributed to the creation of a local feminism.[48]

The CSW provided the discursive framework for the female committee's
petition to promote women's rights, which transcended the oppositional
discourse of imperial feminism. The historical possibility of the Cameroonian Women's Committee represents an example of how the TC produced
a political instrument for the "trust" people to present their grievances
to a global audience. Furthermore, the framework of human rights, often
accused of being a "purely Western creation," showed its advantages in the
anticolonial struggle.[49] The next part shows an even more complex aspect
of the petition machinery which involved the UN in a global scandal.

The Betrothed: Trafficking Women in British Cameroon

A girl was grinding corn in the small space in front of her father's hut.
She was about thirteen years old, a fine child clad in Native dress. Two
or three men walked down the road looking from side to side—they
stopped—looked hard at the girl who, quite unconscious of their looks,
continued her back-breaking task. Then the leader, or "Chinda" as he
is called, stepped forward—dragged the child to her feet and with a
piece of red cam wood put a mark on her forehead—stripped off her
clothes and left her standing naked. The girl howled like a wounded
animal—she was doomed. Her father came out and saw the mark
and knew what it meant. She was branded! Off the "Chinda" and his
men went; their day's work for the King had been done.[50]

This excerpt from a newspaper article titled "Just Cargo" was part of an appeal, dated November 28, 1947, with which St. Joan's International Alliance (hereafter "St. Joan's"), a Roman Catholic NGO, petitioned the TC.[51] St. Joan's aimed to attract international attention to a *scandalous* issue in one of the territories under UN administration: British Cameroons. Titled "Our African Sisters," the text denounced the presumed abuse that young women suffered when betrothed to the Fon of Bikom (a native ruler). The petition became popular because of the ties between St. Joan's and the UN, specifically, the CSW and the TC. Its setting was a small territory in the Bamenda region, but to UN delegates the painful scenario the petition evoked was seen as representative of the general status of women in the colonial world.

This petition created a global cause célèbre through which the status of women in the trust territory of British Cameroons became the focus of multiple actors in a newly formed colonial plot comprising missionaries, feminist activists, UN delegates, and the Western press. With its strong Catholic tradition of women's rights battles, St. Joan's had been active since the struggle for suffrage in Britain. Originally called "Catholic Women's Suffrage Society," St. Joan's changed its name when it acquired the status of international organization. At the LN, and later at the UN, St. Joan's became involved with the status of women in colonial Africa.[52] Since the early meetings of the CSW, St. Joan's—along with other international religious organizations—had condemned some local customs which the NGO deemed responsible for the degradation of women in dependent territories.

This story about the Fon of Bikom is representative of the multiple and complex observers of African women's bodies. The first was Sister Loretta, the Franciscan nun from Chicago, who allegedly witnessed the scene and wrote an article about it for a British Franciscan publication. The second was St. Joan's itself, which used the article as a piece of evidence to evoke a response from the Human Rights Commission. Once the petition passed into UN official channels, the council transferred it to the CSW, as it was a "women's matter."

The title "Just Cargo" implied the presumptive devaluation of girls' bodies in the Bamenda region and "Our African Sisters" reflected an assumed commonality and familiar defense of African women against African men and against local customs. At a higher level, the appeal symbolized the international networks comprised by both women and men who observed, monitored, and aimed to rescue African bodies. Rescuing had a new and different valence as compared with the high stages of colonialism: it was at that point in time part of the much more complex technocratic mechanism of measuring progress toward self-government. At stake was the UN in its debut years, as well as in its own creation: the trust system.

The sensationalist language of the petition includes fairy-tale categories such as the innocent child in a bucolic scenario contrasted with the sudden intervention of evil men. It depicts a pastoral, idyllic life in a remote African village where a thirteen-year-old child was duly contributing to her family chores. A group of men suddenly interrupted this peaceful scene to claim the laboring child as "property" of the ruler. The narrative highlights the violent treatment of the young girl and the public ritual intended to turn a woman into property. "She was branded," (the petition states), and the father, helpless, immediately realized what that brand meant.

The author then presents a different setting (the ruler's compound) in order to describe how the father of the abducted/chosen girl completed the ritual by dragging his daughter in front of the king, an eighty-year-old man who declared, "I accept this piece of cargo." The petition then provides more detail about what the father finds in the king's compound: "One hundred of his six hundred wives stand round him in a semi-circle—naked—as is the privilege and custom of the 'king's own.'"

The story ends with an appeal to the Human Rights Commission to take action against this practice. Although the petition was formally directed to the TC, by concluding with the alert "Human Rights Commission take note!" the author provides a direct connection between this story and moral outrage at a violent ritual that, in Sister Loretta's description, resembled kidnapping and trafficking more than courting.

Questions about the author, the audience, and the expected reactions render these accounts problematic to interpret. Similar to cases of contemporary women's trafficking, there is a correspondence between the narration style and the claim about victimization of women.[53] Moreover, the story can reveal or conceal relevant evidence. The intention was to discredit native customs. "Just Cargo" can also be read, however, as a source reflective of what early NGOs aimed to report, how they reported, and how the UN reacted. The story itself thus becomes an historical event.

Two elements are central to the petition: ritual violence and the politics of numbers. The rule of Bikom was responsible for the questionable royal practice that allowed him to meet his future wives and marry far too many. As illustrated below, the context evoked a century-old European disdain for polygamy along with a new international outrage corroborated by the multiple parties that involved themselves with this issue.

The petition discussed the colonial body in pain, a trope that had long existed and that Europeans described and used at different times and in different places. One widely circulated example was the practice of sati and the extensive Western reactions to it, which called attention to, specifically, the female body and the status of women. Furthermore, observations about native women contributed to the colonial archive often through moral concerns and dangers around practices such as prostitution, adultery, and polygamy.[54] With the consolidation of colonial power, the concern for bodies aligned with the concern for native labor.[55] Native bodies "were bodies to be studied, surveyed, disciplined and, when necessary, reformed to ensure their efficiency as parts of the emerging world system."[56] The issue of polygamy—mostly in its polygyny version—combined colonial concerns with both women and labor.

British colonial administrators generally avoided direct disapproval of native practices unless such censure served to reinforce British rule.[57] British missionaries argued for the discouragement of polygamy, especially for African converts who, despite embracing Christianity, tended to blend different traditions. The UN thus found itself at the convergence point of old narratives and new administrative needs.

The Western press followed the case, and among the most authoritative voices, the New York Times reported on the moral outrage at the UN that led to a special mission to "rescue" the multitude of Cameroonian royal wives in distress. According to the New York Times, "The United Nations Trusteeship Council denounced in no uncertain terms today the compulsory— marriage and multiple marriage customs of the Bikom tribe."[58]

As stated above, visiting missions were part of the council's means of measuring local progress toward self-rule. The 1950 visiting mission to

West and Central Africa included a special "investigatory expedition" to count the wives of the Fon of Bikom. After the UN visit, the *New York Times* stated, "A special mission reported back to the United Nations today that it had looked into the marital affairs of West Africa's fame Fon of the Bikom tribe and his 110 wives and had come up with the conclusion that maybe polygamy, at least in Africa, wasn't such a bad idea, after all."[59] The *New York Times* ironically called off the emotional outrage over polygamy that disappeared once the council's representative considered marriage to the Fon as a form of employment.

The critique of the practice of betrothing young women also disappeared once the economic validation was spelled out: given the scarce possibilities of employment for women, being a royal wife constituted a form of sustenance. The UN delegates eventually met the Fon, who complained about having become the center of an international controversy. He further explained the benefits that his 110 wives had due to living within his compound. According to the press, the UN delegates embraced at least part of his rationale, which saw polygamy as a form of social and economic security. The wives themselves later petitioned the UN and claimed their happiness and well-being depended on being part of the royal compound.[60]

The wives' appeal did not stop international concern about this issue. The last stage of the cause célèbre included the adventurous voyage of the American journalist and feminist activist Rebecca Hourwich Reyher, who went personally to Bikom to obtain primary testimony on this issue.[61]

In her account, she depicts a colonial world in transition between traditional European rule and new mechanisms to measure the ability for self-government. Reyher describes a meeting with a British army representative, who suggested that she give a few bottles of gin to the Fon because he really enjoyed it. She met a Western anthropologist who spoke in favor of the "real" Africa and explained that polygamy was necessary to local economies. She argued with the native expert, who accused Reyher of Western intrusion into something she could not understand. Ultimately, she talked to a local British bishop who spoke vehemently against Sister Loretta, the nun-journalist author of the article "Just Cargo," whom he described as "sex deprived" and who, he argued, had made up the story.[62] Even if they were both from the Western world, which often condemned native customs, the bishop and Sister Loretta maintained gender-based separations in the treatment of local issues.

After careful negotiations and timid attempts to get an account of this story from local residents, Reyher succeeded. In a local tale about the scandal, a royal subject illustrated the Fon's interpretation of the UN Visiting Mission:

[The visiting UN representatives] say I have come with a petition against you. They say "you have too many wives." The fon listened carefully, staring into space inscrutably. The man brought out a paper and read it. "There were just 3 things." Marrying too many wives is bad. Taking other men's daughters while they are young bringing them to the Fon's compound and making them wives is bad. That is because it is against the will of women. When a woman is fully grown and she want [sic] to go away, she must go! No one must stop her. The Fon responded that he was old, at the end of his life, and therefore he did not want anything from women.[63]

In April 1950, the Fon communicated directly to the CSW through the council's reports on the status of women in trust territories. He assured the commissioners that "there were no women in his compound who were not there entirely by their own free will and that he was not prepared to accept any new wives except under this same condition." He further stated that "full opportunity had been afforded to any woman who wished to leave his compound to do so and that some forty of his wives had taken advantage of this permission."[64]

Because of the international clamor on this issue, from a violent brander of "human property," the Fon appears, in his conversation with the CSW, as a humanitarian force in favor of women's rights. In this blurry historical moment of transition to self-rule, the fluid language of practicality within a structurally limited society allowed for this type of compromise: polygamy was not that bad, and for the most part women married to the Fon lived comfortably.

St. Joan's brought to the commission two fundamental issues that signaled the direction of its activities for the next fifteen years: the free consent to marriage and the issue of bodily integrity. This work culminated in the creation of the UN Convention on Consent to Marriage, Minimum Age of Marriage and Registration of Marriages (1962).

Conclusion

This chapter confirms the clash between rights and cultural relativism. The condition of the betrothed women of the kingdom of Bikom was highly complex, whether it was true or false that young girls were subjected to violent rituals. Actually, truthfulness and falseness do not function as useful tools to assess the story. What is clear from the ways in which the actors saw themselves and others in the scandal is that a range of institutions directly or indirectly defined the possibilities of women within the realm of rights: NGOs such as St. Joan's with their translation of local dynamics along religious and imperial narratives; commissioners, with their own internal divisions along Cold War and imperial lines, as well as reflecting tensions between international feminists and local interests; and the UN itself through the Trusteeship Council, which tended to reinforce the status quo of gender politics.

With a focus on economics and modernization, the UN sanctioned the passage of dependent territories from colonies to "underdeveloped countries." This shift allowed for a series of realist considerations that condoned the acceptance of policies that could harm women. Simultaneously, bodily pain became an important symbol of imperial feminist rhetoric through which experienced commissioners reinforced their tenet that tradition was the main discriminating force for women in the colonial world. The TC contributed by operating with complacency regarding colonial legacies and by recycling tropes from the colonial era, such as the enlightened spirit of missionary education.

The end of the Bikom story is a well-known one; culture and circumstances justified the nonintervention in the alleged abuse of women's bodies. Gender appeared as a determining factor which differentiated between abuses by the nation-state from cultural practices that, arguably, harmed women. In its early theorization and definition, human rights were conceived as instruments against nation-states' abuses. The private sphere was not contemplated, and the public sphere suggested mostly violations against men perpetrated by governments.[65] The shift from political conceptions of rights (which saw women's civic participation as the main goal) to economic rights—in which financial dependency constituted an impediment to full rights' acquisition—evolved through a close observation of the colonial/ postcolonial world in both Asia (as chapter 3 shows) and Africa. Although commissioners observed the world through an imperial feminist rhetoric, they initiated a larger debate on the forces that produced discrimination against women.

The culmination of the dichotomy between culture and rights happened through a collaborative effort of the CSW and HRC to denounce female genital modifications via a set of problematic frameworks that, nonetheless, show the definite transition to a focus on discrimination in the private sphere.

6. Thirteen African states and Cyprus admitted to the UN, 1960.
© United Nations, reprinted with permission of the United Nations.

5

Bodily Rituals and the Dialectic of Foreign and Local Voices

Depicted in the photograph at left is the celebratory moment for the new independent nation-states that emerged from anticolonial struggle.[1] Much like the image of Bernardino in chapter 1, the UN portrayal here documents restorative justice. The audience can imagine the before and after of a more pluralistic General Assembly. The traditional clothing and the presence of both women and men symbolized a national struggle for independence embraced by everyone. As partially shown in chapter 4, women in dependent territories had to negotiate traditions with the new international framework of women's rights. This chapter explores the negotiation of the CSW and HRC with the WHO on practices that allegedly harmed the female body.

I am referring here to the so-called female genital cutting or mutilation (FGM). There are four types of FGM depending on the scale of modification of the female genitals.[2] Even though the operation had been present in the West, historically these practices represented a set of tensions between the colonizer and colonized, especially in the African context.[3] Ever since colonial administrators first became familiar with FGM in the early nineteenth century, the dialectic of cultural relativism versus humanitarianism dominated the politics around the practice. This chapter traces the background stories that led to the WHO's position on rituals that affected the female body (1959). The intersections between the universalism of human rights and specific bodily practices such as FGM started through debates at the CSW and then inspired a collaborative effort with the HRC. The story ends with the well-known and problematic Hosken Report, presented within the CSW in the mid-1970s.

"Father and mother are circumcised. Are they not Christians? Circumcision did not prevent them from being Christians. I too have embraced the white man's faith. However, I know it is beautiful, oh so beautiful to be initiated into womanhood . . . Surely there is no tribe that does not circumcise. Or how does a girl grow into a woman?"[4]

With this passage from his 1965 novel *The River Between*, the well-known Kenyan writer Ngugi wa Thiong'o depicts the multiple aspects of male and female circumcision along with—and as representative of—the anxiety that colonial change brought to the Kikuyu people. Wa Thiong'o's depiction of circumcision is not straightforward; it serves as a patriarchal reassertion in a male competition over the "female" land; it is precolonial, hence pure and unpolluted, but it is also "pagan" as opposed to the Western-derived Christianity. Wa Thiong'o emphasizes the beauty of community living and how it comes with giving up a part of one's body. Furthermore, in the case of women, the practice is always the topic of discussions of physically uninvolved spectators and actively involved guardians of the practice. There is a historical quest for authentic voices in the matter mostly to confirm what local representatives or foreign experts affirm about the practice: it is necessary, or it is a violation of women's bodily integrity.[5] The young woman in this excerpt from *The River Between* makes initiation a universal rite of passage. Wa Thiong'o's writing highlights the constant dialectic surrounding the issue of FGM, local versus foreign, so central in the modalities with which UN delegates treated the issue.

Figure 6 depicts the delegates of the new UN member states in September 1960. The presence of postcolonial states allowed for a mitigation of the politics of representation so contentious within the CSW. Starting with the work on the Convention on the Nationality of Married Women, marriage, which began as a public matter and later became a blend of public and private spheres, was at the center of the commission's debates. Along with the private sphere, the theories of development and modernization refocused the international interest in the former dependent territories, now new nation-states. Starting in the late 1950s, we see a clean break with the past through the presence of UN delegates from the Global South and their understanding of their own culture, which, as shown in chapter 4, had mostly generated sensationalistic stances within the UN rooms.

The involvement of the United Nations with FGM represents one of the most intense historical intersections between international women's rights and the Global South. FGM had been a Western concern since early imperial times, especially in the context of the British Empire. Incidentally, it was through a Catholic-led debate that the CSW started a concerted action to denounce FGM. To the Catholic NGO responsible for introducing practices detrimental to women, it was African women themselves who rejected such practices. While this point is difficult to prove given the multiple layers that led from the local setting to an international debate, one aspect appears prominent: the legitimacy of the direct testimony of local voices.

This second case of bodies in pain (see chapter 4 for the first case) also involved various elements of the UN system. Controversies and campaigns against rituals that presumably harmed the female body have a history that predates the formation of the UN. Nevertheless, the UN's involvement in this issue provides a unique perspective, one that included international voices, both pro-colonial and anticolonial, in favor of and against international interventions in the private and local sphere.

At a more internal level, the new WHO-based conception of health as "a fundamental human right" increased the connection between the violation of the body and human rights. The WHO, a UN agency created in 1948 and still active today, represented new trends in international health. If health was a human right, as the WHO advocated, international organizations were supposed to aid states in both the prevention and management of factors that affected human health. In the context of rituals, what was at stake was not health per se but rather whether rituals affecting women's bodies were medical or cultural issues, whether culture could affect the body, and whether this pain constituted a violation of fundamental human rights.[6]

The UN story of FGM goes through a progression of steps: first, the contribution of NGOs active in the general African context and their concern for equality in marriage; second, a debate over the practice of FGM, though without direct mention of it; third, a multiparty UN involvement; and eventually, the problematic confirmation that Western "experts" knew the right action to take.

Direct Testimony and The Construction of African Dignity

As stated in previous chapters, the CSW worked on the basis of data provided by the TC and by organizations active in the dependent territories and/or developing ones. The council's reports passed through different organizational levels. Because of their connections with missionary groups, religious NGOs provided a presumably direct account of the local experience in African countries. Along this line and preoccupied about the status of women in the Global South, international women's organizations that participated in the commission's sessions, such as the International Alliance of Women, brought to the UN the issue of equality in marriage, which directly related to bride-price and polygamy.

Contemporary to the Bikom scandal and in the context of the CSW debate on women in private law—one of the original agenda items of the CSW, together with the political rights of women—the International Alliance of Women proposed a debate on article 16 of the Universal Declaration of Human Rights (UDHR), which provides for equal rights in marriage and member states' protection of the matrimonial union. At the CSW's fifth session (1951), the International Alliance of Women had previously asked the HRC to include paragraph 1 of article 16 (equal rights in marriage between men and women) in the draft of the International Covenant on Human Rights (only approved in 1966). This plea, supported by the International Council of Women, became the opportunity to discuss matrimonial union in broader terms and in different places including the colonial world.[7]

In the course of this debate, the International Union of Catholic Women's League reported on the status of married women in dependent territories. During her "study tour" in Africa, the league's delegate, Alba Zizzamia, met with "relatively cultured African women" whose unified desire was "adequate protection" of their "personal dignity through monogamy." Zizzamia reported that African women aimed for the abolition of the practice of the bride-price, which according to her data, had become abusive. She claimed that, although she was aware of the economic and social reasons for such practices, she "was merely expressing the convictions of educated African women." In her opinion, at stake was "the dignity of women as human beings."[8] The Bikom case showed how polygamy was becoming more and more an international concern. In this case, however, Zizzamia claimed that the attack on the practice was coming from educated local women. There is here an obvious problem of location, such that the whole continent was lumped into a general voice. From a small territory in an already small portion of French Cameroon, the commissioners were then engaging with an entire continent.

Zizzamia stated that monogamy was the force that could truly foster "the development of a people as a whole." She highlighted how, in the case of different views about the dignity of women, the charter and UDHR were legally superior to customary laws. Contrary to the TC's delegates, she believed that law was the force that could change the status quo, and that education would follow. Her claim to authority over solutions for African women came, she argued, from the direct testimony of local women. The union had submitted the commission's Questionnaire on Legal Status of and Treatment of Women (The questionnaire was given to member states and NGOs in preparation for the Convention of Political Rights of Women). This instrument allowed African women, as Zizzamia stated, to express "a desire for the recognition of their personal dignity as individuals, of their maternal feelings, and of their potential contribution to the family as responsible individuals."[9] From the union's perspective, "if certain practices or customs entailed social consequences degrading for some and prejudicial to the healthy development of the nation as a whole, or contradictory to the fundamental human rights of women, concern for the common good and respect for fundamental human rights" had to "take precedence over customs."[10] Zizzamia argued that in the discussion of the trust and dependent territories, the tendency was to give more authority to the customs that damaged women's condition and to the economic and political advantages for such customs. Moreover, she contended that politics and economics were implicated in the "respect of inalienable rights and the inherent dignity of women." Zizzamia encouraged an education system where women could discuss "their own problems."[11] The union, which held status B at the UN and could only suggest measures and not resolutions, expressed the desire to encourage the ECOSOC and the TC to "ensure women a complete freedom of choice of a spouse" together with other measures that guaranteed the rights of mothers and the abolition of child marriage and polygamy.

For the Catholic union, women in the dependent territories needed to be aware of the efforts of the commissioners to improve their status. Zizzamia denounced the disconnection between the commissioners' preoccupation with women in the colonies and the colonized women's awareness of being the object of such international concern. As the Bikom scandal showed, for local issues, there was a certain propensity to give more legitimacy to local voices. As illustrated in the petitions' case, the trusteeship system itself created, consciously or not, the chance for African women (from the trust territories) to manifest their dissent about their status, even if mediated by a Catholic organization.

The powerful framework of human rights and the UN's new narrative of democratization of the colonial world provided women from the dependent territories with a space to denounce their own status under colonial rule. Zizzamia spoke about a general "Africa" without locating groups that engaged with practices detrimental to women's dignity. She highlighted the difficult relationship between universalism as dictated by UN principles and political pragmatism when groups in power did not question women's quality of life. Noticeable was Zizzamia's call for "the human rights of women," which shows that this type of language—popularized much later at the 1995 Beijing conference—was already present, though arguably only in cases symptomatic of the hierarchical status of an issue. The engagement of the HRC here might indicate how "human rights of women" was used whenever cases were too important to be relegated to the realm of women only. Zizzamia reinforced a point that commissioners had inaugurated with their discussion and deliberations on the language used in the Universal Declaration of Human Rights (see chapter 1) and, later, with their appeal to the HRC on the linguistic shape of the Human Rights Covenant.[12] The case of the dignity of women, even if highly problematic, created a more unified relationship between women's and human rights.

At the same meeting where Zizzamia expressed the intentions of African women, the British commissioner, Sutherland, reported the words of the governor of Tanganyika (part of the trusteeship system and under British administration): "The status of women <u>constituted</u> the key to the future progress of the territory."[13] The governor believed that only if a powerful "tribe" provided an example of the fair treatment of women would the others follow. Sutherland concluded her speech by reporting the governor's words on women who were to him "the hallmark of civilization."

In question were practices that the Trusteeship Council, St. Joan's International Alliance, and some commissioners denounced: bride-price, child marriage, and polygamy. At the same CSW session, the French delegate, Lefaucheux, encouraged the use of the word "ancient" to define (without going into details) other practices such as female circumcision. She argued that by using "ancient," it was clear that the trusteeship authority was not responsible for such customs.[14] Reinforcing the historical continuity of traditional rituals at a native level condoned European colonial powers and their political and economic reliance on such practices.[15] This type of language considered colonialism (one more time) parenthetical rather than intrinsic to the fabric of the postcolonial state. These statements also show how women's dignity as constructed by UN authorities became a measurement of practical suitability for a postcolonial progressive society.

From Ancient Customs to Circumcision

A few months after the "ancient customs debate" at the CSW, St. Joan's International Alliance (St. Joan's) sent a direct communication to the architect and director of the TC, Ralph Bunche, (see chapter 1) under the form of a petition.[16] In her communication Florence Barry, president of the NGO, refers to a new question that the TC added to the questionnaires that the administrating authority had submitted to local leaders. The question was about the physical integrity of women. In Barry's words, the NGO "expresses its satisfaction that the Trusteeship Council has included in its questionnaire requesting reports from Administrating Authority, a question regarding the violation of the physical integrity of women (female circumcision). We trust that the Trusteeship Council, in collaboration with the Administrating Authority, will take immediately all appropriate measures to promote the progressive abolition of such customs in Trust Territories."

For the first time the word "female circumcision" appeared in official UN documents on FGM. St. Joan's praised itself for being a Catholic feminist organization, and interestingly, Barry overcame the prominent modesty around talking about FGM and declared that the physical violation of women was "female circumcision."[17]

The TC welcomed the petition and acted on it through a resolution dated July 13, 1953. In it, the council acknowledged the lead of St. Joan's in the matter and moved the initiative further up the UN hierarchy. The TC decided "to draw the attention of the Administrating Authorities to the petition (by St. Joan's) and to take up this question during its annual examination of conditions in those trust territories where the custom complained of may exist."[18] In this unique cycle of actions, St. Joan's—an organization with clear missionary ties (see chapter 4)—proposed an initiative and an understanding of female circumcision as eroding dignity; the council then communicated to the countries in charge of measuring self-rule to assess on the basis of what St. Joan's had expressed.

Member countries of the Third Committee, the UN General Assembly committee dedicated to women's rights, (see chapter 2) met in December 1954 to debate the topic of customs, ancient laws, and practices that affected "the human dignity of women."[19] The body is here hidden behind layers of national self-congratulatory remarks regarding progress in deconstructing cultural "oppression." The meeting started with a solemn premise: "In some areas of the world, women were subject to customs, ancient laws and practices . . . which were not consistent with the principles set forth in the United Nations Charter and the Universal Declaration of Human Rights." Since women were the "hallmark of civilization," the Third Committee confirmed that progress meant eliminating such practices, for "the existence of those customs prevented women from enjoying the fundamental rights which should be theirs and subjected some groups of human beings to social injustice, thus impending general progress." Arguably, with these words they meant the integrity and dignity of the body.

The Third Committee debate ended up being focused on gender equality in general with each country proposing a different understanding. For example, Aziza Hussein, the delegate from Egypt who later became the president of Planned Parenthood, made a conscious effort to disentangle Islam from discrimination against women, just as delegates from Iraq and Pakistan had done in the past.[20] The Argentinian delegation argued instead that if women left the domestic sphere, the very fabric of society would dissolve. The general Third Committee consensus was that the main reasons for ancient practices to exist was poverty. The "ancient customs" emerged as stripped by systems, by agents, and by actual groups that benefited from them.

At the General Assembly, no country wanted to be in the group that practiced "ancient customs," so the discussion served not to analyze the problem, per se, but as an opportunity to present national political agendas. The word "ancient" sparked a heated debate, specifically, as to whether the term was supposed to stay in the final resolution or not. Both the UK and the United States abstained from the final vote because of their unwillingness to see the UN interfere with national laws, even ancient ones.

Circumcision made a brief appearance in St. Joan's petition, and then it disappeared again at the General Assembly and at the CSW, where delegates addressed it through multiple names based on their disdain rather than a desire to engage with what it was. They also introduced a new term that represented a step forward from the too-general "ancient customs": ritual operations. It is unclear what the Third Committee delegates of the 1950s knew about the practice of FGM. It is also unclear whether it was the language of emotions and colonial stereotypes that encouraged governments to say something about it. The difficulties in openly debating FGM partly continued at the CSW, which a few years later clashed with the WHO on this issue.

Conflicts of Competencies: The CSW and the WHO

At the CSW's twelfth session in 1958, the French delegate officially brought to the table the issue of female genital modifications.[21] In certain parts of "Black Africa," she claimed, young girls between the ages of eight and fourteen were subjected to "so-called ritual operations" in hidden places and under uncomfortable and harmful circumstances. She declared, "such practices had serious effects on the physiological balance and repercussions on the psychology and intellectual faculties of the victim." The WHO representative at the CSW, Dr. M. H. Hafezi, claimed that he knew about these rituals and argued against international intervention. He instead supported the direct involvement of local governments.

It is useful to read Dr. Hafezi's clear refusal to intervene in the context of the WHO's politics of international health vis-à-vis the colonial world. In its early definition of health regions, the WHO challenged colonial powers, specifically France, by creating zones based on geographical proximity and similarities of ecosystems and health threats. France insisted that Algeria, previously placed within the North African health region, be placed with Europe, as it was one of France's metropolitan territories.[22]

Hafezi's objection to the WHO's involvement in rituals affecting the body has also to be inscribed within a specific direction of the organization: the shift of the WHO from social medicine—an early approach that encouraged the exploration of the structural conditions related to medical issues—to a technocratic approach, where central planning and policies took the place of a social interpretation of medicine. The WHO went from an organization interested in health issues anywhere to one that paid attention to Cold War divisions and colonial powers' demands.[23] The change was probably due to Cold War-induced fear of everything "social." Furthermore, from a jurisdictional point of view, the WHO could only provide help upon request from a specific country's national health administration. Hafezi never mentioned specific rules but spoke in general terms of noninterference, and the language of technocracy with its pretense of objectivity served the purpose of maintaining the status quo.

According to the technocratic approach, "policies could be detached from their specifically colonial context." The WHO's direction denied cultural specificities in its quest for a universal approach to solving medical problems. As historian Sunil Amrith claims, "The very attraction of a techno-centric approach to public health was that it appeared to detach the WHO from the need to intervene deeply, in matters of 'culture' or social transformation."[24]

Undefeated by the definite position of Hafezi, commissioners insisted on the medical emergency that rituals represented, ignoring the homogenizing thrust of the WHO, which aimed to create transcultural policies and approaches. Within this framework, the French delegate, supported by Bernardino, advocated for the WHO's influence on governments in establishing international standards in medical matters. Bernardino argued that, as in the case of malaria and leprosy, where the WHO had been successful in preventing the diseases, for rituals, the WHO could have prevented attacks against women's bodily integrity.[25] Conversely, malaria and leprosy did not involve rituals of passage into adulthood or practices believed to maintain communal order. The language of emotions soon became central in the formulation of this debate. Commissioners started to speak in catastrophic terms of practices such as FGM.

The Polish commissioner aligned herself with France and the Dominican Republic on the involvement of the WHO, but she used a more evocative language. She encouraged the creation of press campaigns against the "mutilation of women." She urged the WHO to work with the CSW, because counting on governmental action alone was not enough to "remedy that revolting state of affairs."[26] This was the first time that commissioners used such strong language to define practices allegedly harmful to women.

The Polish position changed once the Soviet Union expressed its official line on the issue.[27] The Soviet delegate presented the problem of attempting to voice the concerns of the "other," of speaking on behalf of someone else. Because the issue was declared as a cultural experience, the Soviet position claimed that the CSW needed the representatives of *that culture* to bring the information necessary for concrete action.[28] The WHO delegate responded that governments of the countries where such practices were present were reluctant to accept foreign interventions.[29] Poland agreed and declared that the adoption of the CSW resolution on rituals actually gave "the impression that the UN was interfering in . . . domestic affairs." These problems, the Polish delegate continued, "concerned the African states only and [were] not of universal scope." Commissioners, she argued, needed to show more trust in the states' action and, at the same time, needed to wait for more results until African delegates were part of the debate.

Ultimately, the French representative responded that the intention was not to make a final decision in the absence of African delegates but only to request further information on the practices from countries that had not provided it.[30] This part of the debate suggests tensions within the Soviet Bloc representatives as well as the challenges of international cooperation during the Cold War. It is unclear whether the Soviet Bloc's delegates agreed with Hafezi because of their anti-West sentiments or because they truly believed in the self-determination of newly formed states and native cultures. This type of ambiguity was dominant in the Soviet rhetorical interventions in favor of the developing world.

In the context of individual countries reacting to FGM, Bernardino and the early Australian commissioner and international activist Jessie Street (see chapter 1) debated, for example, the case of Sudan, which having achieved independence in 1957 was then communicating with the UN about the topic.[31] Sudan had a unique story with the practice. As anthropologist Janice Boddy argues in her work on the subject, since the 1920s colonial authorities—specifically, British sisters and midwifery trainers Mabel and Gertrude Wolff in Sudan—aimed at inserting FGM within the language of biomedical treatment, alongside expressions and practices such as surgery, hygiene, and the monitoring of the patient. Boddy demonstrates very effectively that medicalization promised safer practice, though with the hidden agenda of eventually eliminating it.[32] Beyond the official spaces of sensationalist debates, single commissioners—as communications with the Sudanese government demonstrated—did make an attempt to understand better the context of the practice.

The last statement delivered during the 1958 debate came from the commission's secretary, the French lawyer Sophie Grinberg-Vinaver.[33] As mentioned in previous chapters, the role of the secretary was to provide the background data necessary for commissioners to formulate fact-based resolutions. Grinberg-Vinaver in this case provided a more accurate and technocratic account, one that did not create a monolithic category of all African women as victims of rituals affecting their bodies. Such practices, Grinberg-Vinaver argued, were present only in a "few limited areas" and were in decline. She also praised the TC for monitoring and measuring the practices. She delivered a description stripped of emotional expressions and the sense of doom that commissioners' testimony had relayed.

The pressing request for WHO intervention, however, remained on the table. Despite the reluctance of many WHO delegates to address these rituals, the commissioners put on record their demands and moved forward to include more UN officials in their campaign to study further FGM. Hafezi finally brought rules to the table and declared that the WHO could act only with governmental instructions and could not give directions to member states. According to him, governments were aware of such practices, but they believed that education could gradually eliminate them; therefore, "no useful purpose would be served by officially condemning them." By specifying the role of the UN agency in this fashion, Hafezi emphasized how commissioners focused more on the outrage of the rituals than on accurate and realistic actions within UN competencies.

The issue of rituals revealed how different elements within the organization articulated divergent opinions on the politically fraught question of whether to adopt policies focused on these rituals or even on whether pain and the scarification of the body were to be regarded as international issues. The UN was a house divided against itself.[34] Clearly the WHO in this case supported proximity versus distance in its medical authority as opposed to the emotional analyses of the other parts of the UN.

Ultimately, the CSW proposed a resolution to officially ask the WHO to conduct research on the matter of the rituals in Africa. Hafezi noted again that the WHO could not work without the governments' cooperation and that the research in question faced financial limitations as well as difficulties in finding experts in the field. Commissioners did not give in. Because of the reluctance of the WHO's representatives, they proposed a less assertive resolution and asked the WHO to study the possibility of researching this issue.[35]

The commissioners' insistence did not derive only from an emotional analysis; both the HRC and ECOSOC participated in the CSW/WHO's clash of expertise. Such widespread involvement showed that the powerful language of human rights and the trope of the wounded body created a universal narrative of defenselessness that reinforced a gendered and racialized interpretation of African women. Two dimensions appear evident from this stage in the debate: one is the inclusion of women's rights and human rights under the umbrella term of "human dignity." Treating rituals as a violation of human rights contributed also to the erasure of the specificities of cultures and practices. It is difficult to connect FGM to a specific area and culture, yet "culture" is deemed responsible for it. The creation of new nation-states with new postcolonial geographic borders actually made more difficult identifying a specific practice with a specific culture.[36] This second aspect shows that at the UN, the conflict produced more institutional complexity and raised the question of whether the ECOSOC, along with the General Assembly and the Secretariat, could convince the WHO to act on the basis of their differing considerations.

The ECOSOC supported the CSW's request to the WHO to "undertake a study of the persistence of the customs mentioned above and of the measures adopted or planned for putting a stop to such practices."[37] After approving the CSW resolution, the council invited all the UN's specialized agencies, including the WHO, "to bear in mind in the planning of their programmes and activities the need to a concerted action against the continuance of the practice of ritual operations."[38] Simultaneously, John Humphrey and Egon Schwelb from the Human Rights Commission, with the approval of the secretary-general, wrote a proposal to forward the UN's strategy to the WHO plenary meeting.

At the WHO's twenty-third assembly in 1959, the UN delegate presented the concerted proposal by ECOSOC. The WHO officially responded with resolution EB23.R75, which claimed that "since such practices were of social and cultural rather than of a medical nature, the study requested was outside the organization's competence."[39] Schwelb noted that the WHO dedicated a very small place to such matters. The resolution of the WHO ignored the UN's insistence that circumcision forcefully modified the female body and, more generally, violated the integrity of the human body. Claiming that the practice was cultural and hence outside the range of the WHO created a climate in which culture transcended presumed harm to bodies and minds. At an organizational level, the WHO appeared to be acting outside the realm of human rights, as if such a framework applied only to those commissions directly involved with these matters rather than being, like the charter, part of the overall goals of all entities within the UN. The WHO also created an international legal precedent in which culture did not harm and so was somewhat above international law.

In the CSW's work on women and private law, as in the case of political rights, the agents of discrimination remained blurry as the emphasis was on the state's recognition of women's contribution to society at a public and private level, rather than on identifying the forces that had kept women at the margins. However, according to the CSW, harming women's bodies for cultural reasons was an abusive practice; in this way, the differentiation between victims and perpetrators appeared clear. Even if problematically and within imperial feminist politics, women delegates connected the body to the Universal Declaration of Human Rights, inaugurating what became a strong bond between rights and protests against the violation of bodily integrity.

Only in 1975 did the WHO express itself regarding the "possible" damages linked to the procedure of genital cutting.[40] The language of possibilities with which WHO experts described bodily and reproductive injuries to circumcised women still condoned the procedure. The International Women's Network, created on the occasion of the 1975 UN conference for women, sent a direct communication to the CSW, asking for more concrete intervention in this matter. The author of this long survey, one undertaken in support of the CSW's action on genital cutting, was Fran Hosken, who became known for her popular—yet controversial—research on FGM, the so-called Hosken Report, which asserted a relationship between women's bodies and modernization. The future mothers of Africa, Hosken claimed, must not be subjected to mutilations that damaged them and, consequently, "national development."[41] Hosken made a simple argument against damaging citizens who can contribute to the nation. In this context, her claim is significant because it represents one end of a path that started in sensationalism and finished in pragmatism in the critique of ritual practices. Nonetheless, she highlights the importance of women as fundamental for a country's growth, a quasi-technocratic approach in which the nation, not the female body in pain, is the focus. While the Hosken Report was published in 1975, the UN promoted the inclusion of African women in the global forum of human rights earlier. African women, specifically, emerged as the force to improve newly formed states.

African Matters and African Women: Addis Ababa, 1960

At the second session that CSW held abroad (Buenos Aires, March 1960), commissioners debated the imminent seminar in Addis Ababa. The ILO representative at the Buenos Aires meeting noticed how part of the CSW insisted on the WHO's involvement in fighting rituals against women. Her words showed the reluctance of UN agencies to consider commissioners as experts, as well as an ILO's unexpected support of a Soviet position: "It was obvious that few, if any, members of the Commission had any knowledge whatsoever of what ritual operations they were talking about, the extent to which they were practised and their effects. However, both the

French and the UK delegates took the matter very seriously, to such an extent that the USSR delegate voiced her suspicion that it was all a ploy on the part of the old imperialist powers to discredit the newly independent countries of Africa."[42] A few months later the Addis Ababa Seminar happened and the WHO was again called into question, only this time from a local vantage point.

The Addis Ababa 1960 seminar on the participation of women in public life provided those local voices on African issues that the Soviets had so adamantly demanded. The event, organized under the human rights advisory program, provided the opportunity for a discussion of the status of African women by African women. These discussions, as well as the international setting, reinforced the emerging sense of identity under the notion of Africanness. The host country, Ethiopia, symbolized the continuity of African history since its history was unmarked by colonial interference—with the exception of a brief occupation by the Italian army, 1935–1936—and the enthusiastic climate of freedom and independence from European powers. In the inaugural speeches, the host country's royal family touched on the challenges of modernity, independence, and the importance of international cooperation for newly formed countries. The role of women surfaced as a vital contribution to development and progress. However, the debates of the seminar produced something similar to the UN line on colonialism, including, again, a parenthetical aspect—hence a sort of historical condoning—of what had been foreign rule for centuries.

Princess Tenagne Worg from Ethiopia spoke about the part that women had to play in the resolution of problems brought about by "modern civilization."[43] She mentioned the struggle for independence by many African countries and how women's duty was to "work side by side" with men in the spirit of brotherhood. The princess praised the multiple roles of Ethiopian women in different sectors of public life, in the home, and on the battlefield. Her speech consolidated the image of the newly independent African woman who was to contribute in both private and public. The emperor, in contrast, formulated the role of African women's "relentless vigilance" over African civilization.

Ultimately, the empress presented a more spiritual scenario in which the "disordered hearts and minds" had gathered in Addis Ababa for a "global soul-searching." The princess addressed women as "the mothers of mankind," women's contribution to "world statesmanship," and women as the guides for "Africa's future."[44]

Immediately after the inaugural party, in the gardens of the royal palace, a coup against the royal family erupted in Addis Ababa. For a few days, the seminar participants had to conduct most meetings by candlelight.[45] After order was restored, the emperor, in a public appeal, accused the dissidents of aiming to affect the modernizing process of Ethiopia. He thanked God, the air force, and the army for having stopped a rebellion carried out by the so-called loyalist faction of the government and by other rebels who had joined them.[46] The seminar began under these images that epitomized the political atmosphere of the 1960s. It continued despite the disturbance of what the emperor defended as a free and spiritual Ethiopia. It acknowledged the nation-building desire of new African countries. This coup episode somewhat affected the tone of the seminar, but the carryover of the discussions served as a symbol of women's resilience.

In his inaugural speech, Humphrey (HRC) also confirmed that the status of women was inextricably linked to African development.[47] The Liberian delegate opened the general discussion by saying, "A stronger and united front about all cooperative and sympathetic minds is essential to ease today's 'suspicious', 'fearful' and 'chaotic' world." Women, she declared, "are powerful," and their participation in public life could "greatly influence society."[48] The women's rights framework not only served as a code for the fair treatment of women's hearts and bodies but also signaled the connection between the treatment of women and the challenges of modernity.

The delegates from Africa represented the highly educated female population of the continent. In more informal discussions on suffrage, few delegates praised local women and presented a range of issues still affecting their countries. For Example, the Togolese delegate accused the male population of being "backward," as opposed to women who in Togo voted in high numbers. Although she was proud of national female voters too, the Cameroonian representative denounced the persistence of colonial practices for education and opportunities.[49] Interestingly, both countries, part of the trust system, showed how national realities differed even under the same administering authority.

The seminar contributors defined participation "as the active and co-operative service given by individuals and by groups in the interest of human betterment," which started "with the immediate environment," to conclude with "the right to vote, to be elected to office and to take part in other forms of community activity."[50] The participants agreed that education was instrumental to the participation of women in public life. Educated women, even in small numbers, were seen as potential leaders for other women in the community. The association between education and voting rights produced impossible outcomes for women because formal education was not widespread, but they wanted to participate in the creation of the new democratic state.

For the debate on voting and education, most participants agreed that even simple awareness could help with choosing a candidate in case of an election. Furthermore, it was established that women possess a "natural political instinct" developed through other activities, such as trade. Still, there was a general consensus on the importance of learning voting procedures. Women's direct participation as educated guides of the community or as formal electoral candidates was affected by traditional views that simultaneously distrusted women and politicians.

Participants argued that "psychological factors contributed to this attitude and frequently arose from the opinion that women's only proper sphere was the home."[51] At the same time, specific feminine traits made women politicians more appealing to women voters. It was also noted that political parties assigned only nonchallenging positions to women. Although new states were eager to promote a discourse of equality as opposed to rigid conceptions of colonial separation, they did not guarantee women's centrality in politics. Within this context, even when educated women participated actively in communal lives, the high expectations for their participation pressured them and limited their chances of advancement. The participants did not single out men or patriarchy as responsible for such a bleak scenario; rather, they addressed the more abstract category of "social factors." The lack of leisure time emerged as one of the impediments to women's participation in public life. African women contributed a larger workload in the agricultural sector and in the home.

The participants also advocated for education in the vernacular language as a force to strengthen national culture in countries that had achieved independence. Beyond the opening speeches, this was the first collective reference to colonialism. African women delegates also recognized how "the influence of another civilization" played a great part in the cultural and educational life of Africa. They proposed considering the advantages provided by the encounter of civilizations. Education for women also meant being away from home and being subjected to danger outside parental supervision. Sexual dangers appeared as the main threat, and as a solution, the participants proposed sex education both at home and at school. They preferred for teachers and parents to work together to instruct women in sexual matters.[52]

The seminar included a discussion of social, religious, and legal factors that affected the status of women. Inevitably, the debate led to the issue of African women and local culture. Public life, the delegate from Madagascar argued, depended on women's relationships with their families and society.[53] Both written and unwritten laws affected women's participation in public life. The representative of Madagascar posed a question about the means to limit or suppress the power of legal, religious, and societal impediments. Along with the csw's direction on these issues, she identified the main element that closely impeded women to exercise their rights, rituals that damaged women physically and psychologically.

The participants expressed concerns "at the continuance" of ritual practices, indicating that there was resistance toward such practices in local communities and that the phenomenon was confined only to certain areas. The seminar included medical experts (one medical doctor and one midwife) who described the "mutilation and scarification" of the female body during and after ritual procedures. The possible consequences, the experts explained, were of two types. The first was severe hemorrhaging and septicemia in cases in which the necessary hygienic conditions were not present. The other case, a possible result of the operation, were complications in childbirth because of limitations in dilation and general difficulties with labor. These discussions lacked the emotional, outraged tone that women commissioners had used to treat the topic, a tone that was more alarming than informative.[54]

At the seminar delegates discussed the reasons for such practices, which ranged from men's conviction that it prevented adultery to its "educative value," because through this ritual young women "learned the virtues of courage and endurance." As the young woman in *The River Between* claimed (see introduction of this chapter), in the case of the Kenyan Kikuyus, for example, both female and male circumcision represented the promotion into full communal life and the acquisition of the status of full personhood.[55] This part concluded with a plan for both encouraging African culture "by supporting those rich and varied qualities which were of value" for the continent and for the world in general and denouncing instances of cultural practices that damaged the population and contributed to "backwardness."[56] As in the case of the CSW, the ECOSOC, and the Secretariat, seminar participants called for the WHO's inquiry into this subject in concert with national legislation prohibiting the rituals. Practices that defined women's adulthood necessarily led to a discussion on the dominant element of this stage of women's lives: marriage. In this context marriage was inextricable from customary practices.

The delegate from Madagascar defined marriage as the "keystone of society."[57] Popular topics relating to marriage and customs in the native world were child betrothal, bride-price, and polygamy. In the regulation of marriage, diverse religious codes existed alongside the civic code. In general, the participants spoke against practices that damaged women, transcending religious affiliation. They described child betrothal as an agreement between the girl's family and the future husband that happened when the prospective bride was two or three years old. The actual marriage, that is the consummation of the marriage, happened only when the girl reached puberty. However, the participants were against the forced aspect of the union. They proposed that the girl stay in her family's house until she was physically ready for the matrimonial union.[58]

Levels of education mediated the acceptance of marriage agreements; unschooled girls usually accepted without protesting, whereas girls who had received some form of education resisted, and this disagreement damaged the harmony within their family. While education represented a value for women's lives, it damaged their social relationships. There were also cases of impatient husbands who did not wait for girls to reach puberty and consummated the marriage with children who were nine years old. The participants agreed that in such cases, women could die in childbirth and/ or develop "an abnormal psychology."[59] Attacking child marriage from a medical point of view provided a powerful tool that highlighted how "culture" could damage citizens.

Another controversial topic in this section was dedicated to the practice of bride-price. Something that was originally "symbolic" had been contaminated by "undesirable commercialism" and had "degenerated" into a mere "business transaction." Because of the contractual nature of this practice, the monetary amount was central, and brides' opinions were ignored in the face of high bids. The practice also damaged the prospective husband, who often borrowed the necessary amount to compete with other suitors. The participants agreed that the symbolic value of the practice should be restored to avoid further damage until education could eliminate it.[60]

Ultimately, the delegates discussed the issue of polygamy. The participants differentiated between Muslim and animist polygamy. In the case of Islamic law, the husband was bound to support all his wives and the children born of those unions. In the case of animist law, the husband was bound to support only the first wife. The reason for animist men to have more wives was the need for more women to work in the fields. However, for animist women, a polygamous marriage still represented *a marriage* and a conferred status on women in communities where nonmarried women were disempowered. Polygamy presented further complications independent from women's consent; wealthy men usually married all the suitable women, which forced young men to go to towns where "prostitution flourished."[61]

African women had to imagine their own individual national culture as well as a unified category of "African woman" that, although semantically identical to the colonial category of "African" as racially and discursively opposite to European, had to represent something new that aspired to collective strength and modernization. The trope of "civilization" that was so prominent in colonial rhetoric became, in the emperor's words, purely "African." Although this aspect constituted political and spiritual independence from Europe, it also relegated the colonial period to a parenthesis whose ramifications were rarely mentioned.

Conclusion

This chapter shows how the CSW participated in the formulation of the relationship between the African states and the UN. Women's rights and local culture emerged as the most contested elements to define the role of the UN within decolonization and within the postcolonial state. The ever-contentious issue of FGM served as a further test to universalism. A few salient aspects resulted from this debate: the importance of authentic voices, the conflict of competencies between the UN agencies and the CSW, and the intrinsic dialectical aspect of debates of FGM, the foreign and the local.

At the GA debate for the ratification of the Convention on Consent to Marriage, Minimum Age of Marriage, and Registration of Marriages (1965), the Nigerian ambassador asked for a resolution that promoted fair treatment in marriage "according to traditional and religious practice."[62] Although the convention codified the fight against cultural aspects that damaged women in the international legal arena, delegates from member states imposed limitations that significantly restricted the status of women.

In this transitional moment from dependency to self-rule, the status of women became a strong symbol of national unity, where women were seen as the "guardians of tradition." Simultaneously, women became the symbol of the new Africa and modernization. Two competing yet comple-mentary images emerged as African women themselves saw continuity, a straight line, from tradition to modernization. As chapter 6 shows, saving a traditional role while participating in the modernization of the country proved to be a difficult process. The CSW represented the spatial and con-centric dimension of these debates. Commissioners' observations and international legal work for women in dependent territories first and in "developing countries" later contributed to identifying agents of discrimi-nation against women. From an abstract conception of discrimination that sounded ahistorical and hence difficult to fight, the commissioners built a more concrete concept inscribed in the UN's ambivalent attitude toward the colonial and postcolonial.

7. Status of Women in Family Law seminar, Lomé, Togo, 1964.
© United Nations, reprinted with permission of the United Nations.

6

Bodies in Captivity, Gender Equilibrium, and the Shift from Liberal Politics

In dialogue with the image from chapter 1, with its layers of guardians and flags, the photograph on the left presents similar elements but with a different meaning. Whereas flags at the 1945 San Francisco Conference symbolized postwar internationalism, in 1964 Togo they represent the independent nation-states that emerged from the end of colonialism. The second layer is here embodied by women themselves (anonymous in the didascaly of the photo) but standing as the guardians of the proceedings of the Togo seminar and as the symbol of the topic treated. Ultimately, the presence of the host country delegates confirmed Togo as both independent nation and contributor to internationalism. The French inscription on the map of Africa reinforces not only the heritage of colonialism but also the association with a general Africa as opposed to showing the single map of Togo. Margaret Bruce (in the photo next to Rana Ombri, minister of social affairs of the Togolese government) participated as the then secretary of the Division of the Status of Women, elucidating here the direct presence of the CSW at the meeting.

At the 1964 United Nations seminar on family law in Togo, the discussion turned to polygamy, a trope that had historically preoccupied Western observers of the Global South and, as shown in previous chapters, had been at the forefront in the debates on women's rights.[1] At the seminar, participants agreed that polygamy was detrimental to women's dignity, but they confirmed that it was unavoidable in situations involving poverty and a lack of growth. They argued that this unfortunate compromise could change only at more advanced stages of development in which women reached financial independence.[2] In Lomé it was also agreed that economic development determined the place of women in society and that, conversely, more advanced stages of socioeconomic development for women led to progress for society as a whole.[3] Discrimination based on gender, therefore, appeared to be antimodern and even anti-internationalism, whereas development represented the new force that not only could improve individual lives but also increase international cooperation.

The Togo seminar speeches also encouraged a slow pace for women to reach progress as if sudden change could affect the new postcolonial state. This position was similar to what some delegates had suggested at the Third Committee voting session of the 1952 Convention on the Political Rights of Women. In the postcolonial moment, at stake was an international definition and understanding of macro categories such as democracy and postcolonial citizenship: who was to be included in the newly born nation-state, what gender equality meant in this context, and ultimately, what the role of women's bodies was in the postcolonial setting.

Other elements irradiated from the Togo seminar's discussion on development and the family. One that was especially connected to the body was slavery. This issue emerged because of the General Assembly's review of the 1956 Convention on Slavery. Commissioners read slavery as a constraint on the female body and the result of underdevelopment. The trafficked body appears again and again with familial implications as in the case of parents who allegedly had to give up their daughters to indentured slavery. Along with the trafficked body, African commissioners associated slavery with apartheid because, they argued, it denied dignity and therefore produced the conditions for unpaid labor. In their understanding, development unaccompanied by racial and gender equality led to oppression.

This chapter shows that within the CSW the discourses of development and gender equality occurred simultaneously. This close tie was representative of the interconnections between the heritage of colonialism and postcolonial nation building. Since the early stages of the commission's work, delegates highlighted how under colonialism, political and economic dependency were detrimental to the status of women. Colonial powers had called for "civilization" as the force that would lead to improvement in the status of women. Instead, as this chapter contends, commissioners advocated for economic growth and democracy in postcolonial states. Therefore, along with plans for development, they worked to find a comprehensive tool to fight discrimination against women; gender equality was to be a constitutive element of a democratic state. Within this framework, commissioners pioneered the debate on the inclusion of women in development, a theme that later became popular through economist Ester Bosrap's influential text.[4] Along with the insertion of women in development policies, it was the discrepancy between law and practice in matters of women's rights that encouraged the commissioners to focus more on discrimination and culture than on national laws.

As I showed in previous chapters, the CSW engaged with the intersections of Cold War and decolonization narratives. For example, to the socialist bloc, the United States, France, and the UK were all parts of the same capitalist imperial project. Countries that had reached independence in the immediate postwar period (Indonesia, India, and Pakistan) seldom expressed direct disdain for European imperialism. Instead, the clashes between nationalist China and the Soviet delegates over issues of who represented "real" China and spoke on behalf of Chinese women were more open. In the midst of all these dimensions and secure of their own sex equality with men, Western commissioners sought to apply the UN principle against gender discrimination in other countries.

The 1960s saw a change of tone as compared to a few years earlier. As illustrated in chapter 5, at the CSW session in Buenos Aires, traditional colonial powers had been accused of not supporting the newly independent African states. A few years later, at a 1962 Trusteeship Council meeting, the British delegate said "that the emergence of a large number of independent States was perhaps the most significant advance in what was otherwise a depressing period of history. Most of the newly independent States were in Africa; some of them were former dependent territories of the United Kingdom, and their newly acquired nationhood was therefore a source of pride to her country."[5] While independence had become a fact that former imperial masters rhetorically welcomed in order to create UN voting alliances, colonialism became equated with Western elements that interfered with the newly created nation-states, especially in the case of women.

The complex historical moment and especially women's activism, which emerged forcefully at the end of the 1960s at a global level, complicated the advancement of women's rights within the UN. The fear of second-wave feminism was widespread; to some postcolonial leaders, feminism was a Western import like colonialism, so women delegates from the Global South had to negotiate again between local traditions and women's rights.

This chapter discusses the relationship between international development and post-decolonization nation building, the CSW's debates around the creation of an international provision to end discrimination against women, and the interconnections between slavery and the status of women. What tied these topics together was the ambition of attaching an international logic of development to a "universal" concept of rights, which when applied to the Global South appeared divisive. Ultimately, UN representatives widely discussed development and gender equality in conceptual terms, but this was a highly contentious area because contributors were coming at this problem from diverging political, economic, and social positions.

Decolonization and Development: Local and Global Perspectives in the African Case

The assumptions at the basis of the UN politics of women's rights were that international provisions in favor of women were especially useful for those countries in which the status of women was low. The creation of new states that happened to emerge from a well-known scenario of colonial inequality shaped the opportunity to combine women's rights and the politics of development. Sex equality and development were both principles expressed in the UN Charter and at the basis of multiple international legal instruments.[6] At the local level, instead, countries had to negotiate the aftermath of decolonization and the place of women within new nations. It is important to present this dimension because delegates from the Global South used their own understanding of the local woman to test universalism.

While the participants of these debates came from different areas, which comprised Asia, Africa, and the Middle East, it was only when delegates from the post-1960 wave of African anticolonialism joined the UN that debates became more heightened and the UN acquired a central role in the Global South's politics.

Asian and Middle Eastern women's activism had a longer history of women's advocacy as compared to the then more recent rise of concern for the status of women in sub-Saharan Africa.[7] Decolonization and the consequent formation of new nations highlighted more differences between north and south, in terms of industrial growth, infrastructure, and conceptions of women's rights. In the case of colonialism in Africa and the consequent lack of growth, the responsibility of European countries was not easily spelled out because of the specific politics that saw it as Soviet propaganda and because often the new postcolonial state had important economic ties with the former master.[8]

The struggle for independence had included women with different results. In some local instances, anticolonialism transcended the usual narrative of the *evolues*, Western-educated male politicians who became the symbol of anticolonial struggle.[9] At times it was actually the educated male elite that, in the realm of women's rights, just perpetrated the old imperial scheme.[10] Nevertheless, transformational leaders such as Amílcar Cabral aimed instead to involve everyone in the revolution that he envisioned to create the new nation, providing a more complex and diversified scenario on the role of women in the immediate postcolonial period.[11] In his speeches, Cabral highlighted how anticolonialism was not enough to build a new state. In his goal of an independent Guinea-Bissau, in "a new society" as he called it, men and women were to prioritize work and duty useful to the cause. While he considered the armed struggle important, the base of the new country was to be the "tool" and not the gun.

Right after independence women's groups focused on the constitution of clubs dedicated to practical aspects of everyday life, such as farming or handicraft. This activity aligned with the Women in Development approach, a simplistic understanding of economic growth that did not consider the local structural barriers.[12] The First Development Decade (1960–1970) officially inaugurated the centrality of development in the UN policymaking; in General Assembly (GA) resolution 1719—the document stating the principles of the decade—ideas of peace, prosperity, and cooperation were predominant. The GA's language reframed the growth of underdeveloped countries into an international goal, advantageous to the international community for "faster and mutually beneficial world prosperity."[13]

In the first phase of the development era, UN agencies such as the UNESCO, the ILO, and the WHO continued their prominent roles because aid mostly consisted of technical assistance programs.[14] The GA officially asked agencies to build programs to involve individual men and women in the economic and social development of their countries.[15] Local initiatives emerged instead from a combination of international politics that encouraged such participation as well as specific local demands.[16] An example was the case of small countries like Lesotho, where local groups aimed to build a local industry "far from mines, factories, and farms in South Africa."[17] Overall, anticolonial politics were based on promoting a better quality of life after independence, and this meant being employed under fair conditions, close to home, and in opposition to colonial policies that had dismembered communities and promoted unfair practices.

Discrimination and Gender Equilibrium

In 1965 the socialist countries Poland, Hungary, and the USSR asked the GA to start working on an instrument against female discrimination.[18] Only two years before, as the result of the Non-Aligned Movement's promotion of a tool to eliminate racism (Belgrade 1961), the UN Sub-Commission on Prevention of Discrimination and Protection of Minorities had written a declaration on racial discrimination (which became convention in 1965) that led to the GA's welcoming of the socialist countries' proposal on women.[19] In resolution 1720, the GA acknowledged both the work of the CSW and the UN agencies in support of gender equality and women's more prominent role in society.

Ultimately, the GA connected its request to both the desire of translating the principle of sex equality of the UN Charter and Universal Declaration of Human Rights (similarly to the preamble of the International Convention on all Form of Racial Discrimination) into a unified legal provision and the denouncement of still-existing discrimination against women.[20] The eighteenth session (1965) debate over a general instrument to fight discrimination against women forced commissioners to come to terms with both their own past work that instituted instruments in favor of equality and their own local-based conceptions of discrimination.

Annie Jiagge, the representative from Ghana, claimed that discrimination was an "obstacle to good relations in the world." Within this debate Jiagge symbolized the emerging voice from the Global South which aimed to promote UN principles along with a firm understanding of national culture. Jiagge, like most UN representatives, had international politics experience. Her role in this debate is significant because her background went hand in hand with the history of women and empires. She was a fervent Christian as well as a supreme court justice of independent Ghana. She was originally from the Trans-Volta Togoland region (later annexed to Ghana) where her grandmother had been an able trader. Jiagge was part of the YMCA, which was active in building woman's hostels in Accra, thus presumably she favored female labor mobility and women's economic independence.[21] She referred to types of discrimination that transcended gender differences and spoke of exclusions based on race, color, religion, and political belief.[22] Her opinion reflected her own history as both an active Christian leader and a constitutional judge in a newly independent country. Arguably, the racial tensions that European colonial powers had encouraged and the then recent global civil rights struggle inspired her to look at discrimination as affecting human relations.

The Hungarian delegate, Hanna Bokor, was more concerned with discrimination directed specifically at women. Bokor was an expert in international law, legal advisor of the Hungarian government in the 1950s, and later, a professor of economics.[23] With her intellectual background along with her role in the administrative establishment of a socialist country, Bokor argued that discrimination against women affected social progress. She advocated for "full equality" in both public and private life. Past instruments dedicated to the equality of men and women, she said, only encouraged the creation of a stronger international provision to encompass all aspects of women's lives. As illustrated in chapter 3, Eastern European delegates referred to a nonsocialist past in which the status of women was low in order to glorify the then contemporary socialist progresses for women. Their strategy consisted of spreading the successful socialist solution to improve women's lives within the new postcolonial states.

These two female delegates clearly expressed modalities of discrimination based on the local realities of their own countries. Jiagge's opinion was connected to the colonial heritage in which discrimination was the most dominant force regulating human relationships. Similarly, Bokor's depiction of discrimination as averse to social progress was representative of socialist thinking. If conceptions of discrimination were local-specific, the "places" of discrimination, instead, highlighted commonalities among commissioners and NGO representatives.

As shown in chapters 4 and 5, the NGOs had the advantage of being active in the field and dealing directly with locally specific cases. Of course, their activism was not isolated from the rescuing thrust of traditional missionary work; nonetheless, they brought to the commission an impression of the areas in which they were active. Contrary to the HRC, the CSW could not deliberate on specific cases, but the NGOs' direct testimony served as background to formulate appropriate and reality-backed international provisions.

Discrimination, Bokor continued, happened mostly within the family. Previous instruments to promote and protect women's rights were concerned with marriage, not the family per se. The focus on the family produced a set of narratives that compressed and limited conceptions of equality. Like Bokor, the Polish delegate Zofia Dembinska claimed that equality started in the family and then extended to the state: full citizenship began within the domestic realm. Dembinska, much like Bokor, had a background in antifascism and women's politics and was part of the state's establishment.[24] She envisioned a path of expanding rights that started in the family and continued on to the state.[25] However, the family could represent a range of different situations and conditions for women.

Jiagge claimed that a declaration against discrimination could not say that parents had equal duties because such a provision would impose an economic burden on women. Her point assumed a situation of poverty in which women were disadvantaged. For Dembinska equality within the family meant that parents had equal responsibility for the "education and upbringing of children." She did not consider the economic aspects of the parental role but only child rearing in the form of education. For Jiagge, in the area of duties and responsibilities for children, the role of men and women "were not interchangeable." She explained how to protect the position of women within the family. Specifically, women played a role as "guardians of their children." For her, the principle of equality could be applied to the administration of children's property but not to the education of children, in which women, she claimed, needed a prominent role.[26]

Commissioners brought to this debate their own local experience and understanding of the status of women within families. As a result, gender equality became a difficult concept to define and to inscribe in the declaration; such difficulty was due to a combination of different women's realities. Specifically, the family was a source of tension because some commissioners advocated for women's traditional powers in familial relationships while claiming to promote a break with tradition. It was also difficult to find a common ground for this debate. For socialist delegates, the family represented the first locus of discrimination against women. For Jiagge, on the other hand, women had power within family settings. This debate is relevant because, in order to define discrimination, commissioners needed to ground their theories within specific places and institutions. However, the family produced a different set of assumptions that questioned equality with men.

NGOs participated in this debate too; usually they added a dimension closer to women's daily experiences rather than following state's lines. The language they used was often more sensationalist. For example, as seen in the case of the "scandal" of Bikom, Catholic NGOs were adamant about showing (what they perceived as) the detrimental status of women in dependent territories in pretty strong terms.[27] In the NGOs' contributions to the DEDAW debate as well as in Jiagge's understanding, mothers emerged as a powerful group, and full gender equality was seen as the element that could threaten their status.

To the delegation from the International Federation of Women in Legal Careers, the declaration had to deemphasize the differences between the sexes: "the International Federation had excluded all reference to protective measures for women that were based on the theory that women were weaker than men and all references to protective measures for mothers as deprived persons."[28] Societies, the representative added, should have closed the gap between motherhood as a social duty and motherhood as a right.[29] According to this point of view, the delegation explained, societies did not recognize the power that women as mothers had within and beyond the family. The emphasis on the "social duty" of mothers obscured the consequences of the rigid gender roles families imposed on women. The federation focused more on a dated conception of motherhood as connected to national goals. While the condition of women within families was not universal and homogeneous, the focus on "maternal power" excluded all those conditions in which women, including mothers, were disempowered within the family.

At the same debate, the delegate of the International Association of Penal Law declared, "Maternal love is capable of changing the world." Women had a special mission in the world connected to "peace and the safeguarding of civilization." Because of the existence of both this role and maternal power, states were supposed to "grant women equal rights with men."[30] Therefore, total gender equality represented a loss of the familial power for women and undermined mothers' roles as the leaders of the children's upbringing. Moreover, the representative of the International Association of Penal Law claimed that the CSW had to act to establish "equilibrium in the world." Within this framework "equilibrium" meant the recognition of power coming from child-rearing rather than sex equality within the family. This concern for the loss of women's status in the family reflected the tension between an agency developed within rigid gender roles and a law-based agency anchored to international provisions. The focus on the family meant that commissioners were concerned with finding a unified voice on where discrimination was formed and reinforced. Ultimately, they approved a declaration article that denounced "discrimination within marital status."[31] As expected, the article they eventually wrote did not question the family per se but focused on balance between partners.

At the sessions that preceded the approval of the declaration, commissioners had come to terms with the discrepancy between law and reality in matters of women's rights. Legal equality highlighted the limitations that rigid cultural constructs imposed on women's lives.[32] Delegates agreed: "Discrimination against women, resulting in the denial or limitation of their equality with men is unjust and constitutes an infringement of human dignity."[33] This language suggests a direct connection to human rights as opposed to gender-based rights, along with a shift away from traditional liberal feminism, with its roots in formal equality. Nevertheless, advocating for balance as opposed to equality partly empowered the same rigid cultural notions that DEDAW aimed to eliminate.

Helvi Sipilä, the Finnish commissioner and future rapporteur for family planning, advocated for "flexible interpretations" of the status of women, discrimination, and equality, especially for developing countries.[34] She meant that rigid interpretations would most likely generate dissent and endanger the common goal: successfully drafting the declaration. Furthermore, a text that put forth simplicity and agreement was instrumental to acquire the majority of votes at the Third Committee. Arguably, commissioners knew that moderation and a blind respect for tradition were detrimental to the status of women and constituted political weapons against women's advancement. However, their priority was to convince the majority of member states to vote for the declaration, and within this process, crafting persuasive language was the fundamental element for gaining or losing votes.

Women and States between the Universal and the Particular

The discussion at the GA Third Committee presented some commonality with the commissioners' understanding of discrimination against women. As mentioned in other chapters, the Third Committee's meetings, beyond voting on UN instruments, were a unique opportunity for countries' representatives to debate on salient issues of the time period. In the case of the DEDAW, colonialism and underdevelopment were interconnected along with the recognition that women were substantially discriminated everywhere, even in places with the most progressive laws.

The legal support of anti-discrimination was not enough because cultures and customs affected the status of women everywhere. Muslim countries, such as Egypt, Syria, and Iraq, produced one more time an important correlation between development and the status of women, colonialism and poor economic conditions, and the problematic Western representation of the assumed disempowered women in the Global South. In the context of this debate, the United States appeared again to be the most conservative in matters of women's rights as a reflection of Cold War politics in which, as stated earlier, socialist countries hailed gender equality. At issue was whether equality between men and women could be an internationally imposed or proposed goal. New nations had to protect themselves from Western interferences; simultaneously and controversially, Western commissioners continued to consider equality as a rescuing tool for the oppressed women of the Global South, but this attitude was soon to be challenged.

Although commissioners searched for commonalities in establishing one international legal instrument to fight discrimination against women, some delegates highlighted how a focus on the law could be ineffective vis-à-vis everyday practices that produced and condoned gender discrimination. This discrepancy also raised the important question of whether laws were enough to change customs and norms. The aforementioned popular Egyptian representative, Aziza Hussein, participated in this discussion.[35] Speaking for the Arab Republic (Egypt's name until 1971), Aziza Hussein argued that the primary problem was "customs."[36] Hussein spoke in general terms without mentioning specific customs; while her words were broad, her activism had been specific: she was a pioneer in the movement to include women in developmental policies in the countryside as well as in the establishment of family planning programs in Egypt.[37] Another admired representative, Jeanne Cissé from Guinea, pointed out that the declaration had to be general enough to bring together women's experiences globally. A member of the Guinean parliament and an expert in women's rights, Cissé later became the first woman elected president of the UN Security Council (1972).[38] In this context, she claimed that only the commission could draft such an inclusive text because if single states were involved, they would only address types of discrimination against women that were specific to their nations.[39] Women's experience from a global point of view meant finding common ground to define discrimination and protect *all* women from it. Generality and specificity created a stumbling block. Arguably, a focus on national practices would have created a series of defensive reactions from anywhere. There was some rhetorical comfort in thinking that customs affected only women in the Global South.

Commissioners did not succeed in finding common principles to insert within the declaration. They then decided to request the assistance of other UN bodies to draft an instrument that would be both effective and aligned with UN principles. Sipilä confirmed that commissioners were experts in matters of women's politics and could alone define the principles to include in the declaration. She forcefully stated that no other UN body was to be involved; the commission was perfectly capable of drafting the text. Those commissioners who did not believe that, Sipilä argued, "were surely taking the Commission's responsibility somewhat lightly."[40] With this statement,

Sipilä challenged the early concern toward the csw: the loss of expertise in its passage from subcommission to full commission (see chapter 1).

As for other conventions on women's issues, at the Third Committee states' representatives expressed their governments' concerns about, resistance to, or agreement on both gender equality and means to achieve it. Mr. Jha from India considered DEDAW revolutionary and therefore dangerous to the national order; he advocated instead for "an evolution" of women's rights.[41] In his opinion "freedom of choice" was "a Western concept" which "in Oriental countries" interfered with traditional gender relationships.[42]

For Glady Avery Tillett, the U.S. delegate and expert politician in the Democratic party, gender equality did not lead to the same roles for women and men. Biological differences, she claimed, could not be ignored. The U.S. position, in this instance, supported an equal right with some ambiguity.[43] In the international realm, equal rights meant discouraging a direct look into U.S. politics of discrimination as well as a pro-Cold War position of disengagement with everything social. The U.S. delegate argued that, although childbearing signaled differences in gender roles, it could not serve to perpetuate discrimination against women. The American stance advocated for women's freedom to decide "the pattern of life which suited them." Women were therefore locked into a biological destiny and according to the American position, when left to freely decide on their lives, women chose "the traditional role of wife and mother."[44] The American assumption was conservative and contrasted with the radical changes that were affecting American society; other countries presented more progressive ideas on the status of women and a strong support of the commission's work.

The Syrian delegate, Mr. Marrache, spoke vehemently against colonialism as the main force that delayed development and therefore gender equality. Development, which he considered to be a historical problem, affected the status of women in former colonies. Only if women from newly formed states considered underdevelopment and discrimination to be related problems could they "assert equality." He supported a declaration's language specifying how foreign forces had contributed to a lack of growth and, consequently, to gender inequality. Specifically, according to Marrache, words such as "economic backwardness, conservative . . . forces, foreign exploitation, colonialism, neocolonialism and aggression" should be used to indicate the forces bearing primary responsibility for delayed or stalled development.[45]

Anticolonial rhetoric not only unified men and women but in the case of the Syrian speech it condemned foreign rule as detrimental to women too. In Marrache's analysis, colonialism emerged as the historical force connected to both dynamics: gender equality and self-rule. Ultimately, the Iraqi ambassador, Mrs. Afnan, fervent supporter of women's political rights at the time of the 1952 Convention on the Political Rights of Women, (see chapter 2), declared that denouncing discrimination against women should be a goal not merely for developing countries but for the entire world.[46] Her point was strong and salient, one aimed at dismantling imperial feminism. The danger of tracing inequality only elsewhere meant, for Western commissioners, condoning their own possible status of inequality. However problematic, the "deal" was set in stone: economic development led to gender equality, lack of development (and colonialism, specifically) had led to inequality and underdevelopment. An opportunity to discuss slavery reinforced this point.

Slavery and Development

At the commission's sessions, colonialism and underdevelopment became two inextricably linked phenomena. A further occasion for this heightened debate was the GA's request to the CSW in terms of implementations of the 1953 Convention on Slavery which commissioners discussed during the twenty-first session (1968). As in any geopolitically tense debate discussed in previous chapters, the commissioners were faced with the opposition of states that supported new configurations of colonial dependencies (specifically, the UK). The formula to discourage this debate was the same as it had been when the Soviet Union had opposed nationalist China (see chapter 3): these topics were deemed to be outside the commission's competency. Delegates from newly formed countries, along with those who were anticolonialist, nonetheless debated colonialism and slavery, within a framework that encouraged women's participation in economic and social development.

Representatives from the decolonized territories agreed that foreign economic interventions obstructed the creation of a just society and "had deleterious effects on the living conditions of women."[47] These economic interests flourished through the payment of minimum wages, bans on trade unions, and a lack of social security systems. Commissioners described a process of impoverishment of colonies and maximum profit for foreign investors, which had often happened with the compliance of colonial administrations. Furthermore, these mechanisms perpetuated colonial rule, racism, and segregation. As Sir Brian Urquhart (former UN cadre) argues, colonialism was responsible for the missed industrialization of dependent territories.[48] It is significant to highlight how commissioners identified such responsibilities at a much earlier stage. Moreover, the work of the UN in general and the commission in particular connected poverty to other limitations of rights.

Slavery became a lens through which many members pushed the urgency of development.[49] The GA's decision to involve the commission in this debate showed a clear understanding of the role of gender in the practice of slavery.[50] The commissioners' contributions also demonstrates their expertise in issues of economics and equality. The Dutch delegate claimed that only a transformation in economic and social development could change the conditions that favored slavery.[51] It was a problem linked to "poverty, hunger and [lack of] education," and so the UN specialized agency had a prominent role in eradicating it.[52] For the Tunisian commissioner, a convention against slavery should "eliminate serious economic underdevelopment" and punish those who exploit other people. The British delegate agreed that poverty and hunger created slavery, but she added that slavery was "a long-standing social custom" tolerated by local populations.[53] Her position is important because it highlights a long-lasting British argument that placed the responsibility of modes of oppression in local "customs." However, the case of apartheid challenged this argument.

It was the Mauritanian commissioner who introduced the link between slavery and apartheid; in her own words, apartheid, much like slavery was "a system that was designed to maintain people of color in inferior status." She argued that, although all governments had regulations against slavery, the practice survived in developing countries because "both masters and slaves" were victims of underdevelopment.[54] The Mauritanian case, still infamous to this day, represents the perfect example of contemporary slavery based on reinforced racial differences.[55] The case of apartheid, she argued, had a detrimental effect on the education of Black children because the system raised them to believe that life meant "humiliation and misery." Apartheid also disrupted the unity of the family because of economic segregation and constraints on movement. The Mauritanian commissioner claimed that the CSW "remain[ed] indifferent to the tragic fate of those women." Moreover, she differentiated between a type of local slavery (in which both the enslaved and the enslaver were victims) from apartheid, a system of white versus Black exploitation and discrimination.

Following this path, the delegate from Malaysia, instead, emphasized how "slavery" in the context of poverty had different meanings for women. For example, adopted daughters could be used as "servants," and prostitutes seldom freed themselves because of the oppressive mechanisms that "controlled" their lives.[56] Although she proposed an interpretation of slavery that affected women and was closer to the interests of the commission, it was the issue of apartheid that acquired a central polemic role in this debate.

The British delegate spoke against the link between slavery and apartheid. She encouraged the commissioners to consider slavery as defined by the International Slavery Convention of 1926 and the Supplementary Convention on the Abolition of Slavery of 1956. Although the UK "abhorred apartheid and racism," she claimed, "it could not agree that such practice were equivalent to slavery as defined in those Conventions."[57] The 1926 convention has no mention of colonialism or poverty; therefore it was convenient for Britain to attach this debate to an earlier definition of slavery that did not call into question South Africa. She did not express an opinion in favor of apartheid, but she aimed to challenge its connections to slavery and colonialism.[58]

The commissioners' debate on slavery and its connections to apartheid symbolizes a unique intervention in a topic that at the UN was popular and contentious already.[59] The UN denounced apartheid from 1960 onward. In 1963 the well-known South African singer Miriam Makeba gave a speech against apartheid which complemented the aforementioned declaration on racial discrimination. What African women delegates did on this occasion, and through the CSW, was to employ a political strategy to confront those countries that supported South Africa. Furthermore, in their little-explored contribution to this struggle, they brought the gender dimension of apartheid to the international podium beyond the case of Makeba, who had lived in the United States and was an internationally renowned artist.[60]

African commissioners shifted the discussion to a direct relationship between slavery and apartheid. The Liberian delegate replied that "slavery could not be discussed independently from one of its most evil and pernicious forms, namely apartheid." Slavery, therefore, represented not only a way to discuss underdevelopment from a gendered point of view but also the opportunity to create compact alliances among former colonies against persisting colonial powers. The contentious issue of apartheid as a vestige of the colonial system conflicted with the climate of international cooperation and rhetoric against all forms of discrimination.[61] Sipilä confirmed that slavery had a direct connection to women's lives, and therefore, in addition to the institutional request to address the issue, it was within the commission's frame of reference.[62] Through this instance and the previous one on the principles of DEDAW, Sipilä emerged as an authoritative and progressive voice within the commission.

The Development Decades: Overcoming Imperial Feminism and Unifying the "Women of the World"

The Development Decades (1960–70 and 1970–80) and DEDAW offered commissioners a further means to understand the role of women in development and to reunify the category of women of the world. The Second Development Decade was influenced by second-wave feminism and highlighted those tensions that would fully erupt in Mexico City. The First Development Decade encouraged commissioners to experiment with reaching a wider audience. All the UN milestones that included women were discussed at the CSW as showed in the case of Convention on Slavery.

While debating the First Development Decade, specifically the roles of UN-sponsored seminars, it transpired that international meetings served to find commonalities and solve the rescuer/rescued conundrum that had framed women's international politics within a hegemonic context. The CSW aimed to expand the scope of the seminars as they had been an invaluable source to promote transnational encounters and to reinforce the relationship between gender politics and the UN as a whole. In the case of women, the seminars' priorities aligned with the promotion of political rights and participation in the public sphere.

As chapters 3 and 4 indicate, at past seminars the blurry category of "customs and traditions" was never associated with a specific local group. From the mid-1960s, the commissioners directly addressed male and female roles in the improvement of the status of women. DEDAW and the politics of development provided an opportunity to engage with antipatriarchal discourse along second-wave feminist lines. These efforts were not uncontested: the reaction to this type of progressive discourse arrived from both state members (as in the case of the Third Committee) and from within the UN itself. Inserting women into the politics of development was a difficult process influenced by polarization and states' diverse political interests in development.

At the CSW sixteenth session (1962) the agenda included a report on the progresses of the Advisory Services program.[63] As illustrated in chapter 3, international seminars were part of this program. Women experts, argued the representative from the Pan-Pacific Southeast Asia Women's Association, were more appropriate participants than male state representatives in seminars on women's issues.[64] UN seminars were an opportunity for exchanges on women's experiences across the dividing line between experts and audience, focusing on the commonalities of women's lives across geopolitical lines. Moreover, seminars served as an advertisement tool for the CSW's work at a global level. The Dutch delegate claimed that "more women should be appointed as technical assistance experts, for they would give all the necessary attention to the needs of women in their own fields."[65] In response the delegate from the UK directly called for men to awaken to women's actual power and their deserved place in society. She encouraged the UN agencies to work on this issue.[66]

In the case of the status of women, modernization acquired a gendered character, which reflected the fact that in the West, women's advancement ran alongside traditional women's careers. In developing countries, modernization was intertwined with the colonial past and racial discrimination. Colonialism affected the possibility of the creation of a native middle class trained in the key positions of an effective and modern nation. The UN, mostly the UN agencies, therefore acquired the role of covering the modernization void that colonialism had created and reinforced. They taught women the necessary skill sets to directly participate in development along traditional gender lines.

The WHO coordinated countries' requests with specific training programs. At the commission's seventeenth session, the WHO delegate Dr. Rudolph Coigney presented these programs as opportunities for women. In the case of national health, for example, the training of midwives and nurses contributed both to supply the national system with such necessary positions and to provide women with careers.[67] Coigney was aware of the problematic theory of modernizing along traditional lines; he stated that with the improvement of a country's economic conditions, women could enjoy widening career possibilities. Before that time, Coigney claimed, high-quality training programs in nursing and midwifery would be beneficial to newly formed countries. As discussed earlier, in the case of anticolonial liberation struggles and the discourse of development, there was a similar narrative: women first had to wait for political equality and then for economic opportunities.[68]

Although appreciative of the UN agencies' training programs and seminars, the Ghanaian representative advocated for a larger-scale UN intervention that included seminars and trainings specific to the real needs of local women in developing countries. He said that the "current decade might well be designated the 'United Nations decade for the advancement of women,'" as he recognized well ahead of time the need for a UN decade for women and the prominent role that women played at both the local and global levels. [69]

Other representatives advocated for a space for traditional women's work within development policies. They emphasized that in the passage from rural to industrial economies, women's domestic service provided secure jobs.[70] Along similar lines, commissioners praised rural housewives as contributors to community life.[71] They highlighted the relationship between the status of women and the second-wave "choice" in realistic terms, linked to actual scenarios in developing countries. Although modernization and economic advancement appeared as the main gender equalizer, delegates were adamant to include tangible possibilities for all women in the delicate passage from rural to industrial societies.

The delegates from the Global South looked at development as a positive process involving exchange and encounters but also as a source of tension. The delegate from the Philippines stressed that "seminars" promoted "exchanges between representatives of the highly industrialized and the developing countries" in order "to help the latter to avoid the mistakes made by the former at the time of the Industrial Revolution."[72] The idea was to embrace a common path, a recipe to follow globally to increase growth and implement equality. The common path idea was disrupted by the still-present fragmentation of imperial feminist attitudes.

Even if the West/North was in a position of advantage, some commissioners from the developing countries resisted the idea that requesting aid as sharing knowledge was to be framed within the rhetorical terms of a new "civilizing mission." A vivid example was Hussein from the United Arab Republic. She declared that "while women in developing countries appreciate the advice of women from highly industrialized countries, they resent the use of the adjective 'backward' as applied to a level of development."[73] This type of debate had consequences for women beyond developing countries.

The rigid position of the Global North as helper and Global South as help's recipient eliminated—at least within the UN setting—the possibility of defining and fighting "backwardness" in the industrialized nations. From a second-wave point of view, focusing on the "liberation" of women solely in developing countries produced the assumption that women in the North/West/industrialized world were "liberated" and that protests had no reason to take place.

As mentioned earlier, at the Third Committee voting session the Iraqi representative declared that fighting discrimination against women should be a universal goal and not something relegated to the Global South.[74] Ultimately, the commissioners embraced a clear feminist stance: men represented an obstacle to the advancement of women in society. Specifically, men refused to promote women's roles in economic and social development. The commissioners therefore proposed to include the DEDAW's objectives within the UN long-term program for the advancement of women and the approaching Second Development Decade; this goal included a search for new means to increase development. The commissioners believed that women could represent a new human resource.[75]

The debate on developing countries also produced a critique of industrialized countries and the status of women. The connection between equality and development implied that whereas industrialized countries acted as guides in matters of the policies and instruments of development, they were also supposed to assume leadership in matters of gender equality. However, those countries did not advance the status of women because they took "an attitude of self-satisfaction," which did not lead to concrete policies and examples for developing countries to follow but only hegemonic narratives.

Conclusion

This chapter shows how in the specific moment of the creation of the postcolonial states, the CSW sought to find a way to counteract colonial policies that had left the newly formed nations torn by economic, social, and political problems. A rigid understanding that economic development led to gender equality revealed tensions on what equality meant in different localities.

Global South women representatives discussed an agency that originated from the family, despite the colonial administration. The family home appeared as a space free from colonial interference in which women and men had different powerful roles. Some newly formed countries aimed to be observant of traditions and progress simultaneously. Women's rights were therefore contested and revealed the intricacies of allowing full citizenship to women.

The laboring body that was so central in the construction of World War II women's sacrifice and political rights as a reward (see chapter 1), reappears in the UN debates but this time as the enslaved, trafficked, and indentured body. As chapter 7 shows, the bodily tensions increased in discussions on human reproduction and family planning as a human right.

8. (*Left to right*) Eugenia Stevenson (Liberia), Phoebe Asiyo (Kenya), and Taki Fujita (Japan) at csw 25th session, 1974. © United Nations, reprinted with permission of the United Nations.

7

Reproducing the Nation and the Right to Control One's Destiny

The photograph to the left shows commissioners at work at the 1974 Session, the year before the UN Mexico City conference for women. This photo, in color in its original format, and with a central position of Liberia and Kenya epitomizes of the growing role of women from the Global South. The difference in style of clothing, one contemporary, the other one more traditional, illustrates the complexities of the postcolonial world, its traditions, and a simultaneous call for modernity. Far from a fashion assessment, we can see how the traditional clothing recalls nationhood along with local customs, a sort of continuity between the precolonial and postcolonial period. The Japanese delegate is portrayed too, and one can trace the trajectory from the Japanese "observers" who had to learn democracy (see chapter 2) to the full membership of the Asian country. At this same meeting, the UNESCO representative alerted commissioners that the danger of feminism was rising inside and outside the UN. This announcement was a further stage of the agency's critique to the CSW. If the Soviets saw themselves as the early guardians of women in dependent territories, the UNESCO proclaimed itself the ultimate authority in terms of the relationship between rights and culture in the developing world. Within this framework the problem of overpopulation, present at the UN since the mid-1960s, recentered female bodies of the Global South as a key component to a global issue. Family planning meant the right for women to control their bodies; "overpopulation," conversely, had little to do with rights but more with the accountability that constrained women in the Global South to more ambivalent definitions: responsible and irresponsible. Men featured in these debates as the experts and guardians of women's bodies, both at a local and international level.

The approval of DEDAW, along with its different debates, showed the hybridity of the family as both discriminating institution and place for maternal power. A focus on the family led commissioners to a complex definition of reproduction and a set of human rights that connected the private and public spheres. Different understanding of human reproduction locked women's bodies within rigid and opposite positions. In newly formed nation-states governments favored natal policies to replenish the country. Simultaneously, UN experts claimed that what prevented women from participating in public life was the burden of children. Moreover, a new original perspective, derived from analysis of development trends, looked at the family as the microcosm of a political economy where fewer people could potentially have access to more resources. Consequently, the amount of available means could be adversely affected by the presence of too many children. Spacing children and/or deciding the number of children to have— the plan for a family—was beginning to be framed within human rights, which guaranteed that all children could reach their full potential.[1] The context of these debates was complex as newly formed nations advertised population growth as a national goal while at the same time the politics of development enforced rules regarding population control.

As stated in previous chapters, the UN's sanctioned chronological trajectory of the CSW divides the work into a generational history of rights. A closer look at the different focus of commissioners through the years reveals more intricacy and strategies that, even if problematic, eventually brought an understanding of the private sphere as a place of discrimination as well as a recognition of the nation-state as a place that could both release and suppress rights.

Before the acclaimed series of UN women's conferences in which activists denounced a nation-state that ignored violence within the family, the late 1960s commissioners grappled with the dichotomy between public and private spheres, still with a focus on "the other" but with new tensions.[2] As I show in chapter 6, from the CSW's debates an understanding of the family as connected to colonial history emerged, as well as an idea about the specific role that women were expected to have in the new nations. While feminism appeared as a response to local realities rather than as a Western export,[3] UN women representatives did not self-identify as "feminist," at least not within the UN official sources. Early international feminists had identified as such, but in the following years, the word *feminism* became an accusation to signify antidiplomatic and unruly behavior for Global North women and an accusation of embracing Western interferences—a heritage of colonialism—for women in the Global South (see chapter 6). Furthermore, commissioners from the West had used the language of rescuing when discussing women of the Global South but not without resistance to yet another test to universalism.

Adding to these stories of intersections between gender, internationalism, and the Global South, this chapter shows how the reproductive body served as an important test to the universalism of women's rights and human rights. As showed in chapter 6, including the dimension of the postcolonial state challenged conceptions of gender equality for both female and male representatives of the new nations. A further and more complex challenge to universalism was human reproduction, which placed the "other's" body one more time as a highly contested location by which to measure the applicability of rights. This chapter shows that an attempt to apply universal rights to the newly independent nations was contentious because colonialism had created a defined, tense, and inescapable trajectory.

The family and family planning represent the borders of attempts at universalizing rights, and an examination of them created a more diverse dimension of an otherwise monolithic understanding of gender equality. If in the 1950s, colonialism became an offensive word (see chapter 3), the word "feminism" faced a similar destiny. Margaret Bruce, for example, who was the chair of the Secretariat Women's Division from 1963 and 1973 (see chapter 6), called commissioners "militant feminist" in a derogatory sense, as if politicization conferred them less authority in diplomacy.[4] The wider UN setting produced antifeminist stances through the cultural relativist attitudes of organizations such as the UNESCO and the WHO, all of which fiercely opposed a definition of discrimination that challenged the status quo. While all these organizations included different voices, it is important to highlight how agencies that were supposed to forward the UN's mission did not always agree with the UN's considerations and conclusions as the case of FGM widely showed.

Modernizing Along Traditional Roles

In view of the International Conference on Human Rights in Tehran (1968), the CSW sent a questionnaire (through the Women's Division of the Secretariat) to governments and NGOs to ask about women's roles in economic and social development. The answers—contained in a report—highlighted how the role of women was still limited in both "developed and developing" countries. The data showed a growing trend for women's participation in the social and economic sphere as well as governments' efforts to accommodate societies to the "changing role of men and women."[5] Adaptation to a change in the status of women also involved resistance to change from the conservative sector of the population. Within this setting, the report suggested that a progressive education became the main ally of development and equality.[6]

Women in rural areas represented the differentiating element between tradition and modernity. At a discussion on the report, the Iranian commissioner pointed out that in her country women promoted education as a means to overcome "backwardness, deprivation and frustration."[7] Women in rural areas, she argued, especially needed education, but literacy experts focused only on men. She highlighted, therefore, the discrepancy between the UN studies on the need for education for rural women and the tradition-led reality in which efforts were centered on men's education. On the issue of local traditions that affected women's integration in education, the Iranian delegate confirmed, like other Muslim leaders before her, that Islam showed great respect for women. She blamed "invading tribes" for having created and reinforced discrimination against women.[8]

In the same context the Egyptian activist delegate at the UN, Aziza Hussein, also discussed Islam, specifically "the veil," as detrimental to women's psychology.[9] As chapter 2 illustrates, to the representatives from Middle Eastern, "tradition" usually meant Islam. For some countries, such as Pakistan and Iran, Islam favored women's rights. For some others, such as Egypt and Iraq, some elements of Islam were detrimental to the status of women. The element that generated the fiercest debate was "the veil."

Arguably, in some contexts "the veil" had represented the symbol of anticolonial struggle, but Hussein saw it as affecting women's psychological or psychosocial conditions. Tradition represented both the main weapon against colonial domination and the main foundation of postcolonial states.[10] Hussein also emphasized women's rights activism in rural areas "to make women aware of their rights and to encourage them to contribute to social and economic development, especially in questions of economic production, family planning and consumption, and savings."[11] For Hussein, more development in women's lives meant some sort of aware citizenship attuned to national economic goals. The Ghanaian commissioner said that certain sectors of the population saw tradition as the main reason for women's stagnant status. She advocated for "a happy medium . . . between tradition and change" so that women could fully participate in "the evolving social structure."[12]

Again, the idea that equality threatened the position of women within the family emerged from the commissioners' interactions. The Liberian representative, Eugenia Stevenson (see figure 8), said that Liberian women were both emancipated and extremely relevant within the family.[13] It was evident that two tendencies dominated the debate: one that confirmed women's attachment to their status within the family and therefore questioned gender equality and another that reconfirmed the need for women's "historical compromise" of waiting for other forces to clear the path before they could enjoy full equality.

The communication between the UN and member states on women and development revealed that in developing countries there was a perceived— but often unrecorded—gendered division of labor in contributions to national economies. Women were mostly involved in agriculture, handicrafts, education, health, and social services. Areas in which women's presence was scarce were science and technology, housing and urban development, and education. Industrialized countries did not present a scenario that was much different: women did not participate in their nation's "overall development."

In this latter case, the language of the secretary-general's report indicated that women were expected to participate, thus delineating a stronger agency for women in developed countries as well. The underlined argument was that, because laws and spaces that allowed women's participation existed, it was women's responsibility to participate. The forces affecting women's contributions to development were a lack of training, conservative education, and a traditional view of gender roles. The report suggested that "molding public opinion" was the required step for creating "the necessary changes in the economic and social structure."[14]

Commissioners supported the integration of development programs for women with overall national development. An increase in the status of women, the Australian commissioner suggested, was directly related to economic and social development. Yet such goals were to be customized to each nation so that communities could adjust to their specific level of change.[15] What emerged was a nationally based liberal model of development that ultimately became the standard for Women in Development.[16]

The UN approach to development involved a "close interdependence of the various factors that entered into the development process." The director of the Social Development Division claimed that even programs aimed at multiple sectors and attuned to the specific needs of each country were not successful. The director identified the reason for failure in the ignorance of social factors by those who created development programs. In both the "formulation and execution" of development plans, UN organs had paid little attention to "social and institutional obstacles to economic growth," and therefore the unified effort of the UN and aided countries did not impact the assisted countries' populations.

Women were penalized even more because of "attitudes, traditions and concepts" that affected their role within the family and society. The treatment of women's activities as "of a special nature" within development plans contributed to their inferior status. The director of the Social Development Division supported gender-integrated programs but did not provide specific examples, because considering women as a minority within male-dominated activities perpetuated women's disadvantaged condition. From the commissioners' perspectives, development was supposed to be a force not only to regenerate countries' economies but also to "enable everyone to live a better and more rewarding life."[17]

The commissioners were also worried that integrated development plans could affect women's "duties" within the home and family. The Mauritanian delegate, for example, envisioned the role of women as primary educators of future citizens. If women in search of more satisfactory job opportunities moved to urban centers, their primary role would have changed. She proposed training programs using local resources that would benefit both mothers and older women in their own areas.[18] Viewing women as "guardians of cultural and social values," the Madagascar's representative argued, had a consequence for women themselves because those same traditions did not allow them to fully participate in the public sphere. Because societies in newly formed countries mostly dismantled tribal systems, women lost their positions and were not prepared for new types of social and economic relationships.[19]

Including women was not only a matter of equality but also a call for the entire population to contribute to national growth.[20] Dembinska, the above-mentioned Polish commissioner (see chapter 6), instead emphasized the issue of the exploitation of women within existing economic systems. Women in developing countries already participated in the national economy through their agricultural work. In Dembinska's words, women "helped to feed the nation." In her understanding, the focus was supposed to be on equality and labor relationships within existing industries, such as agriculture, and not on the creation of new ones.[21]

Sipilä reinforced the argument against tradition and how it was even reflected in the data from developing countries. Of the nearly two hundred pages in the UN Report on Women and Development, only six were dedicated to women and six to youth, even if these groups were far more numerous than men. Therefore, cultural and structural forces that affected women's participation along with a lack of infrastructure contributed to women's lower status in societies.[22] The report identified women themselves as responsible for their own subaltern condition. They "lacked self-confidence" and mostly acted to improve their lives "from a strictly feminine point of view and without enlisting the help of the men."

Mainstream analysis at the UN therefore advocated for gender cooperation but did not fully consider structural obstacles that affected women's rights. Both international and local instruments could help women in their endeavors. Specifically, Sipilä focused on how the work for DEDAW encouraged data on changing gender roles and plans to educate local leaders. In her view, the UN seminars were the most effective way for countries with similar problems to exchange knowledge and improve the conditions of women. Ultimately, Sipilä stressed that family planning was the appropriate tool to augment women's participation in development.[23]

The Population Bomb

On the front cover of the 1968 publication *The Population Bomb* by Paul Ehlrich was a special warning: "While you are reading these words four people will have died from starvation. Most of them children." Also pictured was a bomb with the caption: "The population bomb keeps ticking."[24] The successful book connected neo-Malthusian theories to a sensationalist language; the circulation of images of poor children and women in the Global South reinforced this idea. The so-called world population problem emerged in the 1950s, first in regard to South and East Asian countries. Decrease in mortality and high fertility created a concern, especially in the mid-1960s when the annual population increase rate was 3 percent. One of the goals of demography was decreasing population growth in order to provide better living conditions.[25]

Starting in the late 1960s, the UN inscribed population control into the human rights sphere implying that more people led to fewer resources and, therefore, more hardship. As stated earlier, family planning became a human right connected mostly to children and their access to resources.[26] The UN provisions on this topic were also the result of debates among women commissioners from the Global South within the bigger framework of gender equality and development. The unmentioned and indirect issue of this debate was the female body. Even if some representatives hinted at the burden on the female body of carrying too many children, discussions on this topic were mostly asexual. Demography, statistics, and policies stripped reproduction from its bodily materiality. Only later, with the UNESCO's attack on reproductive rights, did the female body emerge, once more, as the locus for contested politics of rights.

In the context of considerations on expanding the scope of DEDAW, the Egyptian commissioner, Aziza Hussein, proposed to include the right to family planning, a right connected to practices that, Hussein said, were emerging in Egypt. She pointed out that the commission had been indifferent to such advancement in her country. She argued that "lack of information on family planning" was "a social and economic handicap to women and constitute[d] an infringement of their individual liberty." Having too many children affected women's participation in community life. In Egypt, Hussein continued, the population was receptive to discussions on family planning. She did not want the declaration to include language opposed to traditions, but on the other hand, she supported family planning, an issue often contested from a traditional point of view.[27]

As mentioned earlier, Hussein had a long history of women's activism in Egypt and internationally. At the same time that this debate was ongoing, she founded the Cairo Family Planning Association (CFPA). She believed that women were to be involved directly in development measures; therefore, rural clinics employed village women in order to be more effective in the territory. To Hussein these women—called "ra'idat"—were truly revolutionary as they had a strong role in an otherwise traditional male-dominated area. Later, from 1977 to 1983, Hussein became the president of the International Planned Parenthood Federation. She was an expert in population and development and participated in multiple high-profile activities. She pioneered a dimension of development geared toward "aided self-help," one that placed the needs of the receivers of aid as a guiding principle of the aid itself. Before 1952 only rural men were "used as vehicle[s] for reform ideas." Alternatively, urban women often decided what rural women needed. After the 1952 Egyptian revolution, with the establishment of the Sindiyun—nursery schools in rural areas—village women could voice their needs and "help themselves" through the tools provided by women's organizations active in the countryside.[28] If Hussein was successful in her own local setting, establishing policies on family planning at the UN was contentious because of the divergent opinions of the deliberating constituencies.

The first challenge for a resolution on family planning was convincing Catholic groups of its value. As showed in previous chapters, these organizations had a good UN record, especially on issues regarding the Global South through a type of activism in which sensationalism and a Western rescuing thrust had prevailed. In the discussions on family planning, the World Union of Catholic Women's Organizations argued that family planning did not necessarily mean birth control. The delegate produced a somewhat neonatalist stance by saying that a fall in the birth rate could have serious economic consequences. Including family planning in the range of women's rights, she claimed, could perpetuate discrimination against women because the responsibility for procreation was supposed to be equally shared between the sexes.[29] Her statement aligned with the provision on this issue later (only a few months after the CSW session) established by the International Conference on Human Rights, Tehran 1968. From that conference emerged a statement in which "parents" had the right to decide the spacing of children.[30] This right was presented as a familial rather than an individual right. The commissioners, however, framed it in different terms.

Planning the number of children allowed women to manage their time more effectively and solved the problems of overpopulation and food scarcity. Commissioners from developing countries were aware of this twofold advantage. Family planning, the Malaysian position argued, "was one of the indispensable means of raising the standard of living." For women's lives, family planning could remove traditional obstacles such as the impossibility of being educated or of finding employment due to child rearing.[31] However, family planning, even within realistic population goals, denoted a problematic topic for most countries. For example, the Chilean delegate argued that a general improvement in the living conditions of the entire population would lower the birth rate; individual family planning would not. She presented the problem as detrimental not only to women but to "governments and individuals": she emphasized the role of the state in educating young couples, providing birth control, and allowing the family to "develop its potential."[32] The position of Chile shows that Catholic countries could bring to the table opinions that conflicted with Catholic NGOs, showing that family planning represented a diversified and contested issue even amongst groups that were supposed to present similar positions.[33]

At the CSW's twenty-second session in 1968, the commissioners voted for a resolution to nominate a special rapporteur to conduct research on women and family planning.[34] The ECOSOC approved the proposal, passing resolution 1326, and selected Helvi Sipilä as special rapporteur. In accordance with her appointment, in 1969 Sipilä concluded a report based on both national statistics and specialized studies on the status of women and family planning. Sipilä's report was ongoing as she began to present parts of it at the CSW's twenty-third session in 1970.[35] The commission's resolution on this topic included concerted actions by the Secretariat, NGOs, and member states. The goal was to collect the most accurate data on the relationship between women and family because little information was available.

Sipilä knew, however, that multiple layers distanced the commission from the data it hoped to obtain. She was aware that the topic of family planning was too general and included many constituencies, such as health specialists, public policymakers, and women's rights activists. In their requests for surveys on the topic, commissioners and the representative from the Secretariat Division on Women had to take these issues into consideration.[36] Many states were reluctant to produce data on this topic; instead of looking at this lack of cooperation as an ideological obstacle, Sipilä adopted a more diplomatic line and convinced the Division on Women that patience was necessary as this topic included many aspects. By doing so, she also kept open the communication between member states and the CSW.

Although it was difficult to acquire concrete data on family planning, it was also difficult to define the topic. Sipilä aimed, as did other commissioners, for a description of family planning that included two different points of view: human rights as well as population size and resources. She claimed that the right to family planning meant a "concern for the dignity and well-being of parents and their children." She enlarged the scope of family planning from an individual to a group's right (the whole family). Framing family planning as a general "human right," as opposed to an individual women's right, problematized the gender-defined conditions that reproduction created for both women and men.

The commissioners mentioned several times that women could not participate in public life because they were overburdened by child-rearing; therefore, the number of children that a woman had *did* affect her life. Yet, the commissioners never questioned the family as an institution but aimed to make adjustments within the rigid roles of the traditional family.[37] The key concept they explored was the role of women in family planning so that "women could better undertake their responsibilities in the modern world both as wives and mothers and as participants in public life." Their proposal suggested extra efforts for women to balance three roles: wives, mothers, and participants in public life. Much like Jiagge's position (see chapter 6), here motherhood gave both power and burdensome responsibility for both private and public life. The purpose of spacing children was supposed to facilitate women's access to the public sphere.

When they considered parents as the beneficiaries of family planning, the commissioners escaped the traditional patriarchal dynamics of reproduction. Their unified voice considered that family planning contributed to parents' "full potential." For women specifically the delegates highlighted the health issue of "unwanted pregnancies." By not questioning the place of women in the family or the forces that kept women on a lower status within the family itself, the right of family planning existed more for population goals than for women's equality.[38]

The commissioners, however, saw a governmental interest in population control as an opportunity to introduce family planning as an advantage for women. The language they used did not consider how a different view of family planning, from individual interest to national goal, could affect the status of women itself. Placing family planning within the nation took away the decision-making power of both women and families. While commissioners wanted to avoid the problematic aspect of reproductive rights (a more contemporary concept), inserting women's reproduction within national goals recalls both early twentieth-century eugenics policies and more recent one-child limitations.

At the commission's twenty-fourth session, Sipilä presented the multiple facets of family planning and the unique work that the CSW was doing for the field. For example, she noted that the commission assisted Asian countries and planned to help African and Latin American countries conduct surveys on family planning. Two different positions emerged at the commission. The first one was that an expansion of the right to family planning within familial gender relationships was necessary to improve the status of women. The commission's guidelines were to include men's education in family planning. The second position supported development goals and the detrimental aspect of high birth rates. The commissioners included here countries with low birth rates and stressed the principle that women had the right to space their children's births. In sum this meant that a general international provision on this topic presented several challenges due to diversified cultural and national goals.[39]

As would be expected for that time period, there were no discussions around sex and sexuality at the commission, only discussions on population control and a woman's right to her own destiny. By *destiny*, the commissioners meant the ability to participate in the public sphere; they made no mention of sexual freedom or pleasure. This was not a right directly connected, as it would be later, to "women's liberation" but was instead associated with the right to be a more active citizen in an economic growth scenario. Yet, and unescapably, this type of right implied ideas of liberation and women's control over their reproductive plans. From a political strategy point of view, framing birth control as a matter concerning development and overpopulation provided a way to create family-planning programs that transcended the controversy of reproductive rights. However, the UN agencies saw in the CSW an intent to promote "dangerous feminist politics" and reproductive rights even in a diversified technocratic understanding of family planning.

Opposition to Reproductive Rights: Reactions to Sipilä's Report on Family Planning

The commission received several responses and reactions to its work on family planning, namely from states and UN agencies. These responses are fundamental to understand the status of women in the context beyond the commission's meetings and the repercussions on the possibility of a unified understanding in favor of women's equality within the United Nations. In a larger context, such opposition revealed the stakes of women's full citizenship in terms of individual autonomy, participation to public life, and rights over their own bodies. Reproductive rights—even if not clearly spelled out—appeared as dangerous for the male-led equilibrium of society.

As stated earlier, specific nations' goals challenged the association of family planning with population control. For example, the Central African Republic delegate complained that his country was already underpopulated and had a problem with infant mortality, and therefore families had a responsibility to increase the population: "The essential objective of the government is economic and social development. All of the active forces of the country, men and women, are mobilized for this goal, which encompasses the condition of women in the sense that she is called to take an active part to development plans."[40] This response suggests that increasing births was a duty foundational to the new nation. Moreover, the Central African Republic delegate highlighted the gender and patriarchal aspects of planning reproduction. Along with such responses, the studies that Sipilä collected represent an invaluable window into an early internationalization of proto-reproductive rights.

The Nigerian government produced evidence of how asymmetrical gender power relationships affected family planning. The Society of Gynecology and Obstetrics of Nigeria (SOGON), for example, wrote that even among "literate couples," the husband decided important issues. Even in cases where a woman had several children and could be adversely affected by another birth, it was common for husbands to forbid their wives to use contraception. Men were "the stumbling block," even when women decided "to space their children." SOGON identified "a feeling of insecurity" as the main cause of men's disdain for family-planning facilities. Men feared that intrauterine birth control methods promoted "promiscuity" among women. In the case of women who received that type of contraception, their husbands insisted that they remove it. Husbands had to approve the procedure, so women often had to lie to their physicians or fabricate false approvals. Reproductive health specialists were attuned to these male-dominated relationships and agreed to insert contraceptive devices only if husbands were present.[41] If women appeared too knowledgeable in the Nigerian testimony, in the context of the UNESCO they did not know enough.

The UNESCO representative Kanwar B. Mathur said that women were ignorant of their rights due to the lack of information about international instruments on women's equality. The agency judged that the fertility rate was related to the extent of communicating new notions stressing equal participation in society and access to information, and the existence of programs to lower the fertility rate. The media were instrumental in helping women decide the "size and space" of their families.[42] The UNESCO had a long record of contrast with the CSW. While the agency was active in the Global South with programs for women's education, the assessment of the commissioners' work seldom attracted the UNESCO's positive judgment. To the UNESCO, the commission was either too polarized, too paralyzed by Cold War conflicts, or too feminist to produce a fair picture of the status of women.[43]

The UNESCO directly attacked Sipilä's report and the connection between family planning and development goals. The study, Mathur argued, confirmed the traditional pronatalist argument: "Demographic trends depend on social and economic factors." According to the same position, contraceptives were a "main factor in development," and in conditions of poverty, sectors of the population did not have access to birth control. Even if development contributed to lowering the birthrate, this did not lead to more equality because other socioeconomic factors were involved. Furthermore, "some countries"—the UNESCO claimed—could use family planning to institute eugenic measures against a specific class or ethnic group. Ultimately, the UNESCO's response added that birthrate decreased as a result of factors independent of state-led programs.[44]

The UNESCO was opposed to gender-based politics, and it directly attacked commissioners on these matters. The inclusion of family planning as a human right provoked a strong and unprecedent reaction that was also representative of the tension between the politics to advance women's rights and the successful theory of cultural relativism. In her analysis of Sipilä's report, the UNESCO delegate Marion Callaghan dismantled the connection between family planning and women's rights. She claimed that family planning was a "universal right" that could be divided into multiple subrights: the right to sexuality, to sex education, to women's control over their own bodies, and to abortion. These rights, the UNESCO analysis argued, were dependent on other rights, specifically "the 'right' of the nuclear family; the 'right' of a particular type of individualist morality; the 'right' of a certain delimitation of 'private,' 'public,' 'religious' and 'secular.'"[45] This arbitrary dissection of the right of family planning led to a clear antifeminist stance. Women as individuals had to give up their rights in the name of the collective, the family.

The UNESCO report claims that the attention on these "'rights'" within a Western-based "concern" arose out of "the nuclear family" and the legalization of abortion. Although these interests were legitimate, the UNESCO delegate contended that placing family planning as a "right" presented "some problems." The enforcement of these rights could lead to a shift from a community to "an individualist culture" that could affect family unity and "the vehicles of socialization" and compromise human relationships. She concluded this part by saying that the "moral stamp" of "human right" could homogenize these changes, ignoring differences in cultures, societies, ideologies, religions, and specific community-based goals.[46] An analysis of the UNESCO's conception of rights contributes to an understanding of the large threat that this report represented for the commission's instruments to promote women's rights.

The UNESCO's fragmentation of family planning into a set of "Western" rights led to a further critique of each single right. The first was the right to sexuality, which the delegate argued was closely prescribed in most cultures. The right to sexuality means here the right to express one's sexual behavior in heteronormative terms. Sexuality could only be expressed under certain circumstances within certain established relationships and even, in some cases, only within certain physical confines. A universal definition of the right to sexuality could erase important cultural factors and impose a universally identical definition. The meaning of incest, for instance, differed from culture to culture. Sexual relationships prior to or outside of marriage were another example of different cultures' acceptance of sexuality-related issues. The social meaning of such practices—the UNESCO claimed—was different in Europe, China, and West Africa.

This UNESCO report ended with a provocative question on who could define rights and for whom. The UNESCO challenged the legitimacy of a definition of the right to sexuality and its limitations. Women's rights over their own bodies had a similar fate in the UNESCO's calculations at that time; the agency claimed that cultures had different ways of approaching the issue.

The most contentious subject in this report was abortion, which in this analysis was the result of both capitalism and feminism. In this understanding of individual versus collective rights, abortion appeared as anti-community, as depriving the community of more children. The UNESCO criticized individual (women's) rights as emerging solely from Western, capitalist traditions, thereby ignoring cultural specificities. The UNESCO declared that the meaning of family planning and its "rights package" came from Western-based feminist struggles and made little sense in other countries, especially in developing ones. The main argument was that women's close connection to local communities could not be lost in a universal definition of rights.

These interventions are fundamental to understand the UN internal opposition to feminist politics through dangerous arguments on cultural relativism. Furthermore, the CSW never mentioned feminism as one of its policies, and so in this case it appeared that the word *feminism* was used as an accusation, something radical and arbitrary that had no place in international diplomacy. The response of the UNESCO rendered vulnerable the careful strategies of all commissioners, including those from developing countries, in associating demographic goals with development. The UNESCO advocated for an endogenous definition of equality, a product of culture, history, and communal goals rather than a definition that challenged local elements. Equality, the report declares, cannot be imposed, "taking as its starting point campaigns begun in countries that have the money and the machinery to export 'universal human rights.'" Ultimately, the UNESCO proposed an interpretation that trapped women in their own cultures, ignoring that other human rights could be considered as having intervened in traditions and that traditions are not infallible. The attack on women's rights went beyond this report, and it later included a direct reference to the "invasion" of feminism within the UN.

In its report to the twenty-fifth session of the CSW (1974, see figure 8), the UNESCO declared the danger of the rise of a strong feminist movement. This was the last meeting before the Mexico City conference, and the UNESCO's representative, Miss Zharan claimed, "The emergence of feminist groups as powers in various countries became evident during the session. This movement will take on greater dimensions in 1975 and the UNESCO will have to keep abreast, if not ahead, of this movement through closer links with NGOs and by spreading its action beyond the official level in Member States."[47] Such opposition went beyond the commission's sessions. The CSW could never "win" in the face of the specialized agencies; first with interference with the ILO over women workers' rights, then with the FGM conflict with the WHO, and ultimately with the UNESCO.[48] Arguably, the internal UN competition over the agencies' expertise and national governments' representation contributed to a constant discrediting of commissioners. Through the years of activities of the CSW, the UN agencies assumed their neutrality and objectivity versus the more politicized and less expert member states' delegates. A further critique by the WHO on the CSW's configuration of family planning reinforced this generally hostile trend.

At the 1974 UN International Forum on the Role of Women and Development, the WHO attacked the commission's position on family planning from a different angle. At the forum, women delegates from 108 countries convened to deliberate on "their status and their active participation in the developmental process." Participants summed up all the commission's instruments for women's equality and denounced the gap between laws and practices. Signed conventions and declarations contrasted with the "actual discriminative status of a large proportion of women in the so-called modern world."[49] Moreover, in some legal systems discrimination was codified, and men were legally defined as superior to women. The forum focused on the direct relationship between gender equality and economic growth and the assumption that political democracy derived from development.

This venue was important to bring commissioners' debates and formulations into a larger setting. Most of the forum's discussions were dedicated to the World Population Plan, which was adopted at the Bucharest World Population Conference immediately after the forum (August 1974). Here, too, family planning emerged as a contested issue, particularly for the WHO representative Dr. S. Plaza de Echeverria who argued that "health" was absent from the discussion on women and reproduction. Health, as opposed to birth control, Plaza de Echeverria claimed, was the most important element in development and population goals.[50]

The responses to Sipilä's work highlighted ideological barriers to this early internationalization of reproductive rights. The UNESCO and the WHO, specifically, saw this as an opportunity to stand their experts' grounds on culture and health in confrontational terms with the CSW. Reading the status of women within these two macrocategories challenged women's control of their own destiny and the work of the commission.

Conclusion

This chapter shows how the intricate negotiations on gender equality, development, and reproduction were foundational to both the passage from formal to substantial equality and the official shift in the politics of the commission, from a focus on law to a focus on practices. The report on women and development showed how women were disempowered at a global level. The early CSW's rescuing thrust lost its effectiveness leaving space for a more pluralist women's rights activism.

Negotiating between tradition and development continued to represent a challenge in the CSW's deliberations; commissioners knew that their position within the UN hierarchies depended also on their help to foster their national goals, which were difficult to support when they undermined the status of women. Illustrated here are also the immediate needs of new nations vis-à-vis the role of women. The private sphere appeared one more time as the place for state-sanctioned discrimination against women.

Over the course of decades, commissioners operated along a path that went from the individual and her right to vote to her communal and, ultimately, family life. They always measured women's lives through a lens in which marriage and male-derivative roles were assumed, as if a woman's inescapable destiny and desire was solely to be a wife and a mother. Family planning concluded the historical crescendo that went from voting to reproductive rights, passing through the colonial setting as the push to consider the private sphere and to reunify the category of women of the world, all women were victims of discrimination even if with variations. While commissioners were finding commonalities in the global struggle for the status of women, the UNESCO refractured the category of women's rights between the industrialized West and the developing world. Cultural relativism appeared as somewhat the enemy of women's rights in the Global South, and as the UNESCO example illustrates, any attempt to challenge traditions that affected women's lives was considered an imposition from the West. Circling around patriarchy without ever challenging it showed how international women's rights were always limited because the real culprit was never mentioned.

The female body was the ultimate test of universalism, and in this context it emerged as the tool to repopulate or the tool to depopulate. Connected to female bodies and tradition was also the overly present discussion on the Islamic veil, for some the embodiment of women's "backwardness," a word and concept dear to imperial feminists who negatively influenced women's activism in the Global North and South. From the late 1960s imperial feminists attitude decreased at the CSW; commissioners realized that women were even more penalized because of "attitudes, traditions and concepts" that affected their role within the family and society everywhere.

The CSW was the world stage onto which these foundational dynamics and debates were deployed. At the twenty-fourth session of the CSW in 1972, the representative from the Women's International Democratic Federation, an organization (discussed in chapter 3) that confronted many Cold War–based challenges within the commission—from the rejection of visas to enter the United States and participate in the commission's meetings to direct attacks about the authenticity of its data on women's oppression—due to its Communist ties, proposed the creation of the International Women's Year. Commissioners unanimously agreed with this idea and moved toward this direction: 1975 was proclaimed the International Women's Year. In this context, following the plan of the WIDF also symbolized a less confrontational political atmosphere. Among the many activities of the year, the UN Mexico City conference emerged as the most memorable.

The issues presented in this chapter are often obscured in the general narrative of the UN and women because of the milestone of the 1975 conference, where representatives of women's international organizations and women's activists confronted one another on geopolitical and hegemonic issues. At Mexico City women's subaltern status within both the private and public spheres was confirmed.[51] Fragmented voices advocated for different groups of rights to improve women's lives, but separations and ideological attacks on politics and sexualities affected the climate of the conference. Women emerged as victims of structural inequalities, but it was impossible to find an agreement on the causes and solutions of such inequalities.

Epilogue

Throughout this book I have tried to provide a counternarrative of a single story. In a 2009 TED talk, Nigerian writer Chimamanda Ngozi Adichie warned her audience against "single stories."[1] In her case, the single story was the one believed by Western audiences regarding the African continent. When linear stories become the only way to describe countries, peoples, and histories, Adichie argues, there is a danger of silencing voices and realities. Single stories are about hegemonic relations and positionality, all elements that a closer look at the CSW reveals.

As I have demonstrated, the commission's historical trajectory from obscurity to recognition did not develop along a clear path but through a series of often problematic definitions of equality, inequality, universalism, and difference. Empire, even in its postcolonial version, was central to such definitions, reflecting the challenges of adjusting universal understandings to locations scarred by inequality and oppression. This process, however, was not anti-colonial per se, as commissioners from the Global North developed a new type of configuration which blended imperial feminist attitudes with Cold War and development narratives. Moreover, the practice of internationalism and its limitations, especially in the politics of aid, created a hierarchy between the givers and receivers of aid. The challenge was whether aid could transcend the asymmetries of power.

The events between 1945 and 1975 show a clear tension between the single institutional story of an ineffective CSW and its actual contribution to the advancement of women's rights. Moreover, in the case of commissioners from the Global North, the single story was the one they promoted about women and tradition in the colonial and postcolonial world. Both stories, in a way, fragment the global women's movement and create a long history of imperial feminism that goes from formal imperialism and the relationship between the colony and the métropole to internationalism and collaborative imperial attitudes that saw the First and Second World's women delegates creating a set of antinomies in which women in the Global South were to be rescued.

This monograph operates through an interdisciplinary methodology and, as such, grapples with the moment of reckoning of interdisciplinarity. The postcolonial studies framework pushes the boundaries of the historical inquiry. Seeking the body in intergovernmental historical sources has meant always looking at the construction of "the other" be it a gendered other, a colonized other, or both. The expansion of rights—complicated by history, culture, locations—implies a metaphorical and theorical movement, and as with any movement it can be smooth, sudden, and painful. The canon toward which "otherness" is defined challenges the universalism of rights and reveals how the only way to escape otherness is revisiting universalism or even questioning its existence. The transnational feminist framework strips rights of their presumed and announced universalism to find male-centric legal constructions in need of a constant labor of insertion. Here such insertion, although it was an imperial feminist insertion, since Westerner commissioners operated through this ideology, revealed the cracks in their assumed superiority and actually showed their own problematic position of oppressors and oppressed hidden behind it.

Because of the complexity of the UN, this book includes many trajectories that run parallel and overlap, and about which I provide reflections in different parts of this epilogue. Part of engaging with the single story of women's activism in the pre-1975 period also involved the choice of the visual material used in this book. Although curated, the images render the UN a livelier presence and show how the organization chose to represent itself as restorative of justice—technocratic, internationalist, and cosmopolitan but also weary of geopolitics and imperial balances.

The visual narrative of this book begins and ends with women of color, in order to depict the foundation of the UN and the moment when sex and racial discrimination was gaining more centrality and more clarity in the definition of the oppressive forces against women. Images also serve to witness the complexities and historical intersections. Bernardino's signing of the charter signaled a moment in which women were not only present physically but made sure their presence was imprinted in the charter. The Palestinian refugee camp epitomizes the still-persistent representation of the archetypal woman refugee as well as a crisis that still pervades global politics. The technical assistance programs in Asia are here the symbol of Cold War strategies of development and the promotion of capitalism. Conversely, the socialist side of the Cold War, even if not represented in photos, is inserted into this narrative. Images of meetings suggest, in one case, the invisibility of women in the trusteeship representation of the labor of internationalism and the later seminars in which local experts spoke for their own communities. The parallel visual story ends with an actual meeting of the CSW which represents only women from African and Asia. This choice symbolizes the centrality of the non-Western world: the fact that the object of policies became the subject of policies.

This epilogue is divided in different sections; a section that discusses the historical background, a section on the women that populated the commission and their collective efforts, and ultimately considerations on feminism and the body.

The Macrohistory

Decolonization affected the Cold War balance of the early decades of the UN. The consequent creation of the nonaligned movement and the 1964 G77 formed a bloc that challenged the power of the United States and USSR.[2] The role of China, emblematic of Cold War conflicts, went through a transformation as well. From late 1971 the PRC took the place of Taiwan at the General Assembly. The legitimate seat of the PRC at the UN went through multiple diplomatic moves and voting procedures. The United States was especially concerned with these changes because of its possible political isolation within the UN with more votes in favor of the USSR by the G77. The 91 versus 22 votes to suspend South Africa for its brutal racial politics in 1974 were an example of the voting power of the nonaligned countries.[3] The Palestinian question was also part of these new voting games and at the forefront of the GA voting blocs of the 1970s. Within this framework, human rights became an important rhetorical tool of the United States, which was eager to regain more international prestige. The same was valid for women's rights for which the United States claimed an international role.[4]

The CSW's success and global recognition started with the Mexico City conference in 1975 and continued with a series of important provisions to promote sex equality, enacted in subsequent conferences in Copenhagen (1980), Nairobi (1985), Vienna (1993), and Beijing (1995). In a commentary of the Beijing conference, Gayatri Spivak highlights the theatrical nature of the UN women's conferences. In her analysis women are used to symbolize the curated unity between the North and the South.[5] Like most critics of the UN, she laments the large use of resources by the organization which then translates to little change for women in the local sphere. Emblematic are the questions that she posed to Bangladeshi women's activists about their attendance at the Beijing conference; she asked them about the danger of being "matronized by white and diasporic feminists." Spivak's warning underscores how numerous separations of class, race, sexuality, and nationality still exist and seem to be endemic in international women's activism.

The Commission on the Status of Women is part of the larger UN Woman (2010), a group which advocates for women's rights. The evolution to UN Women, which put together different UN parts dedicated to the rights of women, emerged from Secretary-General Kofi Annan's reforms in the late 1990s. These initiatives led to the creation of the Branch for the Advancement of Women, which later became part of UN women. A similar institutional trajectory created the United Nations Development Fund for Women which joined the macro-organization for women at the UN. Legal scholars Hilary Charlesworth and Christine Chinkin argue that a more effective institutional architecture does not always have an impact on women's lives: "In any event the goals of coherence, effectiveness and economic efficiency— the drivers of institutional reform—were detached from legal reform and norm development."[6]

Transnational Encounters

Considering the commission through the Cold War perspective confirms anxieties and conflicts, but it also reveals the contrast between propaganda and the "scientific" collection of data. Within the CSW, objectivity became a political weapon and presented challenges when identifying discriminatory aspects of women's lives. In self-reflective operations, Soviet delegates defined themselves against prerevolutionary Russian and capitalist models of womanhood. Capitalism, in this case, transcended the linear Marxist critique of decadence to enter the realm of racial relationships. The Soviet Bloc representatives glorified their own progress to show the benefits of socialist-based gender equality and simultaneously to denounce those countries in which repressive practices based on race threatened the advancement of women's rights. Multiple chapters problematize the issue of propaganda, as when Soviet Bloc commissioners presented a real depiction of racist politics in places such as the United States, South Africa, and European colonies. The problem was not the accuracy of the depiction but the origin of such statements against the West. Arguably, these blatant attacks served also as a shield to American delegates who, eager to take part in the back and forth with the Soviets, did not leave space for a true assessment of their internal racial and gender inequalities. However, the compelling element to this story is that, well beyond propaganda and Cold War schemes, delegates from the Global South voiced their own struggles, first with decolonization and later through international cooperation and development. While these women were part of the elite in their countries, they nonetheless contributed to a critical understanding of women's activism, one in which they had to fight against the hegemony of the "single story."

On multiple occasions, the commissioners from Arab countries, Latin America, and Sub-Saharan Africa provided the most innovative ways to look at conflicts. For example, the different interpretations of Islam challenged a unified dimension of women's rights that was constructed as reactionary. Delegates from the Muslim world provided the most advanced framework to read Islamic law vis-à-vis the women's movement. They claimed that discrimination did not come from Islamic law but from its distorted application. The typical Cold War narrative of conflicts has obscured these fascinating examples happening at the margins of the East-West confrontation.

Postcolonial delegates experimented with innovating conceptions of gender equality because they aimed to legitimize those traditions that gave women a prominent role within the family. Their relationship with colonialism appeared as complex: from one side, the desire of moving forward, on the other, the realization of the structural damages centuries of foreign domination had created. Their status might appear problematic since, from a class point of view, they represented the elite voicing the claims of the subaltern.[7] Within this framework, women from the Global South engaged with the contradictions intrinsic in the relationship between tradition and modernity; they did so in a way that was stripped from sensationalism and was more connected to concrete strategies to insert women in the fabric of the new nation-state. The UN often responded through a blend of cultural relativist and technocratic stances that made women's positions untenable. More importantly, the international meetings in the African continent also showed a collective sense of Africanness that echoed pan-Africanism as well as Leopold Senghor's theory of negritude.

The UN provided a terrain for confrontation that escaped the circular métropole-colony "family romance" and complicated the relationship between colonized women and international politics.[8] The close collaboration of the CSW and the Trusteeship Council represents the unexplored role of gender politics in the UN-led promotion of self-rule. The council's administrating authorities (consisting of UN delegates from different countries including colonial powers) presented an ambivalent image of the status of women: on one hand, they critiqued "customs" as detrimental to women; on the other hand, they did not question such customs but, in some instances, glorified their affinities with bourgeois culture. The Trusteeship Council authorities searched for similarities with Eurocentric models of womanhood, and when they could not find them, they claimed that local forces were responsible for women's inferiority. The council did not contest colonial rule, but it "measured" readiness for self-rule on the basis of a European conception of "equality."

The deliberations over women's rights in the colonial setting allowed for a closer observation of the practice of discrimination in the presence or absence of legal instruments in favor of sex equality. The focus on the nation-state as the guarantor of rights had obscured the possibility of identifying other discriminating forces that existed within the state itself. NGOs brought to the UN setting their concern for the status of native women. Catholic NGOs produced assumptions about sub-Saharan countries; they heavily contributed to the denouncement of what Catholic groups perceived as ritual practices harming the body. Commissioners responded with an association between the violation of human rights and of human bodies.

Transnational encounters also transformed the social and equal divide of an earlier period. During the organization of the International Women's Year, Annie Jiagge highlighted the separation that women's politics caused in the UN context; similar to what Dorothy Kenyon claimed at the early stages of the CSW, Jiagge was concerned with the efficacy of gender equality in conditions of extreme poverty. Helvi Sipilä and Margaret Bruce also sided with different parts of this debate, Sipilä was in favor of development as precursor of equality, Bruce focused on legal equality instead.[9] The background of this ideological conflict was also an internal UN protest of equal opportunities for women within the organization based on article 8 of the charter.

Imperial Feminisms

The CSW played a significant, if unexpected, role at the intersection of women, empire, and the politics of the female body. The controversial aspect was a constant focus on the colonial other in the struggle for women's rights along with the presumption that women in the Global North had reached the peak of emancipation. Therefore, the historicization of the category of imperial feminism through the UN represents another "single story." Feminism was not always progressive as it hid hierarchies under the flag of the "white woman's burden." Imperial feminism allows to trace a trajectory in which the body was first implied—in the genealogy of women's politics at the UN and in the insertion of women within the public sphere—and later became central, in the depictions of the racial and colonial female "other."

While the physical and rhetorical encounters of the commissioners cannot be defined through the contemporary transnational feminist framework, these interactions were both transnational and feminist: formulations emerged from the exchanges of ideas by representatives from different locales who worked on the promotion of women's rights. Arguably, the focus on the private sphere could also mean transcending the nation-state, but in a context like the UN where membership is based on nationhood and international legal instruments were the ultimate goal, the nation-state was the constant point of reference.

At a larger level, commissioners were at the center of the complex relationship between universalism and difference, a conflict that starts with the creation of the commission itself as a preemptive measure to avoid the invisibility of women in the internationalization of human rights. The partial theoretical resolution of the universalism/difference conundrum happened in the 1990s with the formulation of the category of women's human rights.[10] However, commissioners had grappled with the tension between women and human rights, not only in the early days of the UN but in multiple other instances in which the female body and its connections to tradition were contested.

Through the colonial framework, the transnational and contentious aspect of the commission-based category of the "women of the world" became "women of the colonial or developing world," a political project rather than an actual definition of the commission's audience. Due to the relationship between UN membership and sovereignty, not all women could be the subject of UN legal instruments. Nevertheless, the early commissioners' international experience encouraged them to produce policies with the intent of including *especially* the colonial world. The fragmentation of the larger category "women of the world" arguably happened because empire gave commissioners a chance to engage with a topic that was central to global politics during the Cold War and intersected with it.

The end of colonialism also meant a shift to economic politics which, within the CSW, encouraged the final negotiation of formal equality as the ultimate goal for the women of the world. After 1960, commissioners from newly formed countries officially participated in the commission's meetings. These delegates brought to the commission the meanings of a newly constituted citizenship. The foundations of postcolonial citizenship highlighted even more the exclusionary mechanisms of the nation-state, confirming the necessity of international law to include women in universal rights. In the post-1960 period, commissioners were against discrimination, but they were not in favor of total gender equality. Specifically, the African commissioners agreed that mothers had to hold the power they had maintained within the family structure. Total gender equality appeared to threaten this power. They advocated instead for gender balance, which refers to the power women carved within traditional institutions. From a conceptual perspective, gender balance, agreed on by most commissioners, represented the combination of history and politics as it included the recognition of the historical consolidation of women's power within the family. A type of power, they argued, that was specific to women. Therefore, total equality with men appeared as a threat to such power. The focus on the family and mothers encouraged commissioners to start a debate on family planning. First introduced by the Egyptian commissioner Aziza Hussein in the mid-1960s, family planning acquired a central political role that involved global-scale research on the topic and a 1970 UN special report by Commissioner Sipilä on this topic.

Imperial feminism still lingers in global women's activism and presents opportunities to research issues of hegemony and feminisms in different locations and through different conflicts. One prominent trend has been the inquiry on the role of people of color in white settler colonial formations and the types of decolonial alliances that can be built in countries such as the United States, Canada, and Australia.[11] The framework of settler colonialism gives new life to the feminist struggle which today includes numerous other conflicts such as the environmental cause, the war on terror, and the global assault by neoliberal economics.

Corporeal Tensions

Body politics are still salient in women's activism. The body serves as a lens through which to understand the tension at the core of national and international identity politics. In the case of the CSW, casting the gaze on the other's body allowed for scrutiny of the private sphere and for culture-sanctioned discrimination to then circle back to the gazer's own reality. The determining voice, for this circular dimension, came from the Muslim world as both Bedia Afnan and Aziza Hussein, in different decades, warned against the Global North's attitude of self-satisfaction in the realm of women's rights. Commissioners from the Global South clearly spelled out that discrimination and inequality affected women everywhere. The unique aspect of this dialectical process was that provisions on discrimination are therefore based historically on the objectification of women in the Global South. In this story, the body is laborious, constrained, trafficked, and mutilated—mirroring the nation's strength and weakness. Commissioners looked at the body through colonized knowledge.

The attempts to insert family planning within the human rights frame-work represented the last stage of the body politics inaugurated with the charter inclusion of sex equality. In the midst of the 1970s' feminist strug-gles to promote reproductive rights in the public setting, commissioners aimed to reach a similar goal—advocating for women to regulate their own reproductive schedules—but within a different agenda. The csw's unified voice did not frame family planning within the need of sexual freedom but rather as a part of development policies. Commissioners adopted a neo-Malthusian position that conceived increases in population as detrimental for existing resources. Paradoxically, their accurate nonfeminist politics attracted the scorn of UNESCO, which deemed them as militant feminists and Eurocentric agents who did not understand cultural relativist stances in matters of rights.

Bodily pain emerged as the sensory category that initiated the shift from a focus on the law to a focus on culture in order to identify and overcome discrimination against women. I do not condone the Western gaze on col-onized bodies; on the contrary, I have examined the consequences of these problematic dynamics through the UN's interpretations.

While the UN was not a colonial force per se, the inclusion of European colonial powers (and newly imperializing agents like the Soviet Union) allowed for crypto colonial dynamics. Scholars of intimacy and empires are concerned with the proximity of bodies—colonizer and colonized—and with the fluidity of their encounters (in practice) and rigidity of colo-nial states in enforcing separations.[12] The colonial state was indeed based on separation. Applying the category of the "intimate" (for example, sex, bathing, breastfeeding, and cooking) to the international realm and female genital modifications shows how even at distance the Western gaze scruti-nized the local realms, constructing narratives of danger for female bodies. The codification of human and women's rights reinforced the emotional language of pain, helplessness, and imperial feminist dynamics in which Western delegates aimed to rescue African women. Empirically, the intimate is mostly unspoken and then suddenly medicalized because of development politics. No one at the UN from 1950 to 1970 talked about depriving women of sexual pleasure; the ritual of FGM was seen as inflicting pain but not as affecting the sexual act.

The conflict between the UN and WHO showed how all parties involved in both women's and human rights took part in the debates over "ritual operations." In that context, violence became an accusation connected to the practice of modifying women's bodies for coming-of-age rituals. Violence was part of the hegemonic Western agenda of rescuing the other; the pain of others and women as victims of their culture were instrumental to the politics of defining FGM within the human rights discourse. I have presented here both the alleged spectators and actual condemners of bodily violence. The alleged victims were never explicitly present, and this hidden role made the epistemic violence of representation even more prominent. I have formulated here an analysis of narratives that constructed the intimacy of FGM as violent and ergo in need of human rights.[13]

Only in the 1970s did the issue of female circumcision find a more relevant place in the WHO's policies. Decolonization, development, and second-wave feminism contributed to a new treatment of the issue by groups with different agendas. Newly formed nations wanted to manage their resources wisely, and as the WHO regional director said at a Khartoum seminar of 1979, the hospitalization for female circumcision amounted to 1,967 days in countries with already few resources.[14] The director himself traced a history of silence of the WHO, saying, "The interest of WHO in dealing with the practice of female circumcision is neither new nor surprising." But only after the International Women's Year did an interest in improving the status of women in economic and social development become prominent.

The observation of women's bodies in pain within the colonial framework historically generated a set of assumptions about native bodies and cultural hegemonic relationships, but in this context, these tensions created an association between the self-determination of the country and the self-determination of the body. In a perspective of scrutiny as an imperial feminist tool, practices that might seem against women can also be the expression of self-determination. In the background of the Algerian War of Independence (1954–1962), for example, the veil became the symbol of assertion against France. While these traditions might be imposed or freely embraced, they have historically represented a form of resistance, ergo the self-determination of the body according to local and constructed-as-anticolonial traditions. The connection between countries and bodies meant that African women had additional levels of constraints emerging from both the colonial and local settings. The politics of development reinforced the shift to body politics. The practice of modification of the female body brings together violence and intimacy, because the act in itself is cutting or eliminating, but the deliberations and discourse surrounding the practice "cut," too, as they obfuscated all possible understanding, at least historically.

Today the decolonization of knowledge is central to democratic processes, showing how equality cannot be built on a basis of epistemic inequality. The body is central to this counterhegemonic operation, enriched by new formulated identities, new bodily configurations, and the resistance to new hierarchies of which bodies matter and which don't. The constant migrant crises at borderlands, transphobic policies, and attacks to reproductive rights clearly demonstrate an even more rigid understanding of canonical bodies and their respective others. The need and struggle for the self-determination of the body is currently a goal that unites the Global South and North, confirming (as this book has shown) that in the context of feminisms, the South can function as mirror for the North.

Notes

Introduction

1. Meeting Records, Commission on the Status of Women, UN Headquarters, New York, May 1, 1955, document E/CN.6/SR.134.
2. Edgar, "Bolshevism, Patriarchy, and the Nation," 252–72.
3. Gallagher and Robinson, "The Imperialism of Free Trade," 1–15.
4. On this debate see, Normand and Zaidi, *Human Rights at the UN*.
5. Gorman, "Britain, India, and the United Nations," 471–90.
6. Jolly, transcript of interview.
7. Richards, "Transnational Links and Constraints," 149–75.
8. See for example, Galey, "Women Find a Place," 11–28; Reanda, "Commission on the Status of Women," 265–303.
9. Rupp, *Worlds of Women*; Garner, *Shaping a Global Women's Agenda*; Zinsser, "From Mexico to Copenhagen," 139–68.
10. Adami and Plesch, *Women and the UN*.
11. Boris, "Equality's Cold War," 97–120.
12. Boris, *Making the Woman Worker*.
13. Laville, "A New Era?," 34–56; Laville, "'Woolly, Half-Baked and Impractical,?'" 473–95; Lambertz, "'Democracy Could Go No Further,'" 34–51; and Baldez, *Defying Convention*.
14. Jain, *Women, Development, and the UN*.
15. Knop, *Diversity and Self-Determination*.
16. See Von Eschen, *Race against Empire*; Anderson, *Eyes Off the Prize*; Laughlin and Castledine, *Breaking the Wave*. Also, excellent works on transnational Black women are Blain and Gill, *To Turn the Whole World Over* and Cobble, *The Other Women's Movement*.
17. Adami, *Women and the Universal Declaration*, 24, 25.
18. Olcott, *International Women's Year*; Marino, *Feminism for the Americas*.
19. De Haan, "Continuing Cold War Paradigms," 547–73.
20. Ghodsee, "Revisiting the United Nations," 3–12.

21. Morrell, "A Higher Stage of Imperialism?"
22. Thomas, "France Accused," 91–121.
23. Burke, *Decolonization and the Evolution*.
24. Moses, Duranti, and Burke, *Decolonization, Self-Determination*.
25. Gallagher and Laqueur, *Making of the Modern Body*; Canning "The Body as Method?," 499–513. Porter, "History of the Body," 233–60. Here are a few details on these important contributions. In a 1983 special issue of the journal *Representations* on "The Making of the Modern Body," Gallagher and Laqueur summarize the scholarly uses of the body: "Scholars have only recently discovered that the human body itself has a history. Not only has it been perceived, interpreted, and represented differently in different epochs, but it has also been lived differently, brought into being within widely dissimilar material cultures, subjected to various technologies and means of control, and incorporated into different rhythms of production and consumption, pleasure and pain." The articles in the volume show how regimes of truth—often fluid and contradictory—about the body reflected the social orders advocated by the bodily experts in question. Roy Porter's 1991 essay emphasizes the potential abstractness and elusiveness of writings of the body—which he characterizes as "floating through history"—along with more concrete and empirical analyses of statistics on the body. He argues for an approach that unites both routes, the elusive and the concrete. Canning's article highlights, as do the previous two works, how bodies can represent other issues: "Bodies, as signifiers, metaphors or allegorical emblems, promise new understandings of nation or social formation." Drawing on the work of Michel Foucault, she mentions discipline, medicalization, and the more Marxian categories of production and reproduction. When some behaviors are prescribed or rewarded, where norms of hygiene or morality are based on the body, bodies are also representations of the nation-state's power. She includes in her analysis a response to Donna Haraway's manifesto: "The repudiation of sex in favor of gender left sex inextricably linked to the body and stigmatized it with biologism and essentialism." The body as symbol, as construction, hides oppression and social relations. Canning rightly contraposes the works of Foucault on biopolitics and discourse to works on pain such as the monograph by Elaine Scarry; pain cannot be reduced to discourse because it is a vivid and determining experience. Porter, however, mentions Scarry as an example of abstraction, arguing that there are historical accounts that clearly explain pain.
26. Baron and Boris, "'The Body,'" 23–43; Patil, *Negotiating Decolonization*.
27. Baron and Boris, "'The Body,'" 24.

28. Grosz, *Volatile Bodies*, 14.
29. Davin, "Imperialism and Motherhood," 9–66.
30. Hartmann, *Reproductive Rights and Wrongs*, cited in Federici, *Beyond the Periphery of the Skin*, 16.
31. On liberal feminism, see Okin, *Women in Western Political Thought*; MacKinnon, *Toward a Feminist Theory*; Scott, *Only Paradoxes to Offer*; Nussbaum, *Feminist Critique of Liberalism*; Baehr, *Varieties of Feminist Liberalism*; Baehr, "Feminist Politics and Feminist Pluralism," 411–36; and Zerilli, "Feminist Theory," 106–24. On imperial feminism, see Burton, *Burdens of History* and Jayawardena, *White Woman's Other Burden*. In the U.S. context, significant accounts are Hoganson, "'As Badly Off As,'" 9–33; and Sneider, *Suffragists in an Imperial Age*. The most influential texts assessing contemporary imperial feminist attitudes within the women's movement are Amos and Parmar, "Challenging Imperial Feminism," 3–19; Mohanty, "Under Western Eyes," 51–80; and Mohanty, "'Under Western Eyes' Revisited," 499–535. On a response to imperial feminism and theories of transnational feminism see, Narayan, *Dislocating Cultures*; Kaplan, Alarcon, and Moallem, *Between Women and the Nation*; Sinha, Guy, and Woollacott, *Feminisms and Internationalism*; Narayan and Harding, *Decentering the Center*; and Naples and Desai, *Women's Activism and Globalization*.
32. On this topic, see Quataert, *Advocating Dignity*; and Reilly, *Women's Human Rights*.
33. On issues of "otherness" in feminist politics, see Lugones and Spelman, "Have We Got a Theory for You!," 573–81; and Collins, *Black Feminist Thought*. On historical issues of defining the "other," see Sinha, *Colonial Masculinity*; Sears, *Fantasizing the Feminine*; and Proschan, "Eunuch Mandarins," 435–67.
34. Dudziak, *Cold War Civil Rights*.
35. Said, *Orientalism*.
36. Burton, *Burden of History*.
37. Mohanty, "'Under Western Eyes.'"
38. In the revised version of her article, Mohanty proposed solidarity and transnational feminist politics as the solution to hegemonic fragmentation in the women's movement. "'Under Western Eyes' Revisited," 499–535.
39. Grewal and Kaplan, *Scattered Hegemonies*, 19. More contemporary and antihegemonic interventions include McLaren, *Decolonizing Feminism*; and Khader, *Decolonizing Universalism*.
40. Campt, *Listening to Images*. In a presentation of the book *Todd Webb in Africa*, author and art historian Erin Hyde Nolan mentioned Campt's work in reference to Webb's photos. See Africa Is a Country, https://www.youtube.com/watch

?v=h1sGcbVsL8g, accessed February 14, 2021; Bessire and Nolan, *Todd Webb in Africa*.

41. On this topic, see Rosenblum, *A World History of Photography*.

42. Marien, *Photography*, 289. 277.

43. Lange, *Destitute Pea Pickers in California. Mother of Seven Children. Age Thirty-Two. Nipomo, California* (1936). U.S. Farm Security Administration/Office of War Information, Prints & Photographs Division.

44. Sandeen, *Picturing an Exhibition*, 12.

45. Sandeen, *Picturing an Exhibition*, 14.

46. Sandeen, *Picturing an Exhibition*, 26. On the exhibition see also Bair, *The Decisive Network*.

47. On this topic see the popular Alloula, *The Colonial Harem*, and the more recent Behdad and Gartlan, *Photography's Orientalism*.

48. Marien, *Photography*, 311.

49. Sandeen, *Picturing an Exhibition*, 25.

50. Certainly, photos satisfied a specific audience, the one who could subscribe to magazines such as *Life* and had the time to read it or to attend an exhibition. These instruments, beyond their power of emotions and of reinforcing world divisions while claiming to represent "one humanity," were also the product of consumer culture.

51. On Todd Webb see Bessire and Nolan, *Todd Webb in Africa*.

52. Hesford and Kozol, *Just Advocacy?*

53. Hesford and Kozol, *Just Advocacy?*, 5, 6.

54. Hesford and Kozol, *Just Advocacy?*, 5, 6.

55. UNESCO, Office of the Resident Observer to United Nations, New York, Complementary Factual Report # STATWOM/CN6–1/1, Relations with Specialized Agencies, Commission on the Status of Women, 1st Session, February 26, 1947, UNESCO Archives, Paris.

56. Minutes Sheet by C. M. Berkeley (executive assistant of Julian Huxley, UNESCO Director General), UN Commission on the Status of Women, 1955, SHS, box 138, Status of Women, part 1 a, 1946–1959, UDC 3–055.2.

57. Popova was a trade unionist and lawyer. Boris, "Equality's Cold War," 105.

58. I occasionally use the term *sex equality*, which can be associated with the contemporary expression *gender equality*. The term *sex equality* comes from the UN Charter and Universal Declaration of Human Rights, which both declare that sex (masculine and feminine) should not be the basis for discrimination against individuals.

1. Women of the World

1. UNESCO correspondence on the 1954 CSW Session. The UNESCO presented a report on literacy rates and provided incorrect data on the Dominican Republic. Bernardino protested, accusing UNESCO of providing old data that discredited her country. The issue involved a series of confidential back and forth in which UNESCO was concerned with being accused of not supporting the UN. Confidential correspondence between A. V. Arnaldo (UNESCO Representative in New York City) and the director general of UNESCO, April 23, 1954, folder Status of Women part I (A) up to 31/VI/59.

2. DuBois and Derby, "Strange Case of Minerva Bernardino," 43–50.

3. In her autobiography, Bernardino praises Stevens as her patron. Bernardino, *Lucha, Agonia Y Esperanza,* xxiv.

4. UN Charter, article 2.

5. United Nations, Department of Public Information, guide to the United Nations Charter (Lake Success NY: 1947), preamble and chapter 1, article 1.

6. Incidentally, Alger Hiss, the UN's temporary secretary-general, oversaw the work of the conference but later became the victim of a Cold War trial. *United Nations Yearbook,* 1946–1947, 14.

7. Thomas, "France Accused," 91–121.

8. Mazower, *No Enchanted Palace,* 64, 65.

9. *Equal Rights Magazine,* July–August 1945, 45–46 (Washington DC: National Woman's Party). I comment on the National Woman's Party later in the chapter.

10. Gorman, "Britain, India, and the United Nations," 71–490.

11. Gorman, 480.

12. General Assembly, Regional Conferences of Representatives of Non-Self-Governing Territories, December 14, 1946, document A/RES/67 (I).

13. Gildersleeve, *Many a Good Crusade.*

14. Jessie Street to the United Association, San Francisco, June 1945, in Radi, *Jessie Street,* 198.

15. On Lutz see Marino, *Feminism for the Americas,* 14–15; and Boris, *Making the Woman Worker,* 53.

16. Historian Leila Rupp has coined the expression "second wave international" to indicate the common goal of international women's organizations in the post-1945 era. While Street, Begtrup, and Bernardino started their political activities before 1945, I'm using Rupp's expression to highlight their post-1945 political activism. See Rupp, *Worlds of Women.*

17. Miller, "'Geneva—the Key to Equality,'" 218–45.

18. United Nations Economic and Social Council, Commission on the Status of Women, first session, 1947, International Labour Organization, ESC–1004/11/1M.T. ILO Archives, Geneva, Switzerland. Interestingly, commissioners later asserted, limiting women's work shifts affected their career choices and possibilities.

19. For more detail on internationalism and these movements, see Jensen and Kuhlman, *Women and Transnational Activism*.

20. Pietilä and Peoc'h, *The Unfinished Story*.

21. *Equal Rights Magazine*, July–August 1945, 45–46. As these words suggests, the *Equal Rights Magazine* had a specific stance toward women's rights, one that had emerged with the struggle for suffrage in the United States context. The magazine was published by the National Woman's Party, founded by the American suffragist Alice Paul, a supporter of formal equality as opposed to substantive equality. The presence of American equal rights feminists shows how diverse the positions of delegates at San Francisco were, even within the same country. For an overview of this issue, see Cobble, Gordon, and Henry, *Feminism Unfinished*, 10.

22. *Equal Rights Magazine*, July–August 1945, 45–46.

23. *Equal Rights Magazine*, July–August 1945, 45–46.

24. Gildersleeve, *Many a Good Crusade*, 330. Gildersleeve does not specify who came up with the nickname for Lutz.

25. Coltheart, "Citizens of the World," 182–94.

26. *Equal Rights Magazine* 1945, 45–46.

27. Linder, "Equality For Women," 165–208.

28. DuBois and Derby, "Strange Case of Minerva Bernardino."

29. Later in this chapter, I show the ways that some aspects of Bernardino's politics were problematic.

30. Pietilä and Peoc'h, *The Unfinished Story*, 132. Cede and Sucharipa-Behrmann, *United Nations Law and Practice*, 177; Ferree and Tripp, *Global Feminism*, 26.

31. This position was not new as the same rhetoric of war sacrifice and political rights for women was advocated by women activists the end of World War I, even if the participants of the Paris Conference ignored women's requests that suffrage be mentioned as an instrument of peace. See Siegel, *Peace on Our Terms*, 9.

32. De Beauvoir, Borde, and Malovany-Chevallier, *The Second Sex*, 74.

33. General Assembly inaugural meeting, February 12, 1946, document A/46.

34. Document A/46.

35. When the first name is not specified, I use the formula reported in the documents, that is, *Mrs.* and *Mr.*, document A/46. The General Assembly debates

include only the last name. When I mention delegate from these debates it is only through their name. See chapters 6 and 7.

36. Document A/46.

37. Document A/46.

38. The glorification of women who participated in the Resistance conflicted with the persecution of women who in the immediate postwar period were accused of having collaborated with the Nazis. See, for example, François, *Femmes tondues.*

39. Document A/46.

40. Document A/46.

41. Historian Katherine Marino shows how Pan-American women delegates "participated in a cultural construction of whiteness connected to Pan-Hispanism and the Spanish language." Marino, *Feminism for the Americas,* 29. While I am aware of differentiations, even within the Latin American world, Bernardino's words sound defensive of empires, a position that she later changed.

42. Document A/46.

43. DuBois and Derby, "Strange Case of Minerva Bernardino."

44. For an expanded discussion on this issue, see Brown, "Feminism, International Theory," 463.

45. Document A/46.

46. Document A/46.

47. In this context "formal equality" indicates a type of gender equality that is supported by laws but that in practice does not eliminate women's discrimination. Formal equality is therefore the contrary of substantive equality. On this debate, see Parisi, "Feminist Praxis," 571–85.

48. On women and war, see canon texts such as Elshtain, *Women and War*; Higonnet et al., *Behind the Lines.*

49. I am contending here a category of "man" that is dominant and not part of any minority, as historians have widely shown how minorities were not contemplated in the social contract.

50. UN Charter, chap. 10, art. 68. For an assessment of this commission, see Normand and Zaidi, *Human Rights at the UN.*

51. Jolly, transcript of interview of Margaret Bruce

52. Economic and Social Council, meeting 1, Sub-Commission on the Status of Women, April 29, 1946, document E/HR/ST/3.

53. Document E/HR/ST/3,

54. Midtgaard, "Bodil Begtrup," 479–99.

55. Street and Coltheart, *Jessie Street,* 181.

56. Morsink, "Women's Rights," 231.

57. Economic and Social Council, general meeting, document E/PV4, May 28, 1946.

58. Document E/PV4.

59. Document E/PV4.

60. Economic and Social Council, resolution, document E/RES/2/11, June 21, 1946.

61. United Nations Social Committee, chapter 2, report of the first session of the CSW, United Nations, folder S-0991-box 6-file 13. United Nations Archives, United Nations Headquarters, New York.

62. Among them was the Indian commissioner, Hamid Ali, who founded the All India Women's Conference. United Nations Economic and Social Council, biographies data on the members of the Commission on the Status of Women, document E/406, 1947. United Nations Archives, United Nations Headquarters, New York.

63. United Nations Economic and Social Council, Commission on the Status of Women, first session, 1947, International Labour Organization, ESC–1004/11/1M.T., ILO Archives, Geneva.

64. Commission on the Status of Women, report to the Economic and Social Council, first session, document E/281/Rev.1, March 15, 1947.

65. United Nations Social Committee, chapter 2, report of the first session of the CSW, United Nations, folder s0991, box 6, file 13. United Nations Archives, United Nations Headquarters, New York.

66. On the dominant interpretation of Begtrup and this issue see, Reanda, "Commission on the Status of Women," 269.

67. United Nations Economic and Social Council, biographies data on the member of the Commission on the Status of Women, document E/406, 1947. United Nations Archives, United Nations Headquarters, New York, New York.

68. Meeting records, Commission on the Status of Women, Lake Success New York, February 11, 1947, document E/CN.6/SR.2.

69. Document E/CN.6/SR.2.

70. Meeting records, Commission on the Status of Women, Lake Success NY, January 20, 1948, document E/CN.6/SR.38.

71. Document E/CN.6/SR.38.

72. Document E/CN.6/SR.38.

73. Document E/CN.6/SR.38.

74. In his critique of the foundational history of the United Nations, historian Mark Mazover defines the UN as "No Enchanted Palace." Mazower, *No Enchanted Palace.*

75. Document e/cn.6/sr.38.
76. Economic and Social Council, meeting of the Sub-Commission on the Status of Women, May 13, 1946—document e/hr/st/16 May 15, 1946. Some documents list her last name as Kalinowski.
77. Dorothy Kenyon represents, in this context, an exception, as she was not a typical Cold War "warrior" but rather an expert on women's rights and law independent of strong political Cold War positions. Later in her life she was the victim of the Joseph McCarthy's Red Scare politics. On Kenyon see, Weigand and Horowitz, "Dorothy Kenyon," 126–31.
78. Commission on the Status of Women, report to the Economic and Social Council, first session, document e/281/Rev.1, March 15, 1947.
79. Commission on the Status of Women, report to the Economic and Social Council, second Session, document e/615, January 26, 1948.
80. Meeting records, Commission on the Status of Women, Lake Success ny, January 20, 1948, document e/cn.6/sr.28.
81. Document e/cn.6/sr.28.
82. Rebecca Adami shows how non-Western women contributed to the Universal Declaration of Human Rights. See Adami, *Human Rights Learning*.
83. The emphasis on *his* is mine.

2. Imperial Encounters

1. From un Media: "The United Nations Relief for Palestine Refugees (unrpr), assisted by voluntary agencies, is supplying food, clothing, tents, blankets and medical attention to some 750,000 Arab refugees spread throughout the Middle East." The year of the photo is uncertain and reported with a question mark.
2. General Assembly resolution, a/res/181(II) November 29, 1947.
3. Economic and Social Council, meeting records, February 5, 1948, Lake Success ny, e_sr.129-en.
4. In 1950 Kenyon was "the very first victim of Senator Joseph R. McCarthy red-baiting's attacks." Baldez, *Defying Convention*, 62.
5. Furedi, *The Silent War*, 194.
6. Uzbekistan had first been part of the Russian Empire and later turned into a socialist republic. The popular unveiling of the Muslim women in Uzbekistan represented a tool to modernize the country. Historians argued that, contrary to European colonialism—based on the reinforcing differences, hierarchies, and separation for the sake of exploitation—Soviet imperialism aimed to

create Soviet citizens, so as to raise the status of the people in Central Asia to the level of the Soviets. See Northrop, *Veiled Empire*; and Edgar "Bolshevism, Patriarchy, and the Nation," 252–72.

7. United Nations Economic and Social Council, continuation of the discussion on the report of the third session of the Commission on the Status of Women, August 1, 1949, document E_SR.316-EN.

8. Meeting records, Commission on the Status of Women, Lake Success NY, January 12, 1948, document E/CN.6/SR.31.

9. Document E/CN.6/SR.31.

10. Document E/CN.6/SR.31.

11. Document E/CN.6/SR.31.

12. The sources present many instances by commissioners from the Soviet Union, Britain, Haiti, and Mexico. Meeting records, Commission on the Status of Women, E/CN6/SR.25, 31,41, and 48.

13. Document E/CN.6/SR.31.

14. UNESCO, Office of the Representative to the United Nations, New York, "Project de Report de la Commission," Document E/CN.6/L.226–Add. 1–7, UNESCO Archives, Paris.

15. Cooper, *Africa Since 1940*, 40.

16. Cooper, *Colonialism in Question*, 188.

17. Biographical data of Mary Sutherland, ILO, folder ESC-1004–11/M.T. E/406, International Labour Organization Archives, Geneva, Switzerland.

18. Document E/CN.6/SR.31.

19. Document E/CN.6/SR.31.

20. This expression was made popular by literary scholar Spivak, "Can the Subaltern Speak?" 24–28.

21. These tropes that commissioners used and strengthened are part of the long history of the relationship between intergovernmental gender politics and empire which had existed since the era of the LN. As historian Susan Pedersen argues, the mandate system signaled a shift in colonial policies from violence to reform. When LN women delegates became interested in including the colonies in their activism, they highlighted how empires could produce reforms for the welfare of colonial subjects. Pedersen, "Metaphors of the Schoolroom," 188–207.

22. This was a UN regulation. Colonial powers were supposed to communicate the progresses of "their" territories toward self-rule. I explain this point in more detail in chapter 4.

23. Commission on the Status of Women, meeting records, Beirut, Lebanon, March 21, 1949, E/CN.6/SR.40.
24. Document E/CN.6/SR.40.
25. See also, Dunstan, "'Une Nègre de drame,'" 645–65.
26. Document E/CN.6/SR.40.
27. Charles Malik to Bodil Begrtrup, January 14, 1948, United Nations Archives, New York, New York, S-0991-box 6, file 13. Malik participated in the drafting of the UDHR and had multiple important roles in the UN context.
28. Document E/CN.6/SR.44.
29. Meeting records, Commission on the Status of Women, Beirut, Lebanon, March 24, 1949, document E/CN.6/SR.45. Nationalist China and the SSRs had an ongoing issue regarding the principle of representativeness. The SSR had officially declared Zung's representation of Chinese women illegal. The commissioners highlighted a procedural and jurisdictional problem, as the CSW could not intervene in the GA's realm.
30. For an in-depth account on WIDF, see Ilic, "Soviet Women," 157–74.
31. Meeting records, Commission on the Status of Women, Beirut, Lebanon, April 1, 1949, document E/CN.6/SR.59.
32. Document E/CN.6/SR.59.
33. Document E/CN.6/SR.59.
34. Meeting records, Commission on the Status of Women, Beirut, Lebanon, April 2, 1949, document E/CN.6/SR.60.
35. Report to ECOSOC, third session, document E/1316, April 19, 1949, para. 57. Resolution 194 defined the Palestinian question from a UN perspective. According to the resolution, the Security Council was required to nominate three states as members of the Conciliation Commission. The resolution is also important for the demilitarization of the holy places to ensure that all religious communities could access them freely.
36. Document E/CN.6/SR.60.
37. De Haan, "Continuing Cold War Paradigms," 547–73.
38. Meeting records, Commission on the Status of Women, Lake Success NY, May 10, 1951, document E/CN.6/SR.97.
39. Report to UNESCO director general, April 18, 1952. UNESCO, Sector SHS, box 177, part 2.a, UN Commission on the Status of Women 1951–1958, UNESCO Archives, Paris, France.
40. Document E/CN.6/SR.97.
41. Document E/CN.6/SR.97.

42. On women and peace during the Cold War see also, Goedde, *The Politics of Peace*.

43. Economic and Social Council, meeting records, August 27, 1951, Palais des Nations, Geneva, document E_SR.522-EN.

44. International Labour Organization, Registry, UN Commission on the Status of Women, sixth session 1952, ESC-1004-11-6, ILO Archives, Geneva.

45. United Nations, Security Council, resolution 83, June 27, 1950, document S/RES/83.

46. Cronin, "The Two Faces of the UN," 53–71.

47. Report ECOSOC, document E/615.

48. Meeting records, Commission on the Status of Women, Lake Success NY, January 8, 1948, document E/CN.6/SR.27.

49. Document E/CN.6/SR.27.

50. Meeting records, Commission on the Status of Women, Lake Success NY, May 11, 1950, document E/CN.6/SR.71.

51. Document E/CN.6/SR.71. For the U.S. delegate, as this part of the chapter demonstrates, women's political education had a larger international purpose.

52. Document E/CN.6/SR.71.

53. Meeting records, Commission on the Status of Women, Lake Success NY, May 15, 1950, document E/CN.6/SR.75.

54. Section des Relations Extérieures de la part de la Sections des Sciences Sociales, Philosophie et Humanité, 15 Janvier 1947, Re: Commission sur le status des femmes. UNESCO Archive, Paris, SHS, box 138, Status of Women, 1a, 1946–1949. Translation is mine.

55. Document E/CN.6/SR75.

56. *La Mujer Ciduadana* was a pamphlet sponsored by the UNESCO and created along with the International Political Science Association and Unesco Institute for Social Sciences at Cologne, Germany. UNESCO, report on the access to women to education, CSW, 1955.

57. Meeting records, Commission on the Status of Women, Lake Success NY, May 16, 1950, document E/CN.6/SR.76.

58. Document E/CN.6/SR.76.

59. Document E/CN.6/SR.76.

60. Koikari, *Pedagogy of Democracy*, 2.

61. Koikari, *Pedagogy of Democracy*, 5.

62. Northrop, *Veiled Empire*, 22.

63. United Nations Economic and Social Council, official records, fourteenth Session, May 22, 1952, document E_SR.575-EN.

64. Meeting records, General Assembly, third committee, December 12, 1952, 474th meeting, document A/C.3/SR474.
65. Economic and Social Council, August 23, 1948, document E-SR-210–1948. Chapter 3 describes in further details the case of Uzbekistan. The Soviets were referring to the 1920s Soviet campaigns that targeted Uzbek women wearing the veil.
66. Meeting records, General Assembly, third committee, December 16, 1952, 479th meeting, document A/C.3/SR479.
67. Document A/C.3/SR474.
68. Document A/C.3/SR474.
69. Meeting records, General Assembly, third committee, December 15, 1952, 478th meeting, document A/C.3/SR.478.
70. Document A/C.3/SR478. Truly, African American women also participated in international politics and in UN politics. They participated in both center and left politics, even if both were anticolonialist. An example was Eslanda Goode Robeson who actively participated in leftist activism alongside her husband Paul Robeson at the Council on African Affairs, an organization that included Ralph Bunche among its members and that had a brief life (1941–1955) because of Cold War anticommunist politics. On this topic see, Ransby, *Eslanda*.
71. Document A/C.3/SR478.
72. For an overview on this topic, see Gates, *Oxford Handbook*.
73. Liang, "Colonial Clauses," 108–28.
74. Document A/C.3/SR478.
75. Document A/C.3/SR478.
76. On the ambivalent attitude toward the CSW in the UK, see Laville, "'Woolly, Half-Baked and Impractical,'?" 473–95.
77. Document A/C.3/SR474.
78. Document A/C.3/SR478.
79. Document A/C.3/SR478.
80. Meeting records, General Assembly, third committee, December 15, 1952, 477th meeting, document A/C.3/SR477.
81. Document A/C.3/SR477.
82. Document A/C.3/SR478.
83. On the partition of India, see Khan, *The Great Partition* and Menon and Bhasin, *Borders & Boundaries*.
84. An organization with the same name and purpose existed in India. (As stated in chapter 1, Indian commissioner Begum Ali had been the founder of the popular NGO called The India Women's Conference.)

85. Document A/C.3/SR478.

86. Meeting records, General Assembly, third committee, December 16, 1952, 479th meeting, document A/C.3/SR.479.

87. Document A/C.3/SR.479.

88. Document A/C 3/SR.479.

89. Castledine, *Cold War Progressives*.

90. Document E/CN.6/SR.133.

91. General Assembly, resolution December 4, 1950, document 421 (V). Political scientist Daniel Whelan points out how *indivisibility* is a contemporary concept, and the resolution used the words *interdepended* and *interconnected*. Whelan, *Indivisible Human Rights*.

92. Whelan, *Indivisible Human Rights*, 62, 63.

3. Competing Womanhood

1. Boris, *Making the Woman Worker*, 64.

2. Boris, "Equality's Cold War," 97–120. The issue of legal and economic equality had been prominent in the U.S. context. See chapter 1.

3. Boris mentions the issues of mothers too. "Equality's Cold War," 98.

4. Minute Sheet, comments on the meeting of the Commission on the Status of Women, sixth session, Geneva, March 25–April 5, 1952, report by Miss Fairchild, registry ESC 1004-11-6 International Labour Organization Archives, Geneva, Switzerland.

5. Burke, "Disseminating Discord," 589–610.

6. The UN Commission on the Status of Women: A Brief Summary of Progress. A Supplement to the Report of the Conference on the Status of Women Around the World. United Nations, March 30, 1959.

7. The Convention on the Nationality of Married Women was another goal inherited by the League of Nations. See Berkovitch, *From Motherhood to Citizenship*.

8. Guerry and Rundell, "Married Women's Nationality," 73–94.

9. See, for example, Fraser, "Becoming Human," 853–906.

10. Correspondence between Dr. Yuen-li Lian, secretary of the International Law Commission, UNESCO, Paris, and Oscar Schachter, director, general legal division, UN Archives, New York, folder S-0441-0725.

11. Meeting records, Commission on the Status of Women, UN Headquarters, New York, April 2, 1954, document E/CN.6/SR.166.

12. On the UN and the United States, see Forsythe, McMahon, and Wedeman, *American Foreign Policy*. As I illustrate later in the chapter, the Soviets had a similar strategy.

13. Meeting records, Commission on the Status of Women, UN Headquarters, New York, March 23, 1953, document E/CN.6/SR.133. Kristen Ghodsee shows how eventually Cold War politics pushed American women to propose their own understanding/version of women's issues in order to decrease the Soviet influence on this matter, Ghodsee, "Revisiting the United Nations," 3–12.

14. Economic and Social Council, Commission on the Status of Women, report of the eighth session, 1954, document E/2571.

15. Document E/CN.6/SR.133.

16. Document E/CN.6/SR.133. On the issue of intrusion see, Furedi, *The Silent War*.

17. Winslow, *Women, Politics*; Laville, "A New Era?" 34–56.

18. The 1927 Soviet campaign called "hujun" (assault, attack) caused the death of many Uzbek women in public unveiling sessions. Three important works on this topic are the pioneer, Massell, *The Surrogate Proletariat*; Northrop, *Veiled Empire*; and Kamp, *New Woman in Uzbekistan*.

19. Fitzpatrick, *Tear Off the Masks!* 129.

20. See Lorenzini, *Global Development*.

21. Randall, "'Abortion Will Deprive You!'" 13–38.

22. Frederick Engels advocated for women's liberation through labor. See, Massino and Penn, *Gender Politics and Everyday Life*, 2. On the fragmentation of gender along class, race, and colonialism see, Boris, "Equality's Cold War," 119.

23. Meeting records, Commission on the Status of Women, UN Headquarters, New York, March 20, 1957, document E/CN.6/SR.235.

24. UNESCO memo by Philippa Harris, seminar on the equality of women in the USSR Soviet Union, September 15 to October 3, 1956, document EXP/PH/MOB/652461, SHS, box number 138, status of women, part 1 a, from 1946 to 1959, UDC 3–055.2. UNESCO Archives, Paris.

25. United Nations Economic and Social Council, twenty-second session, official records, Palais des Nations, Geneva, August 1, 1956, document E-SR-946-EN.

26. UNESCO memo by Philippa Harris, seminar on the equality of women.

27. Meeting records, Commission on the Status of Women, UN Headquarters, New York, September 3, 1957, document E/CN.6/SR.251.

28. Fitzpatrick, *Tear Off the Masks!*, 125–52.

29. UNESCO memo, report by Pippa Harris to the office of the director general, November 15, 1956.

30. UNESCO memo, November 15, 1956.

31. Petrovich, *Soviet Women Enjoy*.

32. Women's historians have shown a different reality in which Soviet women were relegated to certain professional areas and experienced the so-called double

burden of working both inside and outside the home. See Massino and Penn, *Gender Politics and Everyday Life*. The theory of double burden has a longer history that started with the debates on the nineteenth century "new woman." For an accurate debate on this issue, see Duby and Perrot, *History of Women*.

33. "Russian Colonialism in Perspective," *Times* (London), March 13, 1956. Meeting records, Commission on the Status of Women, UN Headquarters, Geneva, March 14, 1956, document E/CN.6/SR.208.

34. Meeting records, Commission on the Status of Women, UN Headquarters, New York, March 24, 1953, document E/CN.6/SR.134.

35. Tyson and Said, "Human Rights," 589–604.

36. It's important to notice that this was on a voluntary basis and that Portugal, for example, rejected to provide details, arguing that the colonies were not separated entities but part of Portugal.

37. Meeting records, Commission on the Status of Women, UN Headquarters, New York, August 30, 1957, document E/CN.6/SR.231.

38. Meeting records, Commission on the Status of Women, UN Headquarters, New York, March 16, 1956, document E/CN.6/SR.212.

39. Meyerowitz, *Not June Cleaver*.

40. Von Eschen, *Race against Empire*; Anderson, *Eyes Off the Prize*.

41. Dudziak, *Cold War Civil Rights*, 13.

42. Meyerowitz, *Not June Cleaver*, 103–27.

43. Dudziak, *Cold War Civil Rights*, 3.

44. Note on expert working to precede seminar in South East Asia, October 29, 1956. United Nations Archives, United Nations Headquarter, New York.

45. United Nations Headquarters, interoffice memorandum, May 18, 1951.

46. Shibusawa "Ideology, Culture."

47. GA Resolution 729, October 23, 1953, A/PV.453.

48. European Office of the United Nations, interoffice memorandum, July 27, 1956. SOA149/07, UN Headquarters, New York.

49. Correspondence between Mary P. Lord, United States representative on the Commission on Human Rights and Egon Schwelb, deputy director, division of human rights, October 5, 1956, SOA149/07, United Nations Archives, New York.

50. Lorenzini, *Global Development*.

51. Burke, *Decolonization and the Evolution*.

52. Hong "Gender, Race, and Utopias," 156–75.

53. Bier, "Feminism, Solidarity and Identity," 143–72.

54. Hong, "Gender, Race, and Utopias," 156–75.

55. Meeting records, Commission on the Status of Women, UN Headquarters, New York, April 1, 1957, document E/CN.6/SR.250.

56. Burke, "Disseminating Discord."

57. Meeting records, Commission on the Status of Women, UN Headquarters, New York, March 30, 1953, document E/CN.6/SR.142.

58. Document E/CN.6/SR.142.

59. Document E/CN.6/SR.142.

60. Commission on the Status of Women, report to the Economic and Social Council, eleventh session, New York, 1957, document E/2968. For Woods's bio, see, Anne O'Brien, "Mary Cecil Tenison Woods (1893–1971)," Australian Dictionary of Bibliography 12 (1990), https://adb.anu.edu.au/biography/tenison -woods-mary-cecil-8772, accessed April 2022.

61. Final Report on Mission to Attend the Ninth Session of the United Nations Commission on the Status of Women. New York, March 14 to April 1, 1955 UNESCO sector, SHS, box 138, status of women, part 1a, 1946–1959.

62. United Nations, 1957 Seminar on the Civic Responsibilities and Increased Participation of Asian Women in Public Life, document ST/TAA/HR1.

63. Document ST/TAA/HR1.

64. Document ST/TAA/HR1 12, 50.

65. Document ST/TAA/HR1 20, 79.

66. Document ST/TAA/HR1 20, 79.

67. Document ST/TAA/HR1, 24, 96.

68. Document ST/TAA/HR1, 24, 97.

69. Document ST/TAA/HR1, 126, 31.

70. Document ST/TAA/HR1, 131, 32.

4. Sacred Trust

1. From the UN photo archive: "Mr. Pedrueza and Dr. Victor Hoo, Assistant Secretary General for the UN Department of Trusteeship, discussing education with the education officers and teachers of the Yola Middle School." UN Digital Photo Collection.

2. Bessire and Nolan, *Todd Webb in Africa*.

3. The photographic book by Bessire and Nolan clearly shows this discrepancy. The brochure is reported at the end of the book, pp. 244–45.

4. United Nations, *A Sacred Trust*.

5. The case of Italy was unique as Italy lost the war but managed to be the Trusteeship administrator for Somalia, one of its colonies.

6. United Nations, *A Sacred Trust*.

7. United Nations Economic and Social Council plenary meeting, February 28, 1947, Lake Success NY, document, E.SR.51–84. The social commission, renamed in 1960 "Commission for Social Development" assisted the ECOSOC with social issues, United Nations Department of Economic and Social Affairs, accessed March 19, 2021. https://www.un.org/development/desa/dspd/united-nations-commission-for-social-development-csocd-social-policy-and-development-division.html. On this topic, see also Limoncelli, *The Politics of Trafficking*.

8. For a thorough account of this topic, see Reanda, "Prostitution as a Human Rights Question," 202–28.

9. Scarry, *The Body in Pain*, 6, 9.

10. Suchland, *Economies of Violence*, 3.

11. According to article 87 of the UN Charter the people of the trust territories could send petitions to the UN and did so in the hundred thousand.

12. The Secretariat's provision shows that in both cases (trust and colonies), the UN considered foreign rule as temporary.

13. Hovet, "Role of Africa," 122–34.

14. Patil, *Negotiating Decolonization*, 28, 29.

15. United Nations, *Yearbook 1946–47*, 78.

16. I use here "imagine" paraphrasing the theory of Benedict Anderson. See Anderson, *Imagined Communities*.

17. United Nations Charter, article 88.

18. Report, first session 1947 and General Assembly resolution 66 (I). Transmission of information under article 73 of the charter, sixty-fourth plenary meeting, December 14, 1946.

19. Burke, *Decolonization and the Evolution*, 52.

20. Commission on the Status of Women Report to the Economic and Social Council, report of the second session 1949, document E/615.

21. See chapter 2 for a detailed analysis of this issue.

22. Burke, *Decolonization and the Evolution*, 52.

23. Burke, *Decolonization and the Evolution*, 52.

24. Meeting records, Commission on the Status of Women, Palais des Nations, Geneva, Switzerland April 2, 1952, document E/CN.6/SR.117.

25. On Lutz's imperial feminist attitudes see also Boris, *Making the Woman Worker*, 60.

26. See, for example, Wilder, *French Imperial Nation-State*.

27. Canon texts on imperial feminism for European colonialism are Burton, *Burdens of History*; and Jayawardena, *White Woman's Other Burden*.

28. Belhabib, "United Nations Trusteeship System," 51.

29. Commission on the Status of Women Report on the Status of Women in Trust Territories, fourth session, April 7, 1950, document E/CN.6/138.

30. Report, E/CN.6/138.

31. Ibhawoh, *Imperialism and Human Rights*.

32. Report, E/CN.6/138.

33. Report, E/CN.6/138.

34. Report, E/CN.6/138.

35. Thomas, *Politics of the Womb*.

36. Comaroff and Comaroff, *Ethnography and the Historical Imagination*.

37. Commission on the Status of Women Report on the Status of Women in Trust Territories, seventh session, January 27, 1953, document E/CN.6/210. On Victorian culture, see Langland, "Nobody's Angels," 290–304.

38. Report, E/CN.6/138.

39. Report, E/CN.6/138.

40. Knop presents this case as the authorities' strictly European interpretation of gender equality. Knop, *Diversity and Self-Determination*, 7.

41. Report, E/CN.6/138.

42. Commission on the Status of Women, Report on the Status of Women in Trust Territories, tenth session, January 10, 1956, document E/CN.6/273.

43. Enloe, *Bananas, Beaches and Bases*.

44. Thomas, *Politics of the Womb*.

45. Rebecca Hourwich Reyher papers, box 34, folder 9, Schlesinger Library, Harvard University, Cambridge MA.

46. My reading of these texts is cautious, as the subaltern voice is not always authentic. However, considering subaltern voices as constructed generates a set of problematic assumptions on the agency of the colonized within the trust system and questions every written source where the balance of power is uneven.

47. Petition T/Pet.5/60–T/Pet.4/32, TCOR, sixth session, annex vol. 2, agenda item 5 (1950). On women in French Cameroon see also Terretta, *Petitioning for Our Rights*.

48. I draw here from political scientist Kumari Jayawardena's popular work on this topic. Jayawardena, *Feminism and Nationalism*.

49. On this issue see, Statement on Human Rights, the Executive Board, American Anthropological Association, *American Anthropologist* 49 (October-December 1947): 539–43.

50. Petition T/Pet.4/2, November 28, 1947, Trusteeship Council Report (TCOR), third session, agenda item 6. Legal scholar Karen Knop analyzes the same petitions and reports that I present here to explore arguments on self-determination and

minority rights. Her work is about the gender and cultural limitations to the international laws on self-determination. Knop, *Diversity and Self-Determination*.

51. T/Pet.4/2, 1947.

52. St. Joan's International Social and Political Alliance, *A Venture in Faith*.

53. Suchland, *Economies of Violence*.

54. Cited by Allman, "Rounding Up Spinsters," 195–214.

55. Thomas, *Politics of the Womb*.

56. Anderson, "Third-World Body," 245–46, cited by Amrith in *Decolonizing International Health*, 9.

57. Bailkin, *Afterlife of Empire*, 135, 136.

58. "U.N. Favors Inquiry of King's 110 Wives: Trusteeship Council Favors," *New York Times*, July 8, 1948.

59. George Barrett, "The Centenarian Fon of Bikom Convinces U.N. Mission That He Needs His 110 Wives," *New York Times*, February 10, 1950.

60. T/Pet.4/38, TCOR, 6th session, annex vol. 2, agenda item 5 (1950).

61. Similar to Mrinalini Sinha's synergic account of Mayo's book on "scandalous" rituals in India, different "experts" treated the issue of this small territory in British Cameroon. See Sinha, *Specters of Mother India*.

62. Reyher, *The Fon*.

63. Reyher, *The Fon*, 117.

64. E/CN.6/138, 1950.

65. Peters and Wolper, *Women's Rights, Human Rights*, 2.

5. Foreign and Local Voices

1. From the UN Media Archive: "As one of its first acts, the 15th regular session of the UN General Assembly, which opened in New York today, unanimously admitted 14 new States to membership in the United Nations. This brings the total number of States members of the UN to 96, almost double its original membership. Here, between meetings, members of the Ghana delegation pose for a photograph. Several of the delegates' wives were also present. Seen, from the left, are: Mr. J. B. Elliott; Mr. J. A. Braimah; Mr. A. C. Kuma; Mrs. Alex Quaison-Sackey; Mr. Krobo Edusei, Minister of Transport and Communications and Minister of State for Ceremonies; Mrs. Krobo Edusei; Mr. Alex Quaison-Sackey, Permanent Representative to the UN; Mrs. Susana El-Hassan MP; Miss A. Christian; and Mrs. E. Abdallah, September 20,1960, United Nations, New York."

2. I am aware of the fact that *mutilation* is a strong and problematic term. I use here FGM only because the term has become recognizable in international policies.

Also, these are the three types of circumcision according to the WHO, "Female genital mutilation is classified into 4 major types. Type 1: this is the partial or total removal of the clitoral glans (the external and visible part of the clitoris, which is a sensitive part of the female genitals), and/or the prepuce/ clitoral hood (the fold of skin surrounding the clitoral glans). Type 2: this is the partial or total removal of the clitoral glans and the labia minora (the inner folds of the vulva), with or without removal of the labia majora (the outer folds of skin of the vulva). Type 3: Also known as infibulation, this is the narrowing of the vaginal opening through the creation of a covering seal. The seal is formed by cutting and repositioning the labia minora, or labia majora, sometimes through stitching, with or without removal of the clitoral prepuce/clitoral hood and glans (Type 1 FGM). Type 4: This includes all other harmful procedures to the female genitalia for non-medical purposes, e.g. pricking, piercing, incising, scraping and cauterizing the genital area. Deinfibulation refers to the practice of cutting open the sealed vaginal opening of a woman who has been infibulated, which is often necessary for improving health and well-being as well as to allow intercourse or to facilitate childbirth." World Health Organization, Female Genital Mutilation, Key Facts (website), accessed June 4, 2020, https://www.who.int/news-room/fact-sheets/detail/female-genital-mutilation.

3. On issues of territoriality and FGM, see Hernlund and Shell-Duncan, *Transcultural Bodies*.

4. Wa Thiong'o, *The River Between*, 30.

5. I contend that the nature of the debate as pro and against, local versus foreigner, is problematic and does not leave space for more nuanced positions.

6. Amrith, *Decolonizing International Health*, 2.

7. Meeting records, Commission on the Status of Women, Lake Success NY, May 10, 1951, document E/CN.6/SR.98.

8. Document E/CN.6/SR.98.

9. Document E/CN.6/SR.98.

10. Document E/CN.6/SR.98.

11. Document E/CN.6/SR.98.

12. Commissioners appealed the Human Rights Commission on the use of the masculine language which, in their opinion, would have prevented women to claim rights on the basis of the covenant. See United Nations Economic and Social Council, Statement of the Representative of the Commission o the Status of Women to the Commission on Human Rights made at the 153rd Meeting on April 11, 1950, and circulated at the request of the Commission, document E/CN.4/418.

13. Meeting records, Commission on the Status of Women, Lake Success NY, May 10, 1951, document E/CN.6/SR.98. UN Depository Collection, Cornell University, Ithaca NY.

14. E/CN.6/SR.98, 1951.

15. Thomas, *Politics of the Womb*, 13.

16. Petition from St. Joan's International Social and Political Alliance Concerning all Trust Territories T/PET.General/22, October 30, 1952.

17. St. Joan's, *A Venture in Faith*.

18. Trusteeship Council Resolution 865 XII. Petitions from St. Joan's International Social and Political Alliance (T/PET.General/22).

19. General Assembly, ninth Session, official records, A/C.3/SR.620, December 14, 1954.

20. I provide more details about Hussein in chaps. 6 and 7.

21. Meeting records, Commission on the Status of Women, Palais des Nations, Geneva, March 21, 1958, document E/CN.6/SR.266.

22. Farley, *Brock Chisholm*, 95.

23. Cueto, Brown, and Fee, *World Health Organization*, 55, 62.

24. Amrith, *Decolonizing International Health*, 12, 17.

25. E/CN.6/SR.266, 1958.

26. E/CN.6/SR.266, 1958.

27. In 1949 the Soviet Union, Ukraine, and Byelorussia withdrew from the WHO. Soon they were followed by Bulgaria, Romania, Albania, Poland, Czechoslovakia, and Hungary. The reason was the WHO's withdrawing aid from Eastern Europe and apparently siding with the United States. The Soviet Union joined again in 1955. See Cueto, Brown, and Fee, *World Health Organization*, 62–63.

28. Emphasis is mine.

29. E/CN.6/SR.266, 1958.

30. E/CN.6/SR.266, 1958.

31. Correspondence between Jessie Street and Minerva Bernardino. ILO, folder ESC-1004–11, International Labour Organization Archives, Geneva.

32. Boddy, "Barbaric Custom and Colonial Science," 60–81. Boddy "The Normal and the Aberrant," 41–69.

33. On Sophie Grinberg-Vinaver's life, see her obituary in the *New York Times*, May 27, 1964.

34. At a later date the UNESCO called itself out when commissioners mentioned further research in the topic. Because of the cultural issue, commissioners could ask the UNESCO to conduct research on FGM, but the UNESCO said a priori that this issue was not within their competency. Rapport sur la 13ème

session de la Commission de la condition de la femme (ONU), le 30 mars 1959. UNESCO Archives, Paris, SHS, box number 138, status of women, part 1 a, from 1946 to 1959, UDC 3–055.2. Translation is mine.

35. Meeting records, Commission on the Status of Women, Palais des Nations, Geneva, March 25, 1958, document E/CN.6/SR.271, UN Depository Collection, Cornell University, Ithaca NY.

36. Hernlund and Shell-Duncan, *Transcultural Bodies*.

37. Economic and Social Council, Ritual Operations 1029th Plenary Meeting, July 10, 1958, resolution 680 b II (26).

38. United Nations, Status of Women in Private Law, Ritual Operations SO-244 (5–4), United Nations Archives, New York, NY. The quotation is in British English.

39. World Health Assembly, May 26, 1959, document A12/P&B/5. WHO Archives, World Health Organization, Geneva, Switzerland.

40. Women's International Network, *In News*, General Information on Female Circumcision, folder M 3/180/8, WHO Archives, Geneva, Switzerland.

41. Women's International Network, *In News*, General Information on Female Circumcision, folder M 3/180/8, WHO Archives, Geneva, Switzerland.

42. International Labour Organization, Registry, Economic and Social Council, Commission on the Status of Women, Buenos Aires, 1960, file ESC, 1004-11-14, ILO Archives, Geneva.

43. Proceedings of the 1960 Seminar on Participation of Women in Public Life, Addis Ababa, December 12–23, 1960, United Nations, New York.

44. Proceedings, Addis Ababa, 1960.

45. International Labour Organization Report on Mission, Joint UN-Government of Ethiopia Regional African Seminar on the Participation of Women in Public Life, file ESC, no. 77–102, ILO Archives, Geneva, Switzerland.

46. "Intellectual Atmosphere Pervades Women's Seminar," *Ethiopian Herald* 2, no. 299 (December 14, 1960).

47. Proceedings, Addis Ababa, 1960.

48. "Intellectual Atmosphere Pervades Women's Seminar," *Ethiopian Herald* 2, no. 299 (December 14, 1960).

49. As stated earlier, Togo was the Togoland Trust Territory, and the state of Cameroon was French Cameroon since the British Cameroon had become part of Nigeria.

50. Proceedings, Addis Ababa, 1960.

51. Proceedings, Addis Ababa, 1960.

52. Proceedings, Addis Ababa, 1960.

53. Proceedings, Addis Ababa, 1960.

54. Proceedings, Addis Ababa, 1960.

55. Pedersen, "National Bodies, Unspeakable Acts."

56. Proceedings, Addis Ababa, 1960.

57. Proceedings, Addis Ababa, 1960.

58. Proceedings, Addis Ababa, 1960.

59. Proceedings, Addis Ababa, 1960.

60. Proceedings, Addis Ababa, 1960.

61. Proceedings, Addis Ababa, 1960.

62. Meeting records, General Assembly Plenary Meeting, A/C.3/SR. 1295, 1965.

6. Bodies in Captivity

1. United Nations, *Proceedings of 1964 Seminar*. In the photo are Mr. Rana Ombri (*standing*), Minister of Social Affairs of Togo; *and left to right*: Mr. Edward Lawson, Deputy Director of the Division of Human Rights, Mrs. Margaret K. Bruce, Chief of Section on the Status of Women, and Mr. Henri Laurentie, Regional Representative of the United Nations Technical Assistance Board and Director of Special Fund Programmes in Togo.

2. United Nations, *Proceedings, Togo Seminar*.

3. For an analysis of polygamy and economics, see Boserup, "The Economics of Polygamy," 25–35.

4. Boserup, *Woman's Role*.

5. United Nations Economic and Social Council, assistance to former Trust Territories and other newly independent states. Thirty-second session, July 4–August 4, 1962, meeting E-SR-1150–1186.

6. UN Charter, articles 1 and 55.

7. On this topic see Badran, *Feminists, Islam, and Nation* and Edwards and Roces, *Women's Suffrage in Asia*.

8. In a 2005 interview, Sir Brian Urquhart, former Undersecretary General of the UN, argued that as a result of colonial takeover, African countries "missed" the Industrial Revolution. Uquart traces a clear path between the presence of foreign rule and the causes of underdevelopment. He claims that from a political point of view, Europeans dismantled native systems to import European institutions while suppressing freedoms and spreading violence. Interview with Sir Brian Urquhart, UN Oral History Project, Ralph Bunche Institute for International Studies, 1999–2010.

9. Hunter, *Political Thought*, 16.

10. Urdang, "Fighting Two Colonialisms," 29–34.

11. Urdang interviewed one of Cabral's close activists, Bweta N'dubi, who denounced the twinning nature of women's struggle, one politicizing all women and the other favoring gender equality promoted by both men and women. Carmen Pereira, member of the ruling party and of the state council, brought about another twinning struggle for women, one against Portuguese colonialism and one against local men. (Urdang, "Fighting Two Colonialisms," 32.) To Pereira personal independence went hand in hand with political independence.

12. Tripp, Casimiro, Kwesiga, and Mungwa, *African Women's Movements*, 235.

13. General Assembly resolution 1710 (XVI), December 19, 1961.

14. Burke, "Disseminating Discord," 589–610.

15. General Assembly resolution 1920 (XVIII), December 5, 1963.

16. Tripp, Casimiro, Kwesiga, and Mungwa, *African Women's Movements*, 236

17. Aerni-Flessner, "Development, Politics," 401–21.

18. Chen et al., *Routledge Handbook*, 236.

19. On the Convention (called CERD), see Baldez, *Defying Convention*, 66. The text of the United Nations Declaration on the Elimination of All Forms of Racial Discrimination is in document A/RES/18/1904, November 20, 1963.

20. Document A/RES/1921 (XIII) December 5, 1963.

21. Interview with Annie Jiagge, *The Rotarian*, February 1968, Rotary International.

22. Summary records, Commission on the Status of Women, eighteenth session, Royal Hilton Hotel, Tehran, March 3, 1965, E/CN.6/SR.416.

23. See Crawford, "Role of the United Nations," 183–84.

24. Chen et al., *Routledge Handbook*, 235.

25. Summary records, Commission on the Status of Women, nineteenth session, Palais des Nations, Geneva, March 2, 1966, E/CN.6/SR.452.

26. Summary records, Commission on the Status of Women, nineteenth session, held at Palais des Nations, Geneva, March 8, 1966, E/CN.6/460.

27. See chapter 5, debate over article 16 of the Universal Declaration of Human Rights by Alba Zizzamia, representative of International Union of Catholic Women's League, meeting records, Commission on the Status of Women, Lake Success NY, May 10, 1951, document E/CN.6/SR.98.

28. There is here a reference to social versus equal feminism, a debate prominent in the United States in previous decades. See chapter 1, note 21.

29. E/CN.6/SR.417. On the debate over protection of women and equality with men, see Cott, "What's in a Name?," 809–29.

30. Summary records, Commission on the Status of Women, nineteenth session, held at Palais des Nations, Geneva, February 28, 1966, E/CN.6/449.

31. Document E/CN.6/449.

32. Economic and Social Council, Report of Commission on the Status of Women, twenty-fourth session, 1972, document E/5109 and E/CN.6/568.

33. Report of twenty-fourth session.

34. Report of twenty-fourth session, para. 134, pp. 41–42. For a biography of Sipilä see "Ms. Helvi Sipilä," UN Women, last modified May 20, 2009, https://www .un.org/womenwatch/daw/news/helvi.html.

35. See chap. 5.

36. Summary records, Commission on the Status of Women, nineteenth session, Palais des Nations, Geneva, March 3, 1966, E/CN.6/SR.454.

37. Johnson and Mcintosh, "Empowering Women, Engendering Change," 249–77.

38. UNESCO, African Women.

39. Document E/CN.6/SR.436.

40. Document E/CN.6/SR.436.

41. General Assembly, Third Committee, 1471st meeting, October 4, 1967, A/C.3/ SR.1471 para. 2, p. 33. The Third Committee records report only the last names of UN delegates.

42. General Assembly, Third Committee, 1471st Meeting, October 4, 1967, A/C.3/ SR.1471 para. 2, p. 33.

43. On Tillett, see McGuire, "'Give Us Peace,'" 887–902.

44. Document A/C.3/SR.1471 para. 33, p. 36.

45. Document A/C.3/SR.1471 para. 48, p. 38.

46. General Assembly, Third Committee, October 2, 1967, A/C.3/SR.1468 para. 29, p. 18. See also Waltz, "Universal Human Rights," 799–844.

47. Summary records, Commission on the Status of Women, twenty-first session, February 2, 1968, document E/CN.6/SR.500.

48. See chap. 6 note 8.

49. On women, slavery, and colonialism, see Campbell, Miers, and Miller, Women and Slavery; for an overview on contemporary slavery, see Miers, Slavery in the Twentieth Century; Engerman, "Slavery at Different Times," 480–84. For a relationship between previous and contemporary forms of slavery, see Dodson, "Slavery," 28–29.

50. In her work on slavery, legal scholar Jean Allain shows how the practice was conflated within other practices close to women's lives, such as marriage. Allain, Slavery in International Law.

51. In the UN documents De Vink's name is listed as J.C.H.H.

52. February 2, 1968, E/CN.6/SR.500.

53. Summary records, Commission on the Status of Women, twenty-first session, February 5, 1968, E/CN.6/SR.501.

54. Document E/CN.6/SR.501.

55. For a general discussion on contemporary slavery in West Africa, see Rossi, *Reconfiguring Slavery*.

56. Summary records, Commission on the Status of Women, twenty-first session, February 5, 1968, UN Headquarters New York, E/CN.6/SR.502.

57. Summary records, Commission on the Status of Women, twenty-first session, February 7, 1968, UN Headquarters New York, E/CN.6/SR.505. On women and apartheid see, Lee, *African Women*; for a closer look of the consequence of apartheid in everyday life, see Ginsburg, *At Home with Apartheid*.

58. For a detailed account of the relationship between Britain and South Africa, see Hyam and Henshaw, *The Lion and the Springbok*. The text of the 1926 Convention on Slavery is available at United Nations Human Rights, Office of the High Commissioner for Human Rights, accessed January 2019, http://www.ohchr.org.

59. See Reddy, "The Struggle against Apartheid," 13, New York, United Nations Office of Public Information.

60. Makeba was married to civil rights activist Stokely Carmichael, so she symbolized the transnational struggle against racism. See Feldstein, *How It Feels*.

61. At the 1985 UN Women's Conference, the U.S. official delegation (led by Maureen Reagan) "threatened to pull out if the issue of apartheid was included in the agenda, insisting that the conference should be limited to discussions of 'women's issues.'" Nnaemeka, *Female Circumcision*, 13.

62. Summary records, Commission on the Status of Women, twenty-first session, February 7, 1968, UN Headquarters New York, E/CN.6/SR.506.

63. Economic and Social Council, Report of the Commission on the Status of Women, sixteenth session, March 19–April 6, 1962, documents E/3606/Rev.1 and E/CN.6/403/Rev.1.

64. Summary records, Commission on the Status of Women, sixteenth session, April 2, 1962, UN Headquarters New York, E/CN.6/SR.378.

65. Summary records, Commission on the Status of Women, sixteenth session, April 2, 1962, UN Headquarters New York, E/CN.6/SR.379.

66. Document E/CN.6/SR.379.

67. Document E/CN.6/SR.378.

68. Relevant texts on this widely discussed issue are Thompson, *Colonial Citizens*; Burton and Allman. "Gender, Colonialism and Feminist Collaboration," 198–222; and Himani, Mojab, and Whitehead, "Of Property and Propriety," 262–71.

69. Mr. K. M. Akude from Ghana is listed as an adviser representing Ghana at the CSW sixteenth session, E/3606/Rev. 1 and E/CN.6/403/Rev. 1.

70. Document E/CN.6/SR.379.

71. Document E/CN.6/SR.382.

72. Document E/CN.6/SR.379.

73. Document E/CN.6/SR.379.

74. A/C.3/SR.1468, p. 18, paragraph 29.

75. Economic and Social Council, report of the Commission on the Status of Women report, twenty-second session, document E/4619 and E/CN.6/527.

7. Reproducing the Nation

1. Seltzer, *Origins and Evolution*, 12.

2. On a discussion on the private sphere, the nation-state, and the UN conferences, see Cook, *Human Rights of Women*.

3. Jayawardena, *Feminism and Nationalism*.

4. Jolly, Transcript of interview.

5. Economic and Social Council, Commission on the Status of Women, report of the twenty-third session, 1970, document E/4831 and E/CN.6/546.

6. Report of the twenty-third session.

7. Summary records, Commission on the Status of Women, twentieth session, February 15, 1967, UN Headquarters New York, E/CN.6/SR.467.

8. E/CN.6/SR.467.

9. E/CN.6/SR.467.

10. For an exhaustive discussion on this topic, see Scott, *The Politics of the Veil*.

11. E/CN.6/SR.467.

12. E/CN.6/SR.467.

13. E/CN.6/SR.467.

14. Summary records, Commission on the Status of Women, twenty-first session, February 12, 1968, UN Headquarters New York, E/CN.6/SR.513.

15. Summary records, Commission on the Status of Women, twenty-first session, February 13, 1968, UN Headquarters New York, E/CN.6/SR.514.

16. For an overview of this issue, see Visvanathan et al., *Women, Gender, and Development*.

17. Visvanathan et al., *Women, Gender, and Development*, 514.

18. Summary records, Commission on the Status of Women, twenty-first session, February 14, 1968, UN Headquarters, New York, E/CN.6/SR.515.

19. E/CN.6/SR.515.

20. E/CN.6/SR.515.

21. E/CN.6/SR.515.

22. Summary records, Commission on the Status of Women, twenty-first session, February 14, 1968, UN Headquarters, New York, E/CN.6/SR.516.

23. E/CN.6/SR.516.

24. Ehrlich, *The Population Bomb*.

25. Seltzer, *Origins and Evolution*, 12.

26. Seltzer, *Origins and Evolution*, 13.

27. Summary records, Commission on the Status of Women, nineteenth Session, Palais des Nations, Geneva, March 3, 1966, E/CN.6/SR.455.

28. Johnson and McIntosh, "Empowering Women, Engendering Change," 264–66.

29. E/CN.6/SR.455. After 1975, the Vatican also got involved in this issue. See, Desmazières, "Women's Identities," 74–98.

30. Proclamation of Tehran, April 22 to May 13, 1968, UN Doc. A/CONF. 32/41.

31. Summary records, Commission on the Status of Women, twenty-first session, February 15, 1968, UN Headquarters, New York, E/CN.6/SR.518.

32. E/CN.6/SR.518.

33. As historian Katherine Marino shows, 1930s Latin American feminists advocated for reproductive rights including access to contraception and abortion. Marino, *Feminism for the Americas*, 13.

34. Report, twenty-first session.

35. February 7, 1960, from Bruce Turner, assistant secretary general, controller, office of the controller to March Schreiber, director, division of human rights, United Nations Archives, SO-244 (18).

36. Helvi Sipilä to Margaret Bruce, May 3, 1969, United Nations Archives, New York, SO-244 (18)

37. Economic and Social Council, Commission on the Status of Women, report of the twenty-third session, 1970, document E/4831 and E/CN.6/546.

38. Report of the twenty-third session.

39. Report of the twenty-fourth session.

40. Michel Gallin-Douathe, government representative of the Republique Centrafricaine, to UN Secretary, May 14, 1969. United Nations Archives, New York, SO-244–18.

41. Report by the Society of Gynecology and Obstetrics of Nigeria, December 19, 1968, United Nations Archive, SO-244–18.

42. COM/MC3/4171/1/185 October 28, 1971, To: Mr. A. Obligado, assistant director-general for communication through Mr. Gunnar R. Naeseelund, director, MC, from: Kanwar B. Mathur, MCE. UNESCO Archives, Paris.

43. For a general story of UNESCO, see Duedahl, *A History of UNESCO*.

44. Memo/DASS/74/MOC/107 January 4, 1974, To: Mrs. M.P. Herzog, Director HR, From: Marion O. Callaghan, DASS, Subject: Premier avant-projet de rapport du Rapporteur spécial sur la condition de la femme et la planification familiale. Ref. Memo/HR/73/320 of December 19, 1973, UNESCO Archives, Paris.

45. From here until the end of the analysis of the UNESCO's response to Sipilä's report, instead of repeating the name of the author of the report, I simply say UNESCO to highlight how this represented the official line of this organization.

46. Memo/DASS/74/MOC/107.

47. Letter To: Mr. A. M. M'Bow, ADG/ED, From: Miss Y. Zharan, Ep/EEO— Subject: Participation at the twenty-fifth session of the Commission on the Status of Women, January 14/February 1, 1974. UNESCO Archives, Paris. The first name of Zharan is unspecified in the records.

48. On the conflict between the CSW and ILO, see Boris, "Equality's Cold War," 101.

49. UN International forum on the role of women in population and development, Virginia, May 2–January 3, 1974, folder P 13/86/49, WHO Archives, Geneva.

50. Folder P 13/86/49, UN International forum on the role of women in population and development.

51. Zinsser, "From Mexico to Copenhagen," 139–68. Olcott, *International Women's Year*.

Epilogue

1. Adichie, "The Danger."

2. The G77 consisted (and still consists) of countries from the Global South that promoted collaboration in matters of development as well as more voting power for postcolonial countries. Baldez, *Defying Convention*, 75.

3. Kathleen Teltsch, "South Africa Is Suspended By U.N. Assembly, 91–22," *New York Times*, November 13, 1974.

4. Baldez, *Defying Convention*, 82.

5. Spivak, "'Woman' as Theatre."

6. Charlesworth and Chinkin, "New United Nations," 1–60.

7. This is a common issue as women delegates at the UN are in general highly educated and part of the elite, whether from the Global South or North.

8. Historian Lynn Hunt has historicized the Freudian construct of "family romance" in her account of the French Revolution. See Hunt, *Family Romance*. Historian Françoise Vergès has used the same theory in colonial history. See Vergès, *Monsters and Revolutionaries*.

9. Olcott, *International Women's Year*, 73.

10. On the shift between women's rights and women's human rights as developed in the context of the Vienna Conference (1993), see Reilly, *Women's Human Rights*.

11. See Dhamoon, "A Feminist Approach."

12. See, for example, Stoler, *Carnal Knowledge*.

13. I looked only at a few aspects of violence; I want to acknowledge that armed conflicts, refugee camps, dispossession, economic exploitation, and ecological disasters are part of a history of violence against women but not the focus on this monograph.

14. Traditional practices affecting the health of women and children. Report of the seminar, Khartoum, February 10–15, 1979, WHO Archives, Geneva.

Bibliography

Archives and Manuscript Materials

Reyher, Rebecca Hourwich. Papers. Arthur and Elizabeth Schlesinger Library. Harvard University

UN Commission on the Status of Women. Summery Records, 1947–75. Cornell University Library, Ithaca, New York.

General Assembly. Third Committee Records, 1952–74 (bound volumes). Cornell University Library, Ithaca, New York.

General Assembly. Fourth Committee Records, 1950–60 (bound volumes). Cornell University Library, Ithaca, New York.

UN Trusteeship Council. Petitions and Visiting Missions, 1950–60 (bound volumes). Cornell University Library, Ithaca, New York.

Reports to ECOSOC, 1947–75. Dag Hammarskjöld Library. United Nations. New York. Economic and Social Council Meeting Records, 1946–75. Dag Hammarskjöld Library. United Nations, New York.

United Nations. *Proceedings of 1964 Seminar on the Status of Women in Family Law, Lomé, Togo, 18 to 31 August 1964*. New York: United Nations, 1965. Dag Hammarskjöld Library. United Nations, New York. The UN documents are recognizable through the UN symbol system, for more information see https://research.un.org/en/docs/symbols.

International Labor Organization Archives, Geneva, Switzerland

Economic and Social Council (ECOSOC) / Commission on the Status of Women

General, ESC 1004–11.

1st Session, Lake Success, ESC 1004/11/1M.T.

6th Session 1952, ESC 1004-11-6.

7th session, 1953, ESC 1004-11-7.

8th session, 1954, ESC 1004-11-8.

10th session, 1956, ESC 1004-11-10.

11th session, 1957, ESC 1004-11-11.

12th Session, 1958, ESC 1004-11-12.

13th session, 1959, ESC 1004-11-13.

14th session, 1960 ESC 1004-11-14.

18th Session. Item 3: Economic Development of Undeveloped Countries, ESC 1000-18-3.

United Nations. Joint UN-Government of Ethiopia Regional African Seminar on the Participation of Women in Public Life. Addis Ababa, December 12, 1960, ESC 77–102.

Seminar on the Status of Women in Family Law for Participants from African Countries, August 31, 1964, ESC 77–107.

Newsletter on the Status of Women, ESC 1004–01.

UNESCO Archives, Paris

SHS, 138, Status of Women, 1 a, 1946 to 1959, 1 b, 1959–1961, 2, 1962–1977.

SHS, 167, International Women's Year and Communication for Family Planning, 1, 1974–1975.

SHS, 174, Status of Women, Coordination with UN and Specialized Agencies, 1, 2, 1965–1970.

SHS, 177, UN Commission on the Status of Women, 1947–1951, 1951–1958.

SHS, 178, UN Commission on the Status of Women, 1958–1964, 1964–1970, 1971–1976.

United Nations Archives, New York City

Central Registry Section, Non-Governmental Organizations

S-0441-0039-08. Organization International Union of Catholic Women's League and Consultative Status.

S-0441-0016-08. Organization and Consultative Status—Women's International Democratic Federation.

S-0441–0728, 29, 30, 31, 32. Volume 2, Status of Women, 1948–54, RAG/02/149–04, 05, 06, 07, 08.

Commission on the Status of Women

14190, FF1B-RO02-SU04, Age of Marriage, Consent to Marriage and Registration of Marriage.

14273, FF1B-RO02-SU04, Status of Women, Convention and Arguments, Convention on the Nationality of Married Women.

14237, FF1B-RO02-SU04, Status of Women, Political Rights of Women.

14175, FF1B-RO02-SU04, Measures Taken on the Implementation of the Provisions of the Convention on the Political Rights of Women.

14078, 84, 88, 93, 100, 108, 114, 120, 125, 141, 146, 151, 156, 162, 165, 166, 169, 173, 188, FF1B-RO02-SU04, Commission on the Status of Women, Sessions 11th to 23rd, 1956 to 1969.

14193, FF1B-R002-SU04, Status of Women in Private Law, Ritual Operations.

14216, FF1B-R002-SU04, Status of Women in Trust Territories and Non-Self-Governing Territories,1957 to 1965.

14227, FF1B-R002-SU04, Report on the Relationship of Family Planning and the Status of Women.

Reports on Women on the Trust Territories, 1950–1965.

Department of Economic Affairs

S-0991-0006-14. Central Registry Section Economic and Social Council Secretariat—Status of Women (biographies).

S-0991-0006-13 S-0441-0015-07. Central Registry Section, Economic and Social Council Secretariat—Status of Women.

Department of Social Affairs, Human Rights Division

S-0916-0004-0027. Miscellaneous—Human Rights—Sub-Committee on the Status of Women—1st Session, New York, May 1946—composition, invitations.

S-0916-0004-0022. Miscellaneous—Status of Women—correspondence (general)—commissions.

S-0916-0004-0021. Miscellaneous—Status of Women—representation to meetings.

S-0916-0004-0020. Miscellaneous—Status of Women—commissions—arrangements—constitution.

S-0916-0004-0023. Miscellaneous—Committee on Status of Women—New York.

Department of Technical Cooperation for Development, Population Programmes

S-0128-0003-07 & 08. Status of women and family planning,

S-0445-0133-02, 05, 07, Implementation of the Declaration on the Elimination of Discrimination against Women, 01/01/1968–31/12/1969.

Institute for Training and Research (UNITAR)

S-0369-0036-02. #453 Speeches—Commission on Status of Women, Acc. 92/03.

World Health Organization Archives, Geneva, Switzerland

Programme on the Participation of Women in Health and Development, July 1976–77, W 6/370/1.

Meetings on the Commission on the Status of Women, 1968–1983, W 6/86/15.

UN Inter-Regional Meeting of Experts on Integration of Women in Development, New York, June 1972, N 64/86/55.

UN/Economic Commissions Regional Meeting on the Integration of Women in Development, with Special Reference to Population Factors, P 13/86/54.

UN International Forum on the Role of Women in Population and Development, Virginia, 1974 P 13/83/49.

Collaboration with the Commission on the Status of Women in the Field of Family Planning, P 13/372/4.

ECA Meetings of High-Level Officials of the United Nations and Other Inter-governmental Organizations with Special Responsibility for Development Programmes in the African Region, N 72/86/20

UN World-Wide Seminars on the Status of Women and Family Planning, P 13/440/22.

General Information on Female Circumcision, 1975, M 3/180/8.

Online Sources

Charter of the United Nations: http://www.un.org/en/documents/charter/.

Department of International Law, Organization of American States, Inter-American Convention on the Granting of Civil Rights to Women (The Bogota Convention), Washington DC, 1948, http://www.oas.org/juridico/english/sigs/a-44.html.

The Universal Declaration of Human Rights: http://www.un.org/en/documents /udhr/.

General Assembly Resolutions, 1946–75: http://www.un.org/documents/resga.htm.

United Nations Yearbooks: http://unyearbook.un.org.

"The United Nations and Decolonization": http://www.un.org/en/decolonization /nonselfgov.shtml.

United Nations Digital Archive: https://www.unmultimedia.org/photo/

Published Works

Adami, Rebecca. *Human Rights Learning: The Significance of Narratives, Relation-ality and Uniqueness.* Stockholm: Department of Education, Stockholm University, 2014.

——. *Women and the Universal Declaration of Human Rights.* New York: Routledge, 2019.

Adami, Rebecca, and Daniel Plesch, eds. *Women and the UN: A New History of Women's International Human Rights.* New York: Routledge, 2021.

Adichie, Ngozi Chimamanda. "The Danger of a Single Story." Technology, Entertainment, Design Global Conference (TED Global), July 21–24, 2009, Oxford, UK. http://www.ted.com/talks/chimamanda_adichie_the_danger_of_a _single_story.

Aerni-Flessner, John. "Development, Politics, and the Centralization of State Power in Lesotho, 1960–75." *Journal of African History* 55, no. 3 (2014): 401–21.

Åkermark, Athanasia Spiliopoulou. *Justifications of Minority Protection in International Law*. London: Kluwer Law International, 1996.

Allain, Jean. *Slavery in International Law: Of Human Exploitation and Trafficking*. Leiden: Martinus Nijhoff, 2013.

Allman, Jean Marie. "Rounding Up Spinsters: Gender Chaos and Unmarried Women in Colonial Asante." *Journal of African History* 37 (1996): 195–214.

Alloula, Malek. *The Colonial Harem*. Minneapolis: University of Minnesota Press, 1989.

Amos, Valerie, and Pratibha Parmar. "Challenging Imperial Feminism." *Feminist Review* 17 (1984): 3–19.

Amrith, Sunil S. *Decolonizing International Health: India and Southeast Asia, 1930–65*. Basingstoke, UK: Palgrave Macmillan, 2006.

Amrith, Sunil S., and Glenda Sluga. "New Histories of the United Nations." *Journal of World History* 19, no. 3 (2008): 251–74.

Anderson, Benedict. *Imagined Communities: Reflections on the Origin and Spread of Nationalism*. London: Verso, 2000.

Anderson, Carol. *Eyes Off the Prize: The United Nations and the African American Struggle for Human Rights, 1944–1955*. Cambridge, UK: Cambridge University Press, 2003.

Anderson, Warwick. "The Third-World Body." In *Medicine in the Twentieth Century*, edited by Roger Cooter and John Pickstone, 245–46. Amsterdam: Harwood Academic Publishers, 2000. Cited by Sunil Amrith, *Decolonizing International Health: India and Southeast Asia, 1930–65*. London, UK: Palgrave Macmillan, 2006, 9.

Arias, Arturo, and David Stoll. *The Rigoberta Menchú Controversy*. Minneapolis: University of Minnesota Press, 2001.

Autio, Sari, and Katalin Miklóssy, eds. *Reassessing Cold War Europe*. Milton Park, Abingdon, Oxfordshire: Routledge, 2011.

Badran, Margot. *Feminists, Islam, and Nation: Gender and the Making of Modern Egypt*. Princeton: Princeton University Press, 1999.

Baehr, Amy, ed. "Feminist Politics and Feminist Pluralism: Can We Do Feminist Political Theory Without Theories of Gender?" *Journal of Political Philosophy* 12, no. 4 (2004): 411–36.

———. *Varieties of Feminist Liberalism*. Lanham MD: Rowman and Littlefield, 2004.

Bailkin, Jordanna. *The Afterlife of Empire*. Berkeley: University of California Press, 2012.

Bair, Nadya. *The Decisive Network: Magnum Photos and the Postwar Image Market*. Berkeley: University of California Press, 2020.

Baldez, Lisa. *Defying Convention: US Resistance to the U.N. Treaty on Women's Rights*. Cambridge, UK: Cambridge University Press, 2014.

Barker, Ernest, and Gerard Hopkins, eds. *Social Contract: Essays by Locke, Hume and Rousseau*. London: Oxford University Press, 1947.

Baron, Ava, and Eileen Boris. "'The Body' as a Useful Category for History Working-Class History." *Labor: Studies in Working-Class History of the Americas* 4, no. 2 (2007): 23–43.

Beauvoir, Simone de, Constance Borde, and Sheila Malovany-Chevallier. *The Second Sex*. New York: Vintage, 2012. Originally published 1949.

Beauvoir, Simone de, Constance Borde, Sheila Malovany-Chevallier, and Sheila Rowbotham. *The Second Sex*. London: Vintage, 2012. Originally published 1949.

Behdad, Ali, and Luke Gartlan, eds. *Photography's Orientalism: New Essays on Colonial Representation*. Los Angeles: Getty Research Institute, 2013.

Belhabib, Cherifa. "The United Nations Trusteeship System, 1945–1961." PhD diss., University of Cincinnati, 1991.

Berkovitch, Nitza. *From Motherhood to Citizenship: Women's Rights and International Organizations*. Baltimore: Johns Hopkins University Press, 1999.

Bernardino, Minerva. *Lucha, Agonia Y Esperanza: Trajectoria triunfal de mi vida*. Santo Domingo: Republica Domenicana, 1993.

Bessire, Aimée, and Erin Hyde Nolan. *Todd Webb in Africa: Outside the Frame*. London: Thames & Hudson, 2021.

Bier, Laura. "Feminism, Solidarity, and Identity in the Age of Bandung: Third World Women in the Egyptian Women's Press." In *Making a World after Empire: The Bandung Moment and Its Political Afterlives*, edited by Christopher J. Lee, 143–72. Athens: Ohio University Press, 2010.

Blain, Keisha, and Tiffany Gill, eds. *To Turn the Whole World Over: Black Women and Internationalism*. Champaign: University of Illinois Press, 2019.

Bobo, Lawrence D., Lisa Crooms-Robinson, Linda Darling-Hammond, Michael C. Dawson. " American Conundrum: Race, Sociology, and the African American Road to Citizenship." In *The Oxford Handbook of African American Citizenship, 1865–Present*, edited by Henry Louis Gates Jr., Gerald Jaynes, and Claude Steele. New York: Oxford University Press, 2012.

Boddy, Janice. "Barbaric Custom and Colonial Science: Teaching the Female Body in the Anglo-Egyptian Sudan." *Social Analysis: The International Journal of Social and Cultural Practice* 47, no. 2 (2003): 60–81.

———. "The Normal and the Aberrant in Female Genital Cutting: Shifting Paradigms." *Hau: Journal of Ethnographic Theory* 6, no. 2 (2016): 41–69.

Boris, Eileen. "Equality's Cold War: The ILO and the UN Commission on the Status of Women, 1946–1970s." In *Women's ILO: Transnational Networks, Global*

Labour Standards, and Gender Equity, 1919 to Present, edited by Eileen Boris, Dorothea Hoehtker, and Susan Zimmermann, 97–120. Leiden: Brill, 2018.

——. *Making the Woman Worker: Precarious Labor and the Fight for Global Standards, 1919–2019*. Oxford: Oxford University Press, 2019.

Boris, Eileen, Dorothea Hoehtker, and Susan Zimmermann, eds. *Women's ILO: Transnational Networks, Global Labour Standards, and Gender Equity, 1919 to Present*. Leiden: Brill, 2018.

Boserup, Ester. "The Economics of Polygamy." In *Woman's Role in Economic Development*, edited by Ester Boserup, Nazneen Kanji, Su Fei Tan, and Camilla Toulmin, 37–50. London: Earthscan, 2007.

——. *Woman's Role in Economic Development*. London: George Allen and Unwin, 1970.

Brown, Sarah. "Feminism, International Theory, and International Relations of Gender Inequality." *Millennium—Journal of International Studies* 17 (1988): 461–75.

Burgers, Jan Herman. "The Road to San Francisco: The Revival of the Human Rights Idea in the Twentieth Century." *Human Rights Quarterly* 14 (1992): 447–77.

Burke, Roland. *Decolonization and the Evolution of International Human Rights*. Philadelphia: University of Pennsylvania Press, 2010.

——. "Disseminating Discord and Discovering the World: UN Advisory Services on Human Rights and the Illusory Faith in Specialist Knowledge." *International Journal of Human Rights* 21, no. 5 (2017): 589–610.

Burton, Antoinette. *Burdens of History British Feminists, Indian Women, and Imperial Culture, 1865–1915*. Chapel Hill: University of North Carolina Press, 1994.

Burton, Antoinette, and Jean Allman. "Gender, Colonialism and Feminist Collaboration." *Radical History Review* 101 (2008): 198–222.

Callahan, Michael D. *Mandates and Empire: The League of Nations and Africa, 1914–1931*. Brighton, UK: Sussex Academic Press, 1999.

Campbell, Gwyn, Suzanne Miers, and Joseph Calder Miller. *Women and Slavery*. Athens: Ohio University Press, 2007.

Campt, Tina M. *Listening to Images*. Durham NC: Duke University Press, 2017.

Canning, Kathleen. "The Body as Method? Reflections on the Place of the Body in Gender History." *Gender & History* 11, no. 3 (1999): 499–513.

Castledine, Jacqueline L. *Cold War Progressives: Women's Interracial Organizing for Peace and Freedom*. Champaign: University of Illinois Press, 2012.

Cede, Franz, and Lilly Sucharipa-Behrmann. *The United Nations Law and Practice*. The Hague: Kluwer Law International, 2001.

Charlesworth, Hilary, and Christine Chinkin. "The New United Nations 'Gender Architecture': A Room with a View?" In *Max Planck Yearbook of United Nations Law*, vol. 17, edited by A. von Bogdandy and R. Wolfrum, 2013.

Chen, Jian, Martin Klimke, Masha Kirasirova, Mary Nolan, Marilyn Young, and Joanna Waley-Cohen. *The Routledge Handbook of the Global Sixties: Between Protest and Nation-Building*. New York: Routledge, 2018.

Cobble, Dorothy S. *The Other Women's Movement: Workplace Justice and Social Rights in Modern America*. Princeton NJ: Princeton University Press, 2011.

Cobble, Dorothy Sue, Linda Gordon, and Astrid Henry. *Feminism Unfinished: A Short, Surprising History of American Women's Movements*. New York: Liveright, 2015.

Collins, Patricia Hill. *Black Feminist Thought: Knowledge, Consciousness, and the Politics of Empowerment*. New York: Routledge, 2000.

Coltheart, Lenore. "Citizens of the World: Jessie Street and International Feminism." *Hecate* 21, no. 1 (2005): 182–94.

Comaroff, John L., and Jean Comaroff. *Ethnography and the Historical Imagination*. Boulder: Westview, 1992.

Cook, Rebecca J., ed. *Human Rights of Women: National and International Perspectives*. Philadelphia: University of Pennsylvania Press, 1994.

Cooper, Frederick. *Africa Since 1940: The Past of the Present*. Cambridge, UK: Cambridge University Press, 2002.

———. *Colonialism in Question: Theory, Knowledge, History*. Berkeley: University of California Press, 2005.

Cott, Nancy. "What's in a Name? The Limits of 'Social Feminism' or Expanding the Vocabulary of Women's History." *Journal of American History* 76, no. 3 (1989): 809–29.

Crawford, James. "The Role of the United Nations in International Legislation by Hanna Bokor-Szegö." *British Yearbook of International Law* 50, no. 1 (1979): 183–84.

Cronin, Bruce. "The Two Faces of the UN. The Tension between Intergovernmentalism and Transnationalism." *Global Governance: A Review of Multilateralism and International Organizations* 8, no. 1 (2002): 53–71.

Cueto, Marcos, Theodore M. Brown, and Elizabeth Fee. *The World Health Organization: A History*. Cambridge, UK: Cambridge University Press, 2019.

Davin, Anna. "Imperialism and Motherhood." *History Workshop Journal* 5 (1978): 9–66.

De Haan, Francisca. "Continuing Cold War Paradigms in Western Historiography of Transnational Women's Organisations: The Case of the Women's International Democratic Federation (WIDF)." *Women's History Review* 19, no. 4 (2010): 547–73.

Dekkers, Wim, Cor Hoffer, and Jean-Pierre Wils. "Scientific Contribution Bodily Integrity and male and female circumcision." *Medicine, Health Care and Philosophy* 8 (2005): 179–91.

Desmazières, Agnès. "Negotiating Religious and Women's Identities: Catholic Women at the UN World Conferences, 1975–1995." *Journal of Women's History* 24, no. 4 (2012): 74–98.

Dhamoon, Rita. "A Feminist Approach to Decolonizing Anti-Racism: Rethinking Transnationalism, Intersectionality, and Settler Colonialism." *Feral Feminisms* 4 (2015): 20–37.

Dodson, Howard. "Slavery in the Twenty-First Century." *UN Chronicle* 42, no. 3, (2005): 28–29.

Donnelly, Jack. *Universal Human Rights in Theory and Practice.* Ithaca NY: Cornell University Press, 2003.

Douglas, R. M., Michael D. Callahan, and Elizabeth Bishop, eds. *Imperialism on Trial: International Oversight of Colonial Rule in Historical Perspective.* Lanham MD: Lexington Books, 2006.

DuBois, Ellen, and Lauren Derby. "The Strange Case of Minerva Bernardino: Pan American and United Nations Women's Right Activist." *Women's Studies International Forum* 32, no. 1 (2009): 43–50.

Duby, Georges, and Michelle Perrot, eds. *History of Women in the West.* Cambridge MA: Harvard University Press, 1993.

Dudziak, Mary L. *Cold War Civil Rights: Race and the Image of American Democracy.* Princeton NJ: Princeton University Press, 2000.

Duedahl, Paul, ed. *A History of UNESCO: Global Actions and Impacts.* London: Palgrave Macmillan, 2016.

Dunstan, Sarah C. "'Une Nègre de Drame': Jane Vialle and the Politics of Representation in Colonial Reform, 1945–1953." *Journal of Contemporary History* 55, no. 3 (2020): 645–65.Edgar, Adrienne. "Bolshevism, Patriarchy, and the Nation: The Soviet 'Emancipation' of Muslim Women in Pan-Islamic Perspective." *Slavic Review* (2006): 252–72.

Edwards, Louise, and Mina Roces, eds.*Women's Suffrage in Asia: Gender, Nationalism and Democracy.* London: Routledge, 2004.

Ehrlich, Paul R. *The Population Bomb.* New York: Ballantine, 1968.

Elshtain, Jean Bethke. *Women and War.* New York: Basic, 1987.

Engerman, Stanley. "Slavery at Different Times and Places." *American Historical Review* 105, no. 2 (2000): 480–84.

Engle, Karen. "After the Collapse of the Public-Private Distinction: Strategizing Women's Rights." In *Reconceiving Reality: Women and International Law,* edited by Dorinda Dollmeyer, 143–56. Washington DC: American Society of International Law, 1993.

Enloe, Cynthia H. *Bananas, Beaches and Bases: Making Feminist Sense of International Politics.* Berkeley: University of California Press, 2000.

Fagan, Andrew. *Human Rights: Confronting Myths and Misunderstandings.* Cheltenham, UK: Edward Elgar, 2009.

Farley, John. *Brock Chisholm, the World Health Organization, and the Cold War.* Vancouver: University of British Columbia Press, 2008.

Federici, Silvia. *Beyond the Periphery of the Skin: Rethinking, Remaking, and Reclaiming the Body in Contemporary Capitalism.* Oakland CA: PM, 2020.

Feldstein, Ruth. *How It Feels to Be Free: Black Women Entertainers and the Civil Rights Movement.* Oxford NY: Oxford University Press, 2013.

Ferree, Myra Marx, and Aili Mari Tripp, eds. *Global Feminism: Transnational Women's Activism, Organizing, and Human Rights.* New York: New York University Press, 2006.

Fitzpatrick, Sheila. *Tear Off the Masks!: Identity and Imposture in Twentieth-Century Russia.* Princeton NJ: Princeton University Press, 2005.

Forsythe, David P., Patrice C. McMahon, and Andrew Hall Wedeman, eds. *American Foreign Policy in a Globalized World.* New York: Routledge, 2006.

François, Dominique. *Femmes tondues: La diabolisation de la femme en 1944; Les bûchers de la Libération.* Coudray-Macouard, France: Cheminements, 2006.

Fraser, Arvonne S. "Becoming Human: The Origins and Development of Women's Human Rights." *Human Rights Quarterly* (1999): 853–906.

Furedi, Frank. *The Silent War: Imperialism and the Changing Perception of Race.* New Brunswick NJ: Rutgers University Press, 1999.

Galey, Margaret E. "Women Find a Place." In *Women, Politics, and the United Nations,* edited by Ann Winslow, 11–28. Westport CT: Greenwood, 1995.

Gallagher, Catherine, and Thomas Walter Laqueur, eds. *The Making of the Modern Body: Sexuality and Society in the Nineteenth Century.* Berkeley: University of California Press, 1987.

Gallagher, John, and Ronald Robinson. "The Imperialism of Free Trade." *Economic History Review* 6, no. 1 (1953): 1–15.

Garner, Karen. *Shaping a Global Women's Agenda: Women's NGOs and Global Governance, 1925–85.* Manchester, UK: Manchester University Press, 2010.

Ghodsee, Kristen. "Revisiting the United Nations Decade for Women: Brief Reflections on Feminism, Capitalism and Cold War Politics in the Early Years of the International Women's Movement." *Women's Studies International Forum* 33, no. 1 (2010): 3–12.

Gildersleeve, Virginia C.*Many a Good Crusade*. New York: Arno, 1980.

Gill, Tiffany, and Keisha Blain, eds.*To Turn the Whole World Over: Black Women and Internationalism*. Champaign: University of Illinois Press, 2019.

Ginat, Rami. *Egypt's Incomplete Revolution: Lutfi Al-Khuli and Nasser's Socialism in the 1960s*. London: Frank Cass, 1997.

Ginsburg, Rebecca. *At Home with Apartheid: The Hidden Landscapes of Domestic Service in Johannesburg*. Charlottesville: University of Virginia Press, 2011.

Goedde, Petra. *The Politics of Peace: A Global Cold War History*. Oxford: Oxford University Press, 2019.

Goldschmidt, Arthur, Amy J. Johnson, and Barak A. Salmoni, eds. *Re-Envisioning Egypt 1919–1952*. Cairo: American University in Cairo Press, 2005.

Goodhart, Michael. "Origins and Universality in the Human Rights Debates: Cultural Essentialism and the Challenge of Globalization." *Human Rights Quarterly* 25, no. 4 (2003): 935–64.

Gorman, Daniel. "Britain, India, and the United Nations: Colonialism and the Development of International Governance, 1945–1960."*Journal of Global History* 9, no. 3 (2014): 471–90.

Gorshenin Konstantin Petrovich. *Soviet Women Enjoy Equal Civil Rights with Men: Report to Equality of Women in the U.R.S.S., a Seminar of the Commission on the Status of Women, U.N. Economic and Social Council*. Moscow, Russia: Foreign Language, 1957.

Grewal, Inderpal, and Caren Kaplan. *Scattered Hegemonies: Postmodernity and Transnational Feminist Practices*. Minneapolis: University of Minnesota Press, 1994.

Grosz, Elizabeth. *Volatile Bodies: Towards a Corporeal Feminism*. Bloomington: Indiana University Press.

Guerry, Linda, and Ethan Rundell. "Married Women's Nationality in the International Context (1918–1935)."*Clio* 43 (2016): 73–94.Hartmann, Betsy. *Reproductive Rights and Wrongs: The Global Politics of Population Control*. Boston: South End, 1995.

Hernlund, Ylva, and Bettina Shell-Duncan, eds. *Transcultural Bodies: Female Genital Cutting in Global Context*. New Brunswick NJ: Rutgers University Press, 2007.

Herzog, Dagmar. *Sexuality in Europe: A Twentieth-Century History*. Cambridge, UK: Cambridge University Press, 2011.

Hesford, Wendy S., and Wendy Kozol, eds.*Just Advocacy?: Women's Human Rights, Transnational Feminisms, and the Politics of Representation*. New Brunswick NJ: Rutgers University Press, 2005.

Higonnet, Margaret Randolph, Jane Jenson, Sonya Michel, and Margaret Collins Weitz, eds. *Behind the Lines: Gender and the Two World Wars*. New Haven CT: Yale University Press, 1987.

Himani, Bannerji, Shahrzad Mojab, and Judith Whitehead. "Of Property and Propriety: The Role of Gender and Class in Imperialism and Nationalism: A Decade Later." *Comparative Studies of South Asia, Africa and the Middle East* 30, no. 2 (2010): 262–71.

Hirschmann, Nancy J., and Kirstie Morna McClure, eds. *Feminist Interpretations of John Locke.* University Park: Pennsylvania State University Press, 2007.

Hoffmann, Stefan-Ludwig, ed. *Human Rights in the Twentieth Century: A Critical History* Cambridge, UK: Cambridge University Press, 2011.

Hoganson, Kristin L. "'As Badly Off As the Filipinos': U.S. Women's Suffragists and the Imperial Issue at the Turn of the Twentieth Century." *Journal of Women's History* 13, no. 2 (2001): 9–33.

Hong, Young-Sun. "Gender, Race, and Utopias of Development." In *Women and Gender in Postwar Europe: From Cold War to European Union,* edited by Joanna Regulska and Bonnie G. Smith, 156–75. London: Routledge, 2012.

Hovet, Thomas, Jr. "The Role of Africa in the United Nations." *Annals of the American Academy of Political and Social Science* 354 (1964): 122–34.

Hunt, Lynn A. *The Family Romance of the French Revolution.* Berkeley: University of California Press, 1993.

Hunter, Emma. *Political Thought and the Public Sphere in Tanzania: Freedom, Democracy and Citizenship in the Era of Decolonization.* Cambridge, UK: Cambridge University Press, 2017.

Hyam, Ronald, and Peter Henshaw. *The Lion and the Springbok: Britain and South Africa Since the Boer War.* Cambridge, UK: Cambridge University Press, 2003.

Ibhawoh, Bonny. *Imperialism and Human Rights: Colonial Discourses of Rights and Liberties in African History.* Albany: State University of New York Press, 2007.

Ilic, Melanie. "Soviet Women, Cultural Exchanges and the Women's International Democratic Federation." In *Reassessing Cold War Europe,* edited by Sari Autio and Katalin Miklossy, 157–74. London: Routledge, 2011.

Immerman, Richard, and Petra Goedde, eds. *The Oxford Handbook of the Cold War.* Oxford, UK: Oxford University Press, 2013.

Iriye, Akira. *Global Community: The Role of International Organizations in the Making of the Contemporary World.* Berkeley: University of California Press, 2002.

Jain, Devaki. *Women, Development, and the UN: A Sixty-Year Quest for Equality and Justice.* Bloomington: Indiana University Press, 2005.

Jayawardena, Kumari. *Feminism and Nationalism in the Third World.* New Delhi: Kali for Women, 1986.

———. *The White Woman's Other Burden: Western Women and South Asia during British Rule.* London: Rutledge, 1995.

Jensen, Kimberly, and Erika A. Kuhlman, eds. *Women and Transnational Activism in Historical Perspective*. Dordrecht, Netherlands: Republic of Letters, 2010.

Jensen, Steven L. B. *The Making of International Human Rights: The 1960s, Decolonization, and the Reconstruction of Global Values*. Cambridge, UK: Cambridge University Press, 2016.

Johnson, Amy J., and Scott David Mcintosh. "Empowering Women, Engendering Change: Aziza Hussein and Social Reform in Egypt." In *Re-Envisioning Egypt 1919–1952*, edited by Arthur Goldschmidt, Amy J. Johnson, and Barak A. Salmoni, 249–77. Cairo: American University in Cairo Press, 2005.

Jolly, Richard. Transcript of interview of Margaret Bruce, Mount Kisco, October 25, 2003. Oral History Collection of the United Nations Intellectual History Project, Graduate Center, City University of New York. Available through the CD-ROM version of UN *Voices: The Struggle for Development and Social Justice*, edited by Thomas George Weiss. Bloomington: Indiana University Press, 2005.

Kamp, Marianne. *The New Woman in Uzbekistan: Islam, Modernity, and Unveiling Under Communism*. Seattle: University of Washington Press, 2006.

Kaplan, Caren, Norma Alarcon, and Minoo Moallem, eds. *Between Women and the Nation: Nationalism, Transnational Feminisms, and the State*. Durham NC: Duke University Press, 1999.

Khader, Serene J. *Decolonizing Universalism: A Transnational Feminist Ethic*. Oxford: Oxford University Press, 2019.

Khan, Yasmin. *The Great Partition: The Making of India and Pakistan*. New Haven CT: Yale University Press, 2007.

Knop, Karen. *Diversity and Self-Determination in International Law*. Cambridge, UK: Cambridge University Press, 2002.

Koikari, Mire. *Pedagogy of Democracy: Feminism and the Cold War in the U.S. Occupation of Japan*. Philadelphia: Temple University Press, 2008.

Kunz, Diane B. *Butter and Guns: America's Cold War Economic Diplomacy*. New York: Free Press, 1997.

Lambertz, Jan. "'Democracy could go no further': Europe and women in the early United Nations." In *Women and Gender in Postwar Europe: From Cold War to European Union*, edited by Joanna Regulska and Bonnie G. Smith, 44–61. London: Routledge, 2012.

Lange, Dorothea. *Destitute Pea Pickers in California. Mother of Seven Children. Age Thirty-Two. Nipomo, California*. 1936. U.S. Farm Security Administration/Office of War Information. Prints & Photographs Division.

Langland, Elizabeth. "Nobody's Angels: Domestic Ideology and Middle-Class Women in the Victorian Novel." PMLA 107, no. 2 (1992): 290–304.

Laughlin, Kathleen A., and Jacqueline L. Castledine, eds.*Breaking the Wave: Women, Their Organizations, and Feminism, 1945–1985*. London: Routledge, 2011.

Lauren, Paul Gordon. *The Evolution of International Human Rights*, Philadelphia: University of Pennsylvania Press, 1998.

Lavigne, Marie. *The Soviet Union and Eastern Europe in the Global Economy*. Cambridge, UK: Cambridge University Press, 1992.

Laville, Helen. *Cold War Women: The International Activities of American Women's Organisations*. Manchester, UK: Manchester University Press, 2002.

———. "A New Era in International Women's Rights? American Women's Associations and the Establishment of the UN Commission on the Status of Women." *Journal of Women's History* 20, no. 4 (2009): 34–56.

———. "'Woolly, Half-Baked and impractical'? British Responses to the Commission on the Status of Women and the Convention on the Political Rights of Women 1946–1967." *Twentieth Century British History* 23, no. 4 (2012): 473–95.

Lee, Rebekah. *African Women and Apartheid Migration and Settlement in Urban South Africa*. London: Tauris Academic Studies, 2009.

Liang, Yuen-Li. "Colonial Clauses and Federal Clauses in United Nations Multilateral Instruments." *American Journal of International Law* 45, no. 1 (1951): 108–28.

Limoncelli, Stephanie A.*The Politics of Trafficking: The First International Movement to Combat the Sexual Exploitation of Women*. Stanford CA: Stanford University Press, 2010.

Linder, Doris H. "Equality For Women: The Contribution of Scandinavian Women at the United Nations, 1946–66." *Scandinavian Studies* 73, no. 2 (2001): 165–208.

Lister, Ruth. "Citizenship: Towards a feminist synthesis." *Feminist Review* 57, no. 1 (1996): 28–48.

Lorenzini, Sara. *Global Development: A Cold War History*. Princeton NJ: Princeton University Press, 2020.

Lugones, Mary C., and Elizabeth V. Spelman. "Have We Got a Theory for You! Feminist Theory, Cultural Imperialism and the Demand for 'The Woman's Voice.'" *Women's Studies International Forum* 6, no. 6 (1983): 573–81.

MacKinnon, Catherine. *Toward a Feminist Theory of the State*. Cambridge MA: Harvard University Press, 1989.

Marien, Mary W.*Photography: A Cultural History*. London: Laurence King, 2019.

Marino, Katherine M. *Feminism for the Americas: The Making of an International Human Rights Movement*. Chapel Hill: University of North Carolina Press, 2019.

Massell, Gregory J.*Surrogate Proletariat*. Princeton NJ: Princeton University Press, 1974.

Massino, Jill, and Shana Penn, eds. *Gender Politics and Everyday Life in State Socialist Eastern and Central Europe.* New York: Palgrave Macmillan, 2009.

Maul, Daniel. *Human Rights, Development and Decolonization: The International Labour Organization, 1940–70.* New York: Palgrave Macmillan, 2012.

Mazower, Mark. "The Strange Triumph of Human Rights, 1933–1950." *Historical Journal* 47, no. 2 (2004): 379–98.

———. *No Enchanted Palace: The End of Empire and the Ideological Origins of the United Nations.* Princeton NJ: Princeton University Press, 2009.

McGuire, John Thomas. "'Give Us Peace': Gladys Avery Tillett and the Search for Women's Political Activism in the United States, 1945–1950." *Women's History Review* 25, no. 6, (2016): 887–902.

McLaren, Margaret A. *Decolonizing Feminism: Transnational Feminism and Globalization.* Lanham: Rowman & Littlefield, 2017.

Menon, Ritu, and Kamla Bhasin. *Borders & Boundaries: Women in India's Partition.* New Brunswick NJ: Rutgers University Press, 1998.

Meyerowitz, Joanne, ed. *Not June Cleaver: Women and Gender in Postwar America, 1945–1960.* Philadelphia: Temple University Press, 1994.

Midtgaard, Kristine. "Bodil Begtrup and the Universal Declaration of Human Rights: Individual Agency, Transnationalism and Intergovernmentalism in Early UN Human Rights." *Scandinavian Journal of History* 36, no. 4 (2011): 479–99.

Miers, Suzanne. *Slavery in the Twentieth Century: The Evolution of a Global Problem.* Walnut Creek CA: AltaMira, 2003.

Miller, Carol. "'Geneva—the Key to Equality': Inter-war Feminists and the League of Nations." *Women's History Review* 3, no. 2 (1994): 218–45.

Mohanty, Chandra Talpade. "Under Western Eyes: Feminist Scholarship and Colonial Discourses." In *Third World Women and the Politics of Feminism*, edited by Chandra Talpade Mohanty, Ann Russo, and Lourdes Torres, 333–58. Bloomington: Indiana University Press, 1991.

———. "'Under Western Eyes' Revisited: Feminist Solidarity through Anticapitalist Struggles." *Signs* 28 (2002): 499–535.

Morrell, Gordon. "A Higher Stage of Imperialism? The Big Three, the NUN Trusteeship System and the Early Cold War." In *Imperialism On Trial*, edited by R. M. Douglas, Elizabeth Bishop, and Michael D. Callahan, 111–37. Lanham MD: Lexington, 2006.

Morsink, Johannes. "Women's Rights in the Universal Declaration." *Human Rights Quarterly* 13, no. 2 (1991): 229–56.

Moses, A. Dirk, Marco Duranti, and Roland Burke. *Decolonization, Self-Determination, and the Rise of Global Human Rights Politics.* Cambridge, UK: Cambridge University Press, 2020.

Moyn, Samuel. *The Last Utopia Human Rights in History*. Cambridge MA: Belknap, 2010.

Naples, Nancy A., and Manisha Desai. *Women's Activism and Globalization: Linking Local Struggles and Transnational Politics*. New York: Routledge, 2002.

Narayan, Uma. *Dislocating Cultures: Identities, Traditions, and Third-World Feminism*. New York: Routledge, 1997.

Narayan, Uma, and Sandra Harding, eds. *Decentering the Center: Philosophy for a Multicultural, Postcolonial, and Feminist World*. Bloomington: Indiana University Press, 2000.

Nnaemeka, Obioma, ed. *Female Circumcision and the Politics of Knowledge: African Women in Imperialist Discourses*. Westport CT: Praeger, 2005.

Normand, Roger, and Sarah Zaidi. *Human Rights at the UN: The Political History of Universal Justice*. Bloomington: Indiana University Press, 2008.

Northrop, Douglas T. *Veiled Empire: Gender & Power in Stalinist Central Asia*. Ithaca NY: Cornell University Press, 2004.

Nussbaum, Martha Craven. *The Feminist Critique of Liberalism*. Lawrence: University of Kansas Press, 1997.

Okin, Susan Moller. *Women in Western Political Thought*. Princeton NJ: Princeton University Press, 1979.

Olcott, Jocelyn. *International Women's Year: The Greatest Consciousness-Raising Event in History*. Oxford: Oxford University Press 2017.

Parisi, Laura. "Feminist Praxis and Women's Human Rights." *Journal of Human Rights* 1, no. 4 (2002): 571–85.

Patil, Vrushali. *Negotiating Decolonization in the United Nations: Politics of Space, Identity, and International Community*. New York: Routledge, 2008.

Pedersen, Susan. *The Guardians: The League of Nations and the Crisis of Empire*. Oxford: Oxford University Press, 2018.

———. "Metaphors of the Schoolroom: Women Working the Mandates System of the League of Nations." *History Workshop Journal* 66, no. 1 (2007): 188–207.

—. "National Bodies, Unspeakable Acts: The Sexual Politics of Colonial Policymaking." *Journal of Modern History* 63, no. 4 (1991): 647–80.

Peters, Julie Stone, and Andrea Wolper. *Women's Rights, Human Rights: International Feminist Perspectives*. New York: Routledge, 2008.

Pierce, Steven, and Anupama Rao, eds. *Discipline and the Other Body: Correction, Corporeality, Colonialism*. Durham NC: Duke University Press, 2006.

Pietilä, Hilkka, and Beth Peoc'h. *The Unfinished Story of Women and the United Nations*. New York: UN, Non-Governmental Liaison Service, 2007.

Porter, Roy. "History of the Body Reconsidered." In *New Perspectives on Historical Writing*, edited by Peter Burke, 233–60. Cambridge: Polity, 2001.

Proschan, Frank. "Eunuch Mandarins, Soldats Mamzelles, Effeminate Boys, and Graceless Women: French Colonial Constructions of Vietnamese Genders." *GLQ: A Journal of Lesbian and Gay Studies* 8, no. 4 (2002): 435–67.

Quataert, Jean H. *Advocating Dignity: Human Rights Mobilizations in Global Politics.* Philadelphia: University of Pennsylvania Press, 2009.

———. *The Gendering of Human Rights in the International Systems of Law in the Twentieth Century.* Washington DC: American Historical Association, 2006.

Radi, Heather, ed. *Jessie Street, Documents and Essays.* Broadway NSW: Women's Redress, 1990.

Randall, Amy E. "'Abortion Will Deprive You of Happiness!': Soviet Reproductive Politics in the Post-Stalin Era." *Journal of Women's History* 23, no. 3 (2011): 13–38.

Ransby, Barbara. *Eslanda: The Large and Unconventional Life of Mrs. Paul Robeson.* New Haven: Yale University Press, 2014.

Reanda, Laura. "The Commission on the Status of Women." In *The United Nations and Human Rights: A Critical Appraisal*, edited by Philip Alston, 265–303. Oxford: Clarendon, 1992.

———. "Prostitution as a Human Rights Question: Problems and Prospects of United Nations Action." *Human Rights Quarterly* 132 (1991): 202–28.

Reddy, Enuga "The Struggle against Apartheid: Lessons for Today's World." *UN Chronicle* 44, no. 3 (2007): 13.

Reilly, Niamh. *Women's Human Rights: Seeking Gender Justice in a Globalizing Age.* Cambridge, UK: Polity, 2009.

Reyher, Rebecca. *The Fon and His Hundred Wives.* Garden City NJ: Doubleday, 1952.

Richards, Yevette. "Transnational Links and Constraints: Women's Work, the ILO and the ICFTU in Africa, 1950s–1980s." In *Women's ILO: Transnational Networks, Global Labour Standards and Gender Equity, 1919 to Present*, edited by Eileen Boris, Dorothea Hoehtker, and Susan Zimmermann, 149–75. Leiden: Brill and ILO, 2018.

Rosenblum, Naomi. *A World History of Photography.* New York: Abbeville, 2007.

Rossi, Benedetta, ed. *Reconfiguring Slavery: West African Trajectories.* Liverpool, UK: Liverpool University Press, 2016.

Rupp, Leila J. *Worlds of Women: The Making of an International Women's Movement.* Princeton NJ: Princeton University Press, 1997.

Sa'dāwī, Nawāl, and Ḥaṭātah Sharīf. *Woman at Point Zero.* London: Zed, 1983.

Said, Edward W. *Orientalism.* New York: Pantheon, 1978.

Sandeen, Eric J. *Picturing an Exhibition: The Family of Man and 1950s America.* Albuquerque: University of New Mexico Press, 1995.

Scarry, Elaine. *The Body in Pain: The Making and Unmaking of the World.* New York: Oxford University Press, 1985.

Schmidt, Heike. "Colonial Intimacy: The Rechenberg Scandal and Homosexuality in German East Africa." *Journal of the History of Sexuality,* 17, no. 1 (2008): 25–59.

Scott, Joan Wallach. *Only Paradoxes to Offer French Feminists and the Rights of Man.* Cambridge MA: Harvard University Press, 1996.

———. *The Politics of the Veil.* Princeton NJ: Princeton University Press, 2007.

Sears, Laurie. *Fantasizing the Feminine in Indonesia.* Durham NC: Duke University Press, 1996.

Seltzer, Judith R. *The Origins and Evolution of Family Planning Programs in Developing Countries.* Pittsburgh PA: Population Matters, 2002.

Shibusawa, Naoko. "Ideology, Culture, and the Cold War." In *The Oxford Handbook of the Cold War,* edited by Richard H. Immerman and Petra Goedde, 32–49. Oxford: Oxford University Press, 2013.

Siegel, Mona L. *Peace on Our Terms: The Global Battle for Women's Rights After the First World War.* New York: Columbia University Press, 2021.

Sinha, Mrinalini. *Colonial Masculinity: The "Manly Englishman" and the "Effeminate" Bengali in the Late Nineteenth Century.* Manchester: Manchester University Press, 1995.

———. *Specters of Mother India: The Global Restructuring of an Empire.* Durham NC: Duke University Press, 2006.

Sinha, Mrinalini, Donna J. Guy, and Angela Woollacott. *Feminisms and Internationalism.* Oxford: Blackwell, 1999.

Sneider, Allison L. *Suffragists in an Imperial Age: U.S. Expansion and the Woman Question, 1870–1929.* New York: Oxford University Press, 2008.

Snyder, Margaret C., and Mary Tadesse. *African women and development: A History.* Johannesburg: Witwatersrand University Press, 1995.

Sontag, Susan. *Regarding the Pain of Others.* New York: Farrar, Straus and Giroux, 2003.

Spivak, Gayatri Chakravorty. "Can the Subaltern Speak?" In *Marxism and the interpretation of Culture,* edited by Cary Nelson and Larry Grossberg, 271–313. Champaign: University of Illinois Press, 1988.

———. "'Woman' as Theatre: United Nations Conference on Women, Beijing 1995." *Radical Philosophy* 75 (January-February 1996): 2–4.

Stienstra, Deborah. *Women's Movements and International Organizations.* New York: St. Martin's, 1994.

St. Joan's International Social and Political Alliance. *A Venture in Faith: A History of St. Joan's Social and Political Alliance Formerly Known as the Catholic Women's Suffrage Society 1911–1961*. London: St. Joan's Alliance, 1961.

Stoler, Ann Laura. *Carnal Knowledge and Imperial Power: Race and the Intimate in Colonial Rule*. Berkeley: University of California Press, 2002.

Street, Jessie M. G., and Lenore Coltheart. *Jessie Street: A Revised Autobiography*. Annandale NSW: Federation Press, 2004.

Suchland, Jennifer. *Economies of Violence: Transnational Feminism, Postsocialism, and the Politics of Sex Trafficking*. Durham NC: Duke University Press, 2015.

Sullivan, Donna. "The Public/Private Distinction in International Human Rights Law." In *Women's Rights, Human Rights: International Feminist Perspectives*, edited by Julie Peters, and Andrea Wolper, 126–34. New York: Routledge, 1995.

Teltsch, Kathleen. "South Africa Is Suspended by UN Assembly, 91–22." *New York Times*, November 13, 1974.

Terretta, Meredith. *Petitioning for Our Rights, Fighting for Our Nation: The History of the Democratic Union of Cameroonian Women, 1949–1960*. Bamenda, Cameroon: Langaa Research, 2013.

———. "'We Had Been Fooled into Thinking that the UN Watches Over the Entire World': Human Rights, UN Trust Territories, and Africa's Decolonization." *Human Rights Quarterly* 34, no. 2 (2012): 329–60.

Thomas, Lynn M. *Politics of the Womb: Women, Reproduction, and the State in Kenya*. Berkeley: University of California Press, 2003.

Thomas, Martin. "France Accused: French North Africa Before the United Nations, 1952–1962."*Contemporary European History* 10, no. 1 (2001): 91–121.

Thompson, Elizabeth. *Colonial Citizens: Republican Rights, Paternal Privilege, and Gender in French Syria and Lebanon*. New York: Columbia University Press, 2000.

Tomlinson, B.R. "What Was the Third World?" *Journal of Contemporary History* 38, no. 2 (2003): 307–21.

Tripp, Aili Mari, Isabel Casimiro, Joy C. Kwesiga, and Alice Mungwa, eds. *African Women's Movements: Transforming Political Landscapes*. New York: Cambridge University Press, 2017.

Tyson, Brady, and Abdul Aziz Said. "Human Rights: A Forgotten Victim of the Cold War." *Human Rights Quarterly* 15, no. 3 (1993): 589–604.

UN Commission on the Status of Women: A Brief Summary of Progress. A Supplement to the Report of the Conference on the Status of Women Around the World. March 30, 1959.

UN Department of Public Information. *Guide to the United Nations Charter*. Lake Success NY: 1947.

UNESCO. *African Women, Pan-Africanism and African Renaissance.* Africa Department, 2015.

United Nations (UN). *A Sacred Trust: The Work of the United Nations for Dependent Peoples.* New York Department of Public Information, 1953.

————. *What the United Nations Is Doing for the Status of Women.* Lake Success NY: United Nations Department of Public Information, 1948.

Urdang, Stephanie. "Fighting Two Colonialisms: The Women's Struggle in Guinea-Bissau." *African Studies Review: The Journal of the African Studies Association* 18, no. 3 (1975): 29–34.

Vergès, Françoise. *Monsters and Revolutionaries: Colonial Family Romance and Métissage.* Durham NC: Duke University Press, 1999.

Visvanathan, Nalini, Lynn Duggan, Laurie Nisonoff, and Nancy Wiegersma, eds. *The Women, Gender, and Development Reader.* London: Zed, 1997.

Von Eschen, Penny M. *Race against Empire: Black Americans and Anticolonialism, 1937–1957.* Ithaca NY: Cornell University Press, 1997.

Walkowitz, Judith R. *City of Dreadful Delight: Narratives of Sexual Danger in Late-Victorian London.* Chicago: University of Chicago Press, 1992.

Waltz, Susan E. "Universal Human Rights: The Contribution of Muslim States." *Human Rights Quarterly* (2004): 799–844.

Wa Ngũgĩ Thiong'o, and Uzodinma Iweala. *The River Between.* London: Penguin Books, 1965.

Weber, Charlotte. "Unveiling Scheherazade: Feminist Orientalism in the International Alliance of Women, 1911–1950." *Feminist Studies* 27 (2001): 125–57.

Weigand, Kate, and Daniel Horowitz. "Dorothy Kenyon: Feminist Organizing, 1919–1963." *Journal of Women's History* 14, no. 2 (2002): 126–31.

Weiss, Thomas George, ed. *UN Voices: The Struggle for Development and Social Justice.* Bloomington: Indiana University Press, 2005.

Westad, Odd Arne. *The Global Cold War: Third World Interventions and the Making of Our Times.* Cambridge, UK: Cambridge University Press, 2005.

Whelan, Daniel J. *Indivisible Human Rights: A History.* Philadelphia: University of Pennsylvania Press, 2010.

Wilde, Ralph. *International Territorial Administration: How Trusteeship and the Civilizing Mission Never Went Away.* Oxford: Oxford University Press, 2008.

Wilder, Gary. *The French Imperial Nation-State: Negritude and Colonial Humanism between the Two World Wars.* Chicago: University of Chicago Press, 2005.

Winslow, Anne, ed. *Women, Politics, and the United Nations.* Westport CT: Greenwood, 1995.

Zerilli, Linda Marie-Gelsomina. "Feminist Theory and the Canon of Political Thought." In *Oxford Handbook of Political Theory*, edited by John Dryzek, Bonnie Honig, and Anne Phillips, 107–24. Oxford: Oxford University Press, 2006.

Zinsser, Judith P. "From Mexico to Copenhagen to Nairobi: The United Nations Decade for Women, 1975–1985." *Journal of World History* 13, no. 1 (2002): 139–68.

Index

Page numbers in italics indicate illustrations

Australia, 49, 112, 117, 184, 207. *See also* Street, Jessie; Tennison-Woods, Mary

backwardness: condemnation of practices of, 152; and discussions of equality, 19; and the Islamic veil, 197; and orientalist attitudes, 35; and rescue, 80; resentment toward use of term, 176; of Soviet societies, 92; UN debates on, 61, 62

Baldez, Lisa, 9

Bandung Conference, 83, 100, 115

Bangkok Seminar: discussion of women's education in, 102–3; founding of, 91; goals and planning of, 101–2; as public performance of equality, 105; and rights models for postcolonial women, 83, 84–85; and women in the public sphere, 27; and women's role in the country-side, 85; working papers resulting from, 104

Baron, Ava, 13

Barry, Florence, 139

Beauvoir, Simone de, 39

Begtrup, Bodil: activism of, 38, 215n16; and affirmations of political equality, 53; concerns over makeup of CSW, 49; and the new commission's agenda, 44–45; and peace, 66; support for a UN group on women's rights by, 6, 36, 45, 46, 54; use of "women of the world" by, 50; on women and peace, 51–52; and women's status as human beings, 50

Beijing conference, 138, 202

Beirut meeting of the CSW, 57, 63–68

Belgium, 25, 95, 117

Bernardino, Minerva: activism of, 25, 38, 215n16; debate on case of Sudan and FGM, 144; and empire, 217n41; and the new commission's agenda, 44; patron of, 215n3; photograph of, 30, 31–32; and representation of a colonized country, 39; signing of the UN Charter by, 200–201; support for a UN group on women's rights by, 6, 36; support for the Convention on Political Rights of Women, 78–79, 215n1; and UNESCO's incorrect data, 215n1; and WHO's involvement in bodily rituals issue, 142, 143; on women as civilizing agents, 41–42

Bissek, Guillaume, 108

Boddy, Janice, 144

bodily pain: assumptions and tensions with self-determination, 209; colonial bodies in pain, 127; and shift from law to culture, 208; victimization of sufferers of, 111. *See also* female genital cutting (FGM); trafficking

body, histories of, 12–14, 212n25

body politics: concept and theoretical constructs informing, 12–13; and constraints on universalism, 15; and defenselessness of African women, 145; in discussions of family planning, 186; and justification of women's rights, 46; proempire rationales in, 122; reinforced by development politics, 210; rescuers and the rescued in, 15; and self-determination, 209, 210; trafficking and, 16; trajectories in, 14; UN Photo Archive images and, 19–23; in women's activism, 207. *See also* family planning; female bodies; female genital cutting (FGM); trafficking

Bokor, Hanna, 163–64

Boris, Eileen, 13; "Equality's Cold War," 9

Bosrap, Ester, 159

Branch for the Advancement of Women, 202

Brazil, 35, 36, 37, 115. *See also* Lutz, Bertha

Breaking the Wave (Laughlin and Casteldine), 10

British Cameroons, 110, 117, 118–19, 124–30. *See also* Cameroons

Bruce, Margaret, 7, 156, 157, 181, 205, 234n1

Bucharest World Population Conference, 196

Buenos Aires meeting, 147, 159

Bunche, Ralph, 35, 223n70

Burke, Roland, 11, 99

Burton, Antoinette, 17–18

Byelorussia, 49, 66–67, 81, 88, 95

Cabral, Amílcar, 161

Cairo Family Planning Association (CFPA), 187

Callaghan, Marion, 193

Cambodia, participation in seminar by, 99

Cameroons, 108, 123–24, 149. *See also* British Cameroons

Campt, Tina, 20

Canning, Kathleen, 12–13, 212n25

capitalism: countries aligned with, 26; victims of, in photos, 20

Caribbean area, 38, 98, 215n1

Carmichael, Stokely, 237n60

Catholic groups, 57, 80, 135, 187–88, 204. *See also* International Union of Catholic Women's League; St. Joan's International Alliance

CEDAW. *See* Committee on the Elimination of Discrimination against Women (CEDAW)

Central African Republic, 191–92

Ceylon. *See* Kotelawala, John

Charlesworth, Hilary, 202

Chile, 67, 188

China (mainland), 94, 159, 201

China (Nationalist), 26, 63, 221n29. *See also* Zung, Cecilia

Chinkin, Christine, 202

Christianity, and decolonization, 26

circumcision, female. *See* female genital cutting (FGM)

Cissé, Jeanne, 168

civic participation: DEDAW and, 185; inclusion of women in, 33, 35, 149–50, 180; rights and responsibilities in, 52, 102; and women's education, 69–72, 97, 149–50; women's labor and, 92

Coigney, Rudolph, 175

Cold War: centrality of ideology during, 94; and the CSW, 86–89; development and capitalism during, 201; and independent nation-states, 9; and photos' messages, 21; and the politics of

197; in UN responses, 4, 204; and
women's rights, 130

Cyprus, 132

Czechoslovakia, 72, 74–75, 232n27

Dalen, Mrs., 40–41

Decade for Women (1975–85), 6, 7–8

Declaration on the Elimination of
Discrimination Against Women
(DEDAW): advancement of women
and aims of, 176; and antipatriarchal discourses, 174; approval
of, 166–67; benefits to women's
civic participation, 185; and cultural
norms, 8, 166; as dangerous, 169;
debate, 165; and slavery, 173;
and women in economic development, 5

decolonization: and African development, 160–62; and Cold War
balance, 201; CSW advocacy for, 10;
and demand for rights, 61; women's
rights and, 12, 154

DEDAW. See Declaration on the Elimination of Discrimination Against
Women (DEDAW)

Dembinska, Zofia, 164, 185

democracy: Cold War politics and,
88–89, 94–95, 97; CSW advocacy
for, 158; definitions and understanding of, 158; development and,
196; gender equality in, 158–59;
India and, 116; Japanese and, 58–59,
70, 71, 179; Trujillo and, 42; use of
term in postwar politics, 94–95;
and U.S. hypocrisy, 17. See also
Universal Declaration of Human
Rights (UDHR)

Denmark, 25, 49. See also Begtrup,
Bodil

dependent territories: as de facto
colonies, 59–60; independence
and geographical changes for, 117;
industrialization of, 171; universalism and, 35; and UN membership,
6. See also colonialism; development; economic rights; empire;
modernization; technical assistance; trust system; women in
dependent territories

Derby, Lauren, 31, 32

development: in Asia, 97–101;
and asymmetries of power, 199;
conflicts of tradition with, 197;
demands for, 105; discrimination
and, 5; failures of, 184; gendered
nature of, 7, 28, 83; and gender
equality, 169, 170; and new hierarchies of women, 7–8; progressive
education and, 182; relationship
with nation building, 160; tensions in, 176; and unifying women
of the world, 173–77; and wom-
en's participation in, 183–84. See
also International Forum on the
Role of Women and Development; national development;
nation-states

Development Decades: First Development Decade, 173–76; Second
Development Decade, 173, 176–77

discrimination: beyond gender differences, 163; capitalism and, 75;
responsibility for denunciation of,
62; in Soviet society, 59. See also
racial discrimination

discrimination against women: agents of, 146; in the Cameroons, 123–24; CSW focus on, 159; CSW's opposition to, 206; DEDAW, colonialism, underdevelopment and, 167; and gender equilibrium, 162–67; as global issue, 176; identifying, 154; Islam and, 100–101; nation-states and, 17; persistence of, 68; and the private sphere, 197; provisions to end, 160; socialist countries' request to address, 162; and strength of nation-states, 102; U.S. impact on CSW's work on, 97; Western hegemonic politics and, 3. *See also* International Forum on the Role of Women and Development

displacement, 3, 9, 57, 123

Dominican Republic, 38, 215n1. *See also* Bernardino, Minerva

Dubois, Ellen, 31, 32

Dubziak, Mary, 97

Duranti, Marco, 11

Economic and Social Council (ECOSOC): approval of the convention for political rights by, 72; and clash between CSW and the WHO, 145–46; and the creation of the CSW, 46; CSW dependence on, 5, 47, 57; and CSW involvement in prostitution, 110; and discussions of peace, 67; encouraged to support women's rights, 137; and family planning, 188; and inquiry into female circumcision, 152; and the nuclear commission, 44; proposal to meet in Lebanon, 57–58; Reso-

lution 48, 52; selection of commissioners for CSW by, 49; in the UN hierarchy, 45

economic rights: in the developing world, 84, 100; and the emancipation of women, 119; and the Global South, 105; modernization and, 105; as part of human rights, 81, 104; shift from political considerations to, 6, 7, 130–31; and the Soviet woman, 92; and tensions in expertise on, 9; Western fears about discussions of, 83–84; and women's progress, 86, 87–88, 89

ECOSOC. *See* Economic and Social Council (ECOSOC)

education: and civic participation, 69–72, 97, 149–50, 184, 222n51; in development of nation-states, 118–19, 182; missionary teaching, 119, 130; and strengthening of national culture, 151

Egypt: and correlation between development and women's status, 167; family planning in, 186–87; on inclusion of women in human rights, 76; on Islam and women's status, 182; women's rights in, 182. *See also* Hussein, Aziza

Ehrlich, Paul: *The Population Bomb*, 186

embodiment, theory and politics of, 13–14

empire: the Cold War and, 88; and defining of equality, 199; and reform, 220n21; rescue narratives, 3–4; and the UN Charter, 34; and UN gender politics, 3, 4. *See also*

France (cont)
socialist views of, 26, 159; on Soviet claims of humanitarianism, 115; and support for women's progress, 75; and support of empires, 25; on Trusteeship Council, 109, 117; and the WHO's classification of Algeria, 142; and women's war effort, 41. *See also* colonial powers; Lefaucheux, Marie Helene; Trusteeship Council (TC)
Fujita, Taki, *178*

G77, creation of, 201, 240n2
Gallagher, Catherine, 12–13; "The Making of the Modern Body," 212n25
Gallagher, Ronald, 4
Gaulle, Charles de, 61
gender balance, 206–7
gender equality: ambiguity in proposed declaration, 169; Bangkok seminar's advocacy for, 104; colonialism and, 169; CSW and, 206; and debates around language, 52–53; economic development and, 158, 177, 196; and focus on the family, 164–65, 203; and formal equality, 43, 217n47; freedom of choice and, 169; industrialized countries' leadership in, 177; and the League of Nations, 36; liberal feminism and, 16; as male-derivative goal, 75; poverty and, 164, 205; racial discrimination and, 72; reason and, 43; slavery and, 171; term of *sex equality* and, 214n58; Third Committee debate on, 140; in the Trust

Territories, 109; women representatives and, 11
gender politics at the UN, 3, 28, 31, 111, 130. *See also* bodily pain; body politics; female genital cutting (FGM); imperial feminism; marriage; sexuality
General Assembly: and ancient customs, 141; and the decision to provide reports on territories, 35; direction to agencies by, 162; and FGM debates, 141, 145; and human rights, 81, 224n91; and the indivisibility of human rights, 81; planning of seminars by, 97–98; pluralism in, 133, 230n1; Resolution 181, 57; Resolution 194, 65, 221n35; Resolution 729, 98; Resolution 1719, 161; Resolution 1720, 162; and resolution on equal rights, 63; review of the Convention on Slavery by, 158, 170, 171; and voting power of nonaligned countries, 201; and women as helpers, 43. *See also* Convention on Consent of Marriage, Minimum Age of Marriage and Registration of Marriages; Convention on the Political Rights of Women; Third Committee; United Nations Charter
Ghana, 117, 132, 162, 163, 175, 183, 230n1. *See also* Jiagge, Annie
Ghodsee, Kristen, 11, 225n13
Gildersleeve, Virginia, 35
Global North: backwardness in, 176; representatives' single story about women, 199; and women's rights, 207

Global South: assumptions about women in, 167; attention to voices from, 25; Bernardino as representative of, 31; and contradictions between tradition and modernity, 204; CSW's stronger focus on, 105; family and women's agency in, 177; growing role for women from, 179; images of poor women and children from, 186; and inequality as global issue, 207; and national culture in promoting UN principles, 162–63; new delegates from, 134; objectification of bodies in, 207; UN's role in politics of, 160; visibility of, 201; voicing of their struggles by, 203

Gordon, Beate Sirota, 71

Grewal, Inderpal: *Scattered Hegemonies* (with Kaplan), 18

Grinberg-Vinaver, Sophie, 144

Grosz, Elizabeth, 14

Guinea, 168

Guinea-Bissau, 161

Gula, Sharbat, 22–23

Haan, Francisca de, 11. *See also* International Union of Catholic Women's League

Hafezi, M. H., 141–42, 144, 145

Hamid Ali, Begum, 49, 53, 60, 218n62, 223n84

Haraway, Donna, 212n25

hegemony: and imperial feminism, 207; of men in international governance, 32, 53; and Otherness, 1, 18; photos and, 20, 22; "single stories" and, 199, 203; transnational femi-

nism's challenge to, 18–19; and violence to women through FGM, 209, 239n13. *See also* rescue narratives

Hesford, Wendy, 22–23

Hiss, Alger, 215n6

historiography, the body in, 12–13, 212n25

Hosken, Fran, 147

Hosken Report, 133, 147

HRC. *See* Human Rights Commission (HRC)

humanitarianism, 71, 80, 115, 133

human rights: ambiguity in, 11; and bodily abuse, 204; and commissions of the ECOSOC, 44; family planning as, 193–94; health as fundamental in, 135; indivisibility of, 81; as intervention into cultural traditions, 195; as political tool, 99; and tensions with old order, 62–63; the U.S. and, 201; and WHO's action on FGM, 146; and women's dignity, 145; *versus* women's rights, 3, 5–6, 76, 79. *See also* human rights framework; Universal Declaration of Human Rights (UDHR); women's rights

Human Rights Advisory Program, 28, 91

Human Rights Commission (HRC): Advisory Services, 98, 174; an appeal for action presented to, 126; and collaboration with the CSW on FGM, 133, 146; CSW and, 5–6, 44–45; debates on marriage issues by, 7; director of, 24; and FGM, 131, 133, 145; and the human rights of women, 45, 138; and individual

Museum of Modern Art (MOMA): *The Family of Man*, 21–23

Muslim women. *See* Islam

national development: as focus of CSW, 7; and focus on women's rights, 100; motherhood and, 165–66; and population growth, 180, 188, 191–92

National Geographic, "Afghan girl," 22–23

nation-states: admittance to the UN, 132, 134, 230n1; cultural practices *versus* abuse in, 130; development and women's status in, 197; education for women's civic participation in, 149–50; exclusionary mechanisms in, 206; family planning sited in, 190; gendered divisions of labor in, 183; as guarantors of rights, 39–40, 88, 94, 204; as point of reference for the UN, 205; population growth and, 180, 188, 191–92, 193; restorative justice for, 133; rhetoric as mediator between the UN and women, 42–43; and strengthening of national culture, 151; UN nonintervention in sovereignty of, 33; UN's relationship with African states, 154; Western interference with, 159, 167, 170–71, 181; women's career possibilities in, 175; women's inclusion in, 15

the Netherlands, 171, 174

New York Times on the Fon of Bikom scandal, 127, 128

New Zealand, 112, 113, 117

NGOs: involvement in FGM issue, 135; presentations on fact *versus* propaganda, 64; provision of knowledge about women by, 60, 115, 136, 204; role in CSW, 47; testimony on discrimination by, 164; and women's equality, 165. *See also* International Union of Catholic Women's League; St. Joan's International Alliance

Nigeria, 117, 154, 192, 233n49

occupied countries, 70, 71, 80

Olcott, Jocelyn, 10

Ombri, Rana, *156*, 157, 234n1

Organization of Democratic Women, 64

Otherness: depicted in photos, 23; imperial feminism and, 17–18; and investigation of the body in history, 200. *See also* body politics; discrimination

Pakistan: criticism by, 85; and European imperialism, 159; independence of, 6; Islam and women's rights, 77–78, 101, 140, 182; technical assistance with Western expertise advocated by, 98; and traditional practices, 95; and universal definitions of human rights, 10; women's rights in, 182; women's status and labor in, 100. *See also* Khan, Begum Liaquat Ali

Palestine, 4, 57, 79, 80, 201, 221n35

Palestinian refugees, 80; photograph of, *56*, 57, 201; rights of, 65–66; sympathy for, 68; UN relief for, 219n1

Pan-Pacific Southeast Asia Women's Association, 174

Parmar, Pratibha: "Challenging Imperial Feminism" (with Amos), 17
Patil, Vrushali, 13–14, 32
patriarchy: in attitudes toward emancipation of women, 119; and the Bangkok Seminar, 104, 105; as challenge to women's rights, 197; circumcision as an assertion of, 134; and colonials' focus on women, 122; continued support of, 76; CSW and, 2; and discrimination, 77; and loss of political rights, 86; reproductive rights and, 190, 191, 192; and the USSR, 90
Paul-Boncour, Mr., 41, 42
peace: as precursor to political rights, 66; shift in goals for, 79; women's alliances for, 51
Pedersen, Susan, 220n21
petitions. See female genital cutting (FGM); St. Joan's International Alliance; United Nations Charter; women's rights
Philippines, 35, 117, 176
photographs: and gendered notions of sympathy, 22–23; of modernization and technocracy, 106, 107; and restorative justice, 19–20; select audiences for, 214n50; as testimony, 20
Plaza de Echeverria, S., 196
Plesch, Dan, 8
Poland, 66, 67, 80, 95, 143, 162, 232n27. See also Dembinska, Zofia; Kalinowska, Fryderyka; Wasilkowska, Zofia
political rights: coexistence with colonialism, 116; CSW work on, 6;

and marriage, 86; Muslim support of, 77–78, 80; and political education, 69–70; seminars and, 174; for women in the USSR, 64; women's war sacrifice and, 177. See also civic participation; Convention on the Political Rights of Women; rescue narratives; Roosevelt, Eleanor
polygamy: changing attitudes toward, 4–5, 128, 129; dangers of, 116, 127; as international and UN concern, 136, 137, 139, 153, 157; prohibitions on, 120, 137; and women's status, 119
Popova, Elizavieta Alekseevna, 66, 68; career of, 214n57; on equality in democracies, 63; and fighting for peace, 51–52, 66, 68; on legal and actual equality for women, 87; as strong voice, 25
Porter, Roy, 12–13, 212n25
Portugal, 113, 226n36
poverty: and ancient customs, 141; and birth control, 193; and gender equality, 164; and limitations on rights, 171; and political rights, 72; and polygamy, 157; and slavery, 171–72; and underdevelopment, 100
private sphere: and the dependent woman, 120; and discrimination against women, 84, 131, 180, 197; economic rights in, 6, 84; human rights in, 130, 180; and international interest in former dependent territories, 134; and interventions in, 135; and the nation-state, 205; UN engagement with, 111–12; and violence, 2; visibility through the other's body, 207; working outside

of, 104. *See also* body politics; displacement; family planning; female genital cutting (FGM); marriage; trafficking

propaganda: and facts, 64, 67, 202; and responsibilities of colonizers in nation building, 161; and Soviet assessments of the colonial world, 115; Soviet positions in alignment with, 68; Soviets' use of, 92–93

Questionnaire on Legal Status of and Treatment of Women, 137

race: and colonialism, 94, 109; and discrimination against Cameroonian women, 123–24; Pan-American delegates and whiteness, 217n41; racial motherhood, 41–42; in Western imperialism, 73; and "woman worker," 9. *See also* apartheid; slavery

racial discrimination: and benefits of the Soviet system, 203; economic interventions and perpetuation of, 170–71; and gender equality, 72; modernization and, 174; and Smuts's support of equality in the charter, 34; UN declarations on racial discrimination, 162. *See also* Soviet Bloc; United States; USSR Report on Women and Development, 185

reproductive rights, 191–96, 208, 210, 239n33

rescue narratives: and African women, 208; assumptions in, 58; and backwardness, 62, 80; empire and,

4; equality in, 167; feminism and, 181; and the Fon of Bikom scandal, 126; imperial feminism and, 200; NGOs and, 164; shift from, 118; solutions to the conundrum of, 173; through photography, 22–23; by the Trusteeship Council, 120; Western agenda and, 209

restorative justice and photographs, 19, 20, 22, 31

Reyher, Rebecca Hourwich, 128–29

Robeson, Eslanda Goode, 223n70

Robeson, Paul, 223n70

Robinson, John, 4

Roosevelt, Eleanor, 5, 39–40, 45, 54, 69, 74

Ruanda-Urundi, 117, 121

Rupp, Leila, 215n16

A Sacred Trust (UN), 108–9

Said, Edward, *Orientalism*, 17

Sandeen, Eric, 21

San Francisco Conference: and articulation of UN's goals, 32–33; Bernardino signing charter at, 30, 31–32; empire and anticolonial voices at, 34–35; flags at, 157; and the LN's agenda, 36–37; orientalist attitudes at, 35; and women's participation in the UN, 37–39, 54

Scarry, Elaine, 111, 212n25

Schwelb, Egon, 146

"second wave international" feminism, 35–36, 159–60, 173–76, 209, 215n16

Secretariat: data collection by, 47, 86, 189; and FGM debates, 145; on goals of advisory programs, 101; reports

sex equality in, 59, 162; and women in the dependent territories, 114; and women's dignity, 137

universalism: body politics and constraints on, 15; challenge of human reproduction to, 181; FGM and, 154; and international development, 160; intersection with cultural practices, 133; and neo-Western superiority, 20; and otherness, 200; and photography, 21–22, 214n50; relationship with difference, 44–46, 206; relationship with pragmatism, 138; war photos and, 21–22; women's inclusion in, 28

urban places: as dangerous for women, 103, 105; and flourishing of democratic ideals, 119

Urquhart, Brian, 170–71, 234n8

USSR: and American racial politics, 17, 58, 63; criticism of Western interference with cultures, 148; as emancipatory power, 1; and female discrimination, 162; G77 as challenge to, 201; imperialism of, 219n6; on interference in FGM, 143; as member of CSW, 49; as patriarchal, 90; position on states and women's rights, 88–89, 225n13; promotion of sex equality by, 37, 64; and Soviet woman as model for women's rights, 89–93; and Uzbekistan, 71, 225n18; views of the West, race, and women's rights by, 60, 95; and women from the dependent territories, 59

Uzbekistan: political rights for women in, 73; relationship with the USSR, 59, 71; seminar participants' visit to, 92; and Soviet views of Muslim women, 89; unveiling of Muslim women in, 89, 219n6, 223n65, 225n18

Venezuela, 49, 61

victimhood, 1, 111, 126

Vienna Conference of 1993, 2

Vietnam War, photos of, 21

Wasilkowska, Zofia, 1–2

Wa Thiong'o, Ngugi: *The River Between*, 134, 152

Webb, Todd, 22, 107, 108

West Africa, Trusteeship Council Visiting Mission in, *106*, 107

Western superiority, 21–22, 135

Wolff, Mabel and Gertrude, 144

woman, creation of legal category of, 13, 32, 42

women in dependent territories: CSW category of, 2, 18, 32, 45, 115; CSW interaction with, 112; and education, 61; equality for, 27; isolation of, 58; legal equality and racial practices affecting, 87–88; Soviet and Indian support of, 59, 60. *See also* backwardness; discrimination; political rights; rescue narratives; tradition

Women in Development approach, 161, 184

"women of the world": CSW action on individual cases for, 46–47; CSW category of, 18; in CSW conception of women's rights, 49–53; and CSW institutional paths, 47–49, *48*;

World War II: as gender equalizer, 43; photos from, 21; and questioning of ruling authority, 33; the UN and women's labor during, 39–44, 177

Zharan, Miss, 195
Zizzamia, Alba, 136–37, 138
Zung, Cecilia, 53, 63–64, 221n29

In the Expanding Frontiers series

www.ingramcontent.com/pod-product-compliance
Lightning Source LLC
Chambersburg PA
CBHW020503270326
41926CB00008B/718